'The   Walls':
The Fiction of J. G. Ballard

Liverpool Science Fiction Texts and Studies

General Editor DAVID SEED

Series Advisers
I. F. CLARKE EDWARD JAMES PATRICK PARRINDER
AND BRIAN STABLEFORD

'The Angle Between Two Walls'
The Fiction of J. G. Ballard

ROGER LUCKHURST
Birkbeck College, London

LIVERPOOL UNIVERSITY PRESS

First published 1997 by
LIVERPOOL UNIVERSITY PRESS
Liverpool, L69 3BX

British Library Cataloguing-in-Publication Data
A British Library CIP record is available
0–85323–821–9 cased
0–85323–831–63 paper

Set in Linotron 202 Meridien by
Wilmaset Limited, Birkenhead, Wirral
Printed and bound in the European Union by
Bell & Bain Limited, Glasgow

For Julie,
overdeterminedly

Table of Contents

Acknowledgements

This project was first conceived under the tutelage of two brilliant teachers: Geoff Hemstedt at Sussex University and Bruce Woodcock at Hull University. Advice from Rowland Wymer and Peter Nicholls also helped in the completion of this project. My colleagues at Birkbeck, Claire Marshall and Carol Watts, have offered friendship and assistance. Isobel Armstrong's enthusiasm has been inspirational, and conversations with John Kraniauskas helped along the way.

David Pringle's knowledge of Ballard is legendary; his assistance has been crucial. In the days when the Science Fiction Foundation Library was based in Dagenham, Joyce Day was extremely helpful. I have also had the advantage of friendship with a living science fiction library, Andrew Butler. His knowledge helped fill the gaps of my own.

Thanks too to Chris Greenhalgh, John Lennard, Mary Luckhurst and Alison Mark, who sent me relevant material. My biggest debt is to Julie Crofts, who has managed to pull off a wonderful mix of intellectual and emotional support, remorseless sarcasm and unerring fashion sense throughout my tortured writing process.

Sections of Chapter One have appeared in *Science Fiction Studies* and the material in Chapter Five has been published in *Contemporary Literature* and *Extrapolation*. Although these appeared in very different forms, my thanks go to the editors of these journals for permission to reprint material. Istvan Csicsery-Ronay Jr at *SFS* was particularly supportive at a crucial time, and I thank him for his helpful advice and comments.

Some Framing Questions

On the final descent into Heathrow airport, the ground that first comes into sharp focus below you seems surprisingly rural and criss-crossed by canals and reservoirs, although it soon begins to be carved up by swathes of tarmac and the inelegant architecture of motorway intersections. Patterns of suburban streets become discernable, but speeding past these, thoughts are already directed towards the interminable wait for luggage, the negotiation of customs, and the endless journey into the centre of London by tube. That first view of the edges of London, its suburbs and transport systems, is soon forgotten in the rush for the centre.

This phase of the journey always seems to me to be wryly significant. You have just flown over Shepperton, the home of J. G. Ballard, and have glimpsed, however briefly, the landscape informing texts like *Crash, Concrete Island, High Rise* and *The Unlimited Dream Company*. But the speed of the descent allows you only a momentary view, and this is a landscape soon left behind. There is no reason, as a visitor or even a resident of London, to go to Shepperton 'on the ground' unless you live there.

This fast descent and quick move towards the centre allegorizes, I like to think, the attitude of both 'literary London' and the academy of English studies. Each in turn, when considering the landscape of contemporary British fiction, tends to rush to London's inner city, to the networks and connections between Martin Amis and Julian Barnes, Harold Pinter and Melvyn Bragg, *The London Review of Books* and *The Times Literary Supplement*. Both the London literary scene and the academy feel discomfited by writers who have chosen the edges of the city. That geographical marginality is either taken as wilful perversity or, more threateningly, as an affront to the pretensions of the centre. The affront is no doubt intended: Ballard revels in the banality of the Western suburbs and is splendidly abusive about literary society and academics, just as Iain Sinclair grounds his fictions in the dense histories of the despised East End, and Angela Carter celebrated 'bastard' South London in her last novel, *Wise Children*. The literary centre is hemmed in by these awkward voices who refuse to play the literary game: their off-centre locations echo their ex-centric, discomfiting writings.

This book is an attempt to describe and analyse the unease felt when reading the body of work produced by J. G. Ballard, a corpus compelling to some, repelling to others, yet always provocative for both constituencies. Although I have begun by placing Ballard amongst other writers that occupy the edge (and there are other, less London-centred, sodalities in which his work might be considered),[1] the unease Ballard's work induces derives from quite specific sources. Whereas Angela Carter has been swallowed, since her death, by the academy (the maverick can no longer sarcastically answer back), the resistance to Ballard's work—whether regarded as sometimes pornographic or just morbidly, even comically, obsessive—will always result in part from the tinge of embarrassment associated with a writer operating, however uncertainly, in the genre of science fiction. However inaccurate the stereotype of science fiction now is, it remains a male-adolescent identified genre, its clunking prose and emotional stuntedness occasionally lifted by sociological interest or debased philosophical potential.

It might appear that I am about to rehearse the commonly heard complaint that a writer usually associated with science fiction has been unjustly ignored by the prejudice of general readerships, that his or her work is more complex, more worthy than that. I am not interested in taking this line (indeed, I wish to question the logic of such legitimations), for the science fiction community is just as often prepared to condemn Ballard for his perverse contributions to the genre. Science fiction can feel as uncertain and unhappy with these texts as anyone else. A special issue of Delap's *Fantasy and Science Fiction* magazine ran a symposium in 1977 entitled 'J. G. Ballard: Where Does he Fit?' This question persistently haunts nearly all critical writing on Ballard, for the framings of his work have remained undecided (and undecidable) throughout his career, such that multiple, often incompatible, Ballards have proliferated: the science fiction writer; the mainstream post-war novelist of increasing import; the aberrant foreign body within science fiction; the belated voice of a science fictional modernism; the anticipatory or timely voice of a paradigmatic postmodernism; the avant-garde writer of extreme experimental fictions; the prophet of the perversity of the contemporary world. Such distributions among neatly packaged, discrete frames, however, can only reduce anxiety for a limited time. The contradictions between these Ballards soon become apparent again, as his work slips the frame that has been imposed.

My interest in Ballard comes from the visible discomfort his work produces. I do not wish to neutralize or 'solve' the unease of his texts by insisting he should be brought in from the margin to the centre, or reassessed by a simply fine-tuned set of aesthetic criteria. Rather, I want to describe and sustain the nature of the unease that surrounds Ballard, and which propels either fascination or repulsion. For it seems to me that Ballard renders visible the space *between* frames, exposes the hidden assumptions behind the secure categorizations of literature and literary judgment. These, operating dualistically (science fiction/mainstream, popular/serious, low/high, modernist/postmodernist, literature/theory, autobiography/fiction, and so on), all tend to find their mechanisms troubled when confronting a Ballard text.

Ballard, it might be said, is in the place of *the hinge*, the device which at once joins together and separates two planes or surfaces. *La brisure*, or the hinge, is one of the many quasi-names the philosopher Jacques Derrida gives for the point in any structural system that makes the working of the system at once possible and impossible (*Of Grammatology*, 65). I am suggesting, therefore, that Ballard's work can hold strategic importance in interrogating unexamined categories of literary value. Ballard's 'nonsense' question, cited from *The Atrocity Exhibition*, and which gives me my title, is thus not meaningless at all. 'Does the angle between two walls have a happy ending?' marks out the place of the angle, the hinge, as the place from which Ballard's texts produce their effects. The claim pursued throughout is that the discomfort that Ballard's work produces in numerous critical communities is not simply due to the failure to find the right protocol or the right frame, but that the Ballard oeuvre is nothing other than a prolonged meditation on the question of protocols, boundaries, frames and the evaluations they set in train. The angle between two walls at once allows and frustrates the literary critical distribution of texts between science fiction and mainstream, high and low, avant-garde and popular, and the many other categories that will come into play in the subsequent chapters.

Such a thesis must, of necessity, speak from a structurally similar space of the 'between.' This book both is and is not a work of science fiction criticism. It is not a survey of Ballard's vast output over forty years of writing, for this has been done, very competently, by David Pringle and Peter Brigg. Rather, it aims, where necessary, to contextualize Ballard's fiction within the science fiction genre, but also travels

over many terrains more or less foreign to science fiction: existentialism, Surrealism, Pop Art, psychoanalysis, ethnologies of contemporary
supermodernity, and the theory of autobiography, to name but a few.
Such heterogeneity reflects the bewildering diversity of the intersections made by Ballard's texts, the hinges of the many discourses which
his work can be seen to occupy. The technique adopted is often to place
Ballard's fiction alongside such discourses, to enable them to resonate
more widely. But this is not an attempt to escape the confines of
science fiction. I am anxious not to repeat the structure of argument,
analysed in detail in Chapter One, by which a reading of Ballard is
legitimated by arguing for his transcendence of generic concerns and
generic boundaries, an effect apparent in both science fiction and non-
science fiction critics alike. This would seek to neutralize Ballard's
uneasy non-place between categories, rather than focusing on the
uncanny hinge-effect. Sustaining this place has been difficult, and
perhaps accounts for a certain instability of address in the book. A
critical distance from the approach of science fiction critics has been
necessary and this is, I think, an echo of the persistent distress that
Ballard has caused to science fiction.

Thus far, it might appear that this work is concerned merely with the
problems of 'housing' Ballard within literary categories: a *meta*-critical
work rather than a critical one. The book does indeed begin with a
chapter analysing Ballard's 'unhomeliness' in regard to these housings,
particularly in relation to the denigration of generic literature, and the
effect this has on that vital terminological divide, science fiction and
the mainstream. It is also an occasion to set out the difficulties I have
had with predominant accounts of the genre by science fiction critics.
This is demonstrated by analysing the way in which the name of J. G.
Ballard appears in general accounts of science fiction and its history, for
this evidences his disruptive effect on definitional boundaries. A text
that is devoted to asking framing questions, questions about the frame,
must start 'before' or 'outside' a simple discussion of Ballard's oeuvre.
The determination of a body of work, signed and collected under the
name J. G. Ballard, is an apparently simple act of collation, but reading
does not begin with such a straightforward act. Protocols, generic
codes, and contextual sitings generate the frames of recognition that
allow readability, and this is where the difficulties begin in relation to
Ballard.

Subsequent chapters, however, investigate the manifold ways in
which his work might be said to thematize both the space between and
the peculiar oscillation of the permeability and impermeability of

borders. His fictions, it might be said, unfold in suspensive Zones,[2] in interstices where quotidian logics and causalities are held strangely in abeyance: *Concrete Island*, on a patch of wasteground between motorways; *The Unlimited Dream Company*, in a Shepperton magically transformed, but within strict limits governed by peculiar borders; *Empire of the Sun*, in the anomalous pocket of the International Settlement in Shanghai, its formalized colonial codes suspended in the vacuum between the end of war and the beginning of peace. A short story like 'Zone of Terror' exemplifies this suspensivity: a desert setting on the indeterminate edge of an indeterminate city, a place of retreat 'chosen for its . . . supposed equivalence to psychic zero' (*The Disaster Area*, 123), is the place where Larsen experiences the murderous hiatus of the Zone. In such a place, the identity of self, secured by the co-ordinates of time and space, undergoes slippage: autoscopia produces the startlingly material figure of his own double. This uncanny splitting intensifies; multiple doubles leak into febrile existence through this temporal and spatial fracture, doubles who direct Larsen's death.

Larsen's anguish of waiting in the suspended logic of the Zone embodies the analysis of the catastrophe novels I take up in Chapter Two. These novels all take place, in effect, between two catastrophes. Texts like *The Drowned World*, *The Drought* and 'The Voices of Time' are set long after variably specified global disasters and the dwindling populations that occupy this terminal zone await the second catastrophe of their own deaths, each profoundly disturbed by this intermissive state. The interstitial zone, the pocket at once inside and outside, is a space of sublimity. It hovers between terror of entrapment and the ecstasy of release.

The space of the between in these texts calls for, calls up, ways of bridging their gaps. Readers may find a certain manic productivity of theoretical frameworks to delineate this catastrophic space between: the disaster novels alone call up colonial and post-colonial explanations, Jungian and Freudian movels, Jaspersian and Heideggerian existentialism, as well as the Derridean hinge-effect. In part these are insisted upon by the texts, which embed their own theoretical models of explanation, but in part they are overproduced because the space between is the space of athesis, that is, something which suspends or disallows the operation of thetic, or theoretical, explanations.[3] This contradiction, which makes the texts at once graspable and ungraspable (fascinating and irritating in equal measure), requires elaboration.

Single-thesis explanations of Ballard's oeuvre have been increasingly produced, lulled by what appears to be an obsessively repetitive body of texts. Of late two models have come to predominate. On the one hand, Warren Wagar and Gregory Stephenson explain the entirety of Ballard's work as a narrative of transcendence, the desired escape from the confines of everyday space and time. On the other hand, critical narratives influenced by Baudrillard's reading of *Crash*, argue the reverse—Ballard's texts detail an immanental immersion in a contemporary 'postmodern' order of simulation. If I am wary of both of these models, resisting them is not achieved by replacing them with another single thesis. 'The angle between two walls' may work to isolate a reiterated structure, but it merely describes the architecture of a space, the precise nexus which precipitates a feeling of unease. How that space is traversed is open to multiple, contradictory and divergent theses.

The reader of a Ballard text is often reduced to a feeling of redundancy, of impotent laughter, for the critical thesis haltingly formed in the process of reading the text is often found in the text, over the page, always just down the line. Doctor Nathan in *The Atrocity Exhibition* becomes, effectively, the text's own internal interpretive voice. 'Zone of Terror', interpreted above in terms of Freud's uncanny double, in fact contains a Doctor Bayliss who casually dismisses the Freudian model for his own confident physiological narrative. These meta-commentaries embedded in the text must inevitably direct interpretations. They cannot, however, exhaust the enigmatic space between. The gap between reality and symbol, the event and its narration—or, in other registers, between trauma and abreaction (psychoanalysis), existence and Being (existentialism), the disruptive 'third term' between dualisms (deconstruction)—all hold highly suggestive mechanisms for traversing a Ballard text. There is no dearth, in other words, of ways to read theoretically the space between in Ballard's work.

You can demonstrate a thesis, then, but this strange, suspensive gap also demonstrates *athesis*. The weird discourse that is literature has always been a perplexing object to define: a literary text can make 'philosophical' utterances, but is not subject to the rigour of philosophical argumentation; a literary text (especially a science fiction one) can investigate science, but could not conform to strict scientific protocols without losing its fictivity. Derrida suggests that 'this strange institution called literature' is marked by literature's *'being-suspended'*: it 'neutralizes the "assumption" which it carries; it has this capacity . . . because this capacity is double, equivocal, contradictory, *hanging on*, *hanging between*, *dependent* and *independent*, an "assumption" both assumed and suspended' ('This Strange Institution', 49). The a-thesis of literature, both taking on theoretical statements but also suspending the conditions required of rigorously formed theory, seems to me to capture perfectly the experience of reading Ballard's work, whose interstitial spaces re-double this effect. His work at once constantly activates theoretical models, but it is also awkward, didactic, and overtheorized, tending to evade or supersede the theories meant to 'explain' it. This is to be caught on the horns of readability and unreadability, graspability and ungraspability. It means that his texts at once welcome theoretical 'capture', but always escape it. My five chapters, pursuing different aspects of Ballard's peculiar interstitiality, will demonstrates the need to generate multiple ways of bridging the discomfiting gaps that cleave his fictions.

Having articulated the grounds for my approach in relation to the first two chapters, the first on the frames for science fiction, the second on the strange Zones of his catastrophe novels, summary becomes a little easier. Chapter three devotes all its energies to *The Atrocity Exhibition*, Ballard's most 'thetic' text, at times resembling a text-book of contemporary psychopathology in its clinical, repetitive prose. The extremity of its textual violence (which caused it to be initially withdrawn in America, and a 'chapter' to be involved in a successful prosecution for obscenity in England) makes it a profoundly difficult text to discuss—the one book which Ballard's advocates tend to gloss over or ignore. The frames of reference are necessarily widened in following its densely allusive style. This chapter is, so far as I know, the first sustained consideration of Ballard's debt to a century of avant-garde practice, *The Atrocity Exhibition* referring to figures like André Breton, Hans Bellmer and Max Ernst, as well as to deploying the art techniques of Cubism, Surrealism and Pop Art. My overriding argument here is that *The Atrocity Exhibition*, in its compacted paragraphs, conjoins classically Modernist avant-gardism with the paradigmatic 'postmodernist' devices, and that this profoundly troubles recent theories of the avant-garde, which would keep these two moments rigorously separate. *The Atrocity Exhibition*, in this approach, serves as a deconstructive lever, a hinge once more, which problematizes the monolithic divide between Modernism and Postmodernism, categories which have dictated contemporary critical theory in the last decade. More, since it speaks from the heart of 1960s cross-fertilizations of experimental work, it necessitates a re-thinking of the place of that anomalous decade between what is conceived as avant-garde and post-avant-garde moments. Positioned between these, as its radical writing technique is between the iconic (painterly) and the verbal (writerly), it also tests, to the limit, the feminization of the place of the hinge. The figure of Woman as the modulus, the switching centre between levels, between codifications, between high and low, *between men*, occupies the central concern of *The Atrocity Exhibition*, and the violence directed towards the woman in Ballard is an uncomfortable element that has hitherto been entirely suppressed, yet urgently needs to be addressed.

Chapter four attempts to insert a distance between Ballard's obsession with the effects of the globalization of media technologies and the predominant apocalyptic narratives of postmodernism. The temptation to portray Ballard's work as an immanent performance of postmodern nihilism has too often been taken. Whilst this reading finds some textual support, I move the focus from the gleaming chrome, evacuated interiorities and the ceaseless circulation of traffic in *Crash* to the detritus and overlooked spaces of the contemporary landscape. *Concrete Island*, the derelict gantries of Cape Kennedy, as well as the ruination of America itself in *Hello America*, are read as 'outmoded' spaces (in the terms of Surrealism and Walter Benjamin) which fracture the glazed self-identity of the present, allowing uncanny traces from the past and the future to protrude into the foreclosed postmodern. The sense of the uncanny which hovers over the concrete island, abandoned cities and space technologies, the murderous doubles which come to haunt the vacuous personalities of figures like Pangborn in 'Motel Architecture', is perhaps my most explicit treatment of the thematic of unease that emerges from Ballard's strange urban spaces.

The last chapter circles back to consider the enigma, the core of unreadability, that disturbs definitional frames and propels the interminable work of critical analysis. The cycle of obsessive repetition which generates novel after novel, story after story, allows at least an organization of the oeuvre and a structural design to be discerned. What was gifted by *Empire of the Sun* and *The Kindness of Women*, it seemed, was an autobiographical key which rendered the origins of a compulsive body of texts transparent. Better, for those critics at a loss to explain their fascination with Ballard, they suggested a non-science fictional impetus which could explain the apparently intolerable conjunction of a 'serious' novelist inside a 'popular' genre. Generic productions could be translated into aberrant responses to an unresolved trauma of a childhood spent as a prisoner of war. As autobiographical novels, however, teasingly wavering between creative fiction and apparent psychological truth, *Empire* and *Kindness* hover on the edge of the fictional oeuvre, at once inside and outside, always hinting at, then refusing, the claim that they might finally decode the series. The attempt to place final, determinable meaning in a space outside the texts, in the signature of the authorial body, is as frustrated and frustrating as the attempt to pin down the internal textual signature, the idiomatic specificity of Ballard's work. This is shown in a reading of the maddening *Vermilion Sands*.

Does *The Angle Between Two Walls* have a happy ending? In some ways it does not: it seeks to provide a wide number of theoretical approaches, all unified by the enigma of the space between, but ends with the suggestion that *Vermilion Sands* remains, in some crucial way, 'unreadable'. The oeuvre will not give up its irreducible core, the remainder that escapes analysis, and which locks some into obsessive re-reading and others into exasperation and hostility. If it is obvious by now that I belong to the former of these groups, my aim is nevertheless to provide illumination for all of Ballard's puzzled readers by a process of ceaselessly traversing the space of his novels, in tracking their catastrophic journeys. I have not attempted to provide a complete, exhaustive reading of Ballard's fictions. Whether these five *passings* over the fiction of J. G. Ballard have been useful in delineating the nature of his work can only be adjudged, inevitably, by the assenting or dissenting passages that follow.

CHAPTER ONE
J. G. Ballard and
the Catastrophe of Genre

At the end of Iain Sinclair's novel, *Radon Daughters*, the central characters escape pursuit by slipping aboard a ship on the Thames. This is not the end of their weird, hallucinatory adventures, however. This is a Ship of Fools because it hosts a science fiction convention:

> The decks were awash with determinedly local aliens, anoraks concealing mutant flesh—primitive gills, supernumerary mouths ridged in plasticine. The anoraks themselves were a sort of skin . . . Freakishness was the norm. A normalcy of Asps with carrier-bags on otherwise deserted platforms, returning alone from allnight monster-flick retrospectives. The normalcy of those who grow up nervous, feeding upon their own bodily excretions. (414)

Sinclair's savage, baroque portrait economically draws on the stereotype of the science fiction fan ('Fans? Too mild a word. Rabids.' [415]): dysfunctional, desperately affected, retarded male adolescents.

Ordinarily a critic might dismiss the peculiarities of 'fandom' as epiphenomenal to the task of textual analysis. With popular genre fiction fandom becomes, if not integral, then vital to discussion. Samuel Delany may write that 'science fiction writers have a specific sense of an involved and committed audience' (527), but this positive sense of community is rarely echoed by writers or critics who claim that the popular may, in fact, be 'serious'. Colin Greenland, for instance, laments that the New Wave of the 1960s failed in its attempts to make science fiction a literate and literary genre, and blames 'the tastes of readers [who are] not in the least concerned with serious literary intentions and literary movements' (204). Such attitudes can become hyperbolized, as in the explicit thematization of the fan in Stephen King's *Misery*, who literally imprisons and tortures the writer for deigning to abandon the popular to write 'serious' fiction.

I begin with the fan, because in coming to write about science fiction and J. G. Ballard, a negotiation with embarrassment has to be undertaken. Even at a moment of institutional interrogation of canonical formations and the excavation of literary value, the perception of science fiction remains almost exclusively tied to the stereotype of the fan. To write on science fiction as a cultural critic involves marking a distance, inserting a boundary, between criticism and fandom, and between serious science fiction and the rest of the genre's frivolous or nerdish pleasures. The science fiction text or texts to be discussed are chosen and isolated with the violent inscription of a demarcating line: Fred Pfeil, for instance, marks out the emergence of 'unprecedentedly literary sf' in the 1960s from a genre previously concerned with 'prepubescent techno-twit satisfactions . . . for sexually terrified twelve and thirteen year-old boys' (84). The virulence of this statement merely spells out the anxious proclamation: *I am not that*. Much of the critical work on science fiction contains such surface disturbances, the 'noise' of an anxiety that concerns itself precisely with *legitimation*.

Despite an alleged shift from a singular, vertical hierarchy of cultural value to a horizontal and dispersed set of plural evaluations, it remains the task of 'tastemaking' intellectuals, suggests Andrew Ross, to 'define what is popular and what is legitimate, who patrol the ever-shifting borders of popular and legitimate taste, who supervise the passports, the temporary visas, the cultural identities, the threatening "alien" elements and the deportation orders, and who occasionally make their own adventurist forays across the border' (*No Respect*, 5). Ross's *No Respect* indicates the apparent mutual exclusion of the popular and the legitimate, the need to transpose popular culture into terms that might justify its study. Certain popular genres have codified protocols of legitimation (detective fiction or the horror film spring to mind); science fiction, it seems, still awaits a cohesive formulation, and as such criticism remains 'contaminated' by the image of the uncritical, adulatory fan.

A catastrophe thus appears to await those wishing to claim for Ballard the status of a 'major' writer: the catastrophe of the glutinous adherence of his name to the 'popular', the generic: science fiction. To praise Ballard's name always seems to involve an intensification of the anxiety of legitimation, by strategies that distinctly echo Ross's image of border policing.

But this structure of inside and outside, legitimate and illegitimate may seem an overly simplified dichotomy: science fiction courses, after all, proliferate (especially in America), and the genre has recently

THE CATASTROPHE OF GENRE 3

become central to theorists of postmodernism, in a variety of guises. And yet critical discourse on science fiction is peculiarly enframed, hedged around by borders. Where Pfeil's violent demarcation will quickly become paradigmatic for the critic approaching science fiction from 'outside' its field, marking off a legitimate site, science fiction itself operates its own founding dichotomy. Its topography has been long established. There is, on the one hand, the 'mainstream', that outside of science fiction where the literary/institutional determinations of the category of acceptable taste and the constitution of canons are instituted. On the other lies science fiction, figured at times as a 'ghetto', a site of containment, and often repudiation. Between is a line that determines inclusion and exclusion, a border that is also a screen for fantasmatic projections of the 'other'. Science fiction writers and critics can be just as savage about the 'mainstream' as Sinclair is in his provocative image of the fan.

Multiple and overdetermined borders, then: to write on science fiction is to negotiate a chain of linked binaries—serious/popular, academic/popular, legitimate/illegitimate, mainstream/science fiction. Rather than efface these mechanisms of judgment, I must begin, even before reading Ballard's work, to analyse their logic.

That 'before', however, is strictly inaccurate. Rather, these border mechanisms are announced in the very process of reading Ballard. Indeed his texts offer a sustained and explicit thematization of borders and the transpositions they effect. If this has not been especially noted, its troubling and uncanny effect is everywhere present in the growing body of commentary on his work. Two examples to begin, of which the first is a minor taxonomic incident. Larry McCaffery's introduction to *Storming the Reality Studio* first presents the name J. G. Ballard amongst Thomas Pynchon, William Burroughs and Don DeLillo as 'major "mainstream" literary innovators' who write 'experimental, quasi-SF works' (2). Eight pages later, Ballard reappears, this time with Alfred Bester as largely ignored writers of 'aesthetically radical SF' (10). Little significance, perhaps, should be given to this categorical slippage; then again, it becomes readable as a symptom of a persistent difficulty. Charles Nicol's analysis of two Ballard stories, 'The Drowned Giant' and 'The Voices of Time' confronts a paradox. The former is a fiction that is 'poetic but not necessarily within the poetry of science fiction', the latter is science fiction '[b]ut I doubt that a mainstream reader can appreciate the subtlety and beauty of such SF works, because his own set of literary values is limited by a tradition that excludes them' (156). 'The author's name manifests the appearance of a certain discursive set', Foucault suggests (107), but here the 'author-function' fails to render the oeuvre homogeneous; instead, adjacent stories apparently demand fundamentally incompatible reading protocols. Ballard, it seems, occupies two mutually exclusive constituencies, science fiction and the mainstream, and the effect of the border between them and of the judgments it distributes becomes a crucial factor in any approach to his work.

This is why an explicit foregrounding of frameworks is a necessary first step: Ballard's work insists on attention to their operations. Frames initiate readings, genres, judgments, legitimations. All too often, and especially in relation to science fiction, such frameworks are effaced. My reasons for attentiveness to them here is asserted by Jacques Derrida: 'I am seeking merely to establish the necessity of this whole problematic of judicial framing and of the jurisdication of frames. This problematic, I feel, has not been explored, at least not adequately, by the institution of literary studies in the university. And there are essential reasons for that: this is an institution built on that very system of framing' ('Living On', 88). There is a need to excavate and expose how legitimizing framings can both exclude and strategically incorporate science fiction, as well as how, in a peculiar effect, the framing of the legitimate induces a kind of melancholic introjection of such judgments even into the writing of those who would vigorously defend science fiction as legitimate in its own right.

Judging Science Fiction

The legitimacy of studying popular cultural forms is inseparable from intellectual history; as intellectual formations shift, so does the perception of the nature and terrain of the popular. Recent histories of post-war intellectual attitudes to the popular (Ross, Brantlinger's, *In Crusoe's Footsteps*) display rapid and ongoing transformations, from the 'massification' condemned by the Frankfurt School to the rise of cultural studies and postmodernism.

How to legitimate a study of an adolescent and exuberantly kinetic genre? How to separate the academic stance of distanced or disinterested judgment from the uncritical immediacy of the fan? Engagements with the popular require operative modalities that can 'secure opportunities for intellectuals to sample the emotional charge of popular culture while guaranteeing their immunity from its power to constitute social identities that are in some way marked as subordinate'

(Ross, *No Respect*, 5). Such modalities, in relation to science fiction, have moved from depth to surface.

By depth, I mean those methods that enact a hermeneutic movement from manifest to latent, that articulates the surface as a symptom of larger and more serious concerns. Science fiction is approached as transparent, revealing beneath its embarrassing surface a latent meaning. With the revelation of this meaning comes value and thus legitimation. Patrick Luciano, for example, insists that beneath the 'ridiculous' surfaces of 1950s science fiction films, a repetitive, archetypal structure is revealed to transform these texts into Jungian quest narratives of the phased ascent to individuation. Significantly, it is his Jungian approach which saves the films' 'meaning and value' and allows them to 'transcend their presumed exploitative absurdity' (viii). He approvingly quotes Jung's statement that 'literary works of highly dubious merit are often of the greatest interest to the psychologist' (110) and insists of science fiction that: 'The genre is not childish but childlike, and accordingly its meaning is sophisticated and complex behind a surface of rather simplistic design' (114). Science fiction is infantile: *in-fans*, literally 'without speech', it cannot speak for itself, it must be spoken (up) for, it is not in control of its own bodily functions. The critic thus serves to 'master' manifest, infantile chaos to uncover latent structures of meaning: as such, it performs a distancing from the generic itself.

This is not to deny that the 1950s B-movie boom has proved a productive site for innumerable depth readings, in the sense that they are obviously 'about' the Cold War, or nuclear anxiety, or imperialism, or depersonalization, or post-war gender realignments, often in over-determined ways. What such readings tend to ignore, however, are the very surfaces of the texts, which are largely dismissed in order to focus on their latency. Susan Sontag's essay 'The Imagination of Disaster' in her *Against Interpretation* is another instance that treats this sub-genre. That the projection of depth rescues the critic from a catastrophic imbrication in the genre is evident here, published as it is in a collection which begins with the famous polemic, 'Against Interpretation', refusing the need of 'defending and justifying art' (5), and ends with the announcement that the distinction 'between "high" and "low" culture seems less and less meaningful' (302), that the division of the valued 'individual signature' of the serious work can no longer be opposed to 'group concoctions made for an undifferentiated audience' (297). In the same year as making that claim, Sontag's essay on science fiction insists both on depth reading to move beneath the 'primitive gratifications' (214) and 'unintentionally funny' (225) surfaces of the films, and that their interest lies precisely in the disjunction between high and low, the 'intersection between a naive and largely debased commercial art product and the most profound dilemmas of the contemporary situation' (224). Fulfilling, as she does, the role of influential 'taste-making' intellectual, marking the emergence of a 'new sensibility' in cultural forms in the 1960s, her treatment of science fiction refuses its entry into the new dispensation for dialogues and border crossings between the serious and the popular. Rather, the essay continues the sense that popular or mass entertainment is somehow closer to the national collective unconscious and its neuroses and can offer a simple guide to the historical epoch of its production. The interest lies there, in a depth that is to be interpreted or given speech by the critic, the text being a symptom incapable of performing its own interpretive work.

The paradigmatic textual hermeneutic is psychoanalysis, and standard science fiction narratives—physical, psychic or global 'alien invasions'—can be transcoded into standardized psychoanalytic explanations. Science fiction is thus 'a peculiarly apt site for the return of culture's repressed . . . under seemingly innocent cover' (Kuhn, 92). Even better, of course, is the generic association with male adolescence, for the crude psychoanalytic critic can focus precisely on the genre's 'represented absence': sex. For Vivian Sobchack, then, either the comically inept heterosexual 'moment' is only present to 'answer the unspoken charges of homosexuality which echo around the edges of the genre' (105), or the predominant absence of sexuality is simply retrieved from its condensed or displaced representations elsewhere. Mastery of depth once more precludes textual surface: 'Most American science fiction films play out scenarios which focus on infantile experience,while pretending to adult concerns' (114).

Sobchack's analysis comes from *Alien Zone*, a collection edited by Annette Kuhn, in which the science fiction film is approached through various theoretical modes. Indeed, the text provides a register of registers for theoretical approaches (and containments) of science fiction, moving from reflectionist Marxist accounts, through ideological and psychoanalytic 'symptomal' readings, and ending with postmodernism. Motivated in part by a concern to extend the film genre theory, Kuhn's opening statement nevertheless announces how the science fiction film will be *used*: 'perhaps more interesting, and probably more important, than what a film genre is is the question of what, in cultural terms, it does—its "cultural instrumentality" ' (1). Seeing through surface pleasures is once more integral to uncovering the efficacity of genre: as Kuhn explains in the introduction to the 'Repressions' section, science fiction's 'cultural instrumentality hinges on a working through . . . of cultural taboos and obsessions which cannot be addressed openly' (92–93).

To insist on a reading which reads *through* texts to a ground that lies beyond their own reach is an act of engagement which is also a token of disengagement, an instrumentalization of the generic which displays an ability to master rather than become embarrassingly entangled. Depth ensures distance. Postmodernism, however, with which Kuhn's collection ends, has been associated with a crisis or even disablement of depth hermeneutics. Paradoxically for a critic earlier associated with a passionate defence of the 'symptomal', the resuscitation of the silent speech and present absences of texts in *The Political Unconscious*, Fredric Jameson's influential account of postmodernism announced the loss of 'critical distance' and approached texts which stubbornly refuse or disable the 'hermeneutic gesture' ('Postmodernism', 60).

It would seem, on first glance, that postmodernist theory may offer an escape from the restricted topography of legitimacy and illegitimacy, of 'inside' and 'outside'. Fredric Jameson has argued that postmodernism has as 'one fundamental feature . . . the effacement of the older (essentially high-modernist) frontier between high culture and so-called mass or commercial culture' ('Postmodernism', 54). He continues:

> The postmodernisms have in fact been fascinated precisely by this whole 'degraded' landscape of schlock and kitsch, of TV series and *Reader's Digest* culture, of advertising and motels, of the late show and the grade-B Hollywood film, of so-called para-literature with its airport paperback categories of the gothic and the romance, the popular biography, the murder mystery and science-fiction or fantasy novel . . . ('Postmodernism', 55).

Jameson is speaking here to some extent in the voice of what he argues is a now superseded theoretical approach to popular culture; the value attached to the degraded mass is precisely what has undergone transformation. In postmodernism there is a de-hierarchization of the binary structures of high/low, serious/popular. Although the appearance of science fiction in Jameson's list is as one element amongst a 'landscape' of cultural forms, Kuhn notes that science fiction 'has been hailed as a privileged cultural site for the enactment of the postmodern condition' (178). There is indeed a repeated return to the science fictional as paradigmatic of postmodernism, and its various appearances in this theoretical field allow a closer analysis of the modes of legitimating the study of science fiction.

Announcing the effacement of the boundary between high and low is a consistent element of definitional postmodernism. For Andreas Huyssen, the boundary was erected by a modernism 'constitut[ing] itself through a conscious strategy of exclusion, an anxiety of its contamination by its other: an increasingly consuming and engulfing mass culture' (vii). Postmodernist texts are said to leap the bounds, and in doing so erase the meaning-effects that such boundaries produce. The 'Great Divide' no longer operates. Fiedler, of course, seminally 'crossed the border', seeing the contemporary novel (in 1970) as converting high art into 'vaudeville and burlesque' (478) in an intrinsically post-Modernist political act. This 'contamination' works both ways: it is not just the movement from above, from the high, into the realm of mass art; mass culture also finds its boundaries exposed and erased, a self-consciousness invading the generic and exploding its confines. This '[i]f anything', says Huyssen 'is the postmodern condition in literature and the arts' (ix). This is placed as observable and empirically verifiable in texts and for Huyssen the critics are lagging behind, still hegemonically insisting on the divide between the high and the mass.

Despite this claim, Huyssen finds it necessary to re-inscribe a border: 'my argument . . . will not deny the quality differences between a successful work of art and cultural trash (Kitsch)' (ix). The necessity of that line is to avoid the 'mindless pluralism of anything goes', even as the reinscription of quality to some extent reinstates the divide. Aware of this problem, Huyssen places its solution in the future tense: further work 'will have to explore this dimension'; right now, 'it is time for the critics to catch on' (ix). Equally, Fiedler's 'Cross the Border' begins with 'the unconfessed scandal of contemporary literary criticism' (461) and demands of it a new language. The central point, that the new novel moves into mass cultural forms as a political act, yet again reinscribes the border at a different line: this move 'can be mitigated without essential loss by parody, irony—and even critical analysis' (465). This is not, or never simply, the acceptance of mass culture.

In definitional postmodernism this borderline or divide is consistently removed only to be reinscribed somewhere else: Linda Hutcheon, for example, insists on the distinction between 'genuine' critical postmodernist architecture, and the kitsch imitations of it in popular forms (*The Politics of Postmodernism*). This is not, then, the announcement of a general erasure, but is an analysis directed, codified and selectively constructed by the cultural critic.

Science fiction appears in this new cultural category in guises that depend on the formulation of what constitutes postmodernism. If taken as an attempt to describe the contemporary moment, increasingly hyperbolic claims attend the genre. The sense that genre study could be spatially marginalized from canonical culture is entirely reversed: where Jameson suggests that genres have 'now spread out and colonized reality itself' (*Postmodernism*, 371), Istvan Csicsery-Ronay Jr specifically proposes that 'SF has ceased to be a genre of fiction per se, becoming instead a mode of awareness about the world' (308). Gaining legitimacy from the evident fascination of key postmodernists like Jameson and Baudrillard with the genre, the implication is that the 'Real', or at least critical apprehension of reality, has become science fictional itself. This presumably lies behind Jameson's passing comment that cyberpunk is 'the supreme literary expression, if not of postmodernism, then of late capitalism itself' (*Postmodernism*, 419). Scott Bukatman, too, in his proclamation of a new, profoundly disorienting ontology, marked by the immersal of subjectivity into transnational electronic networks, produces a conception of postmodernism that reads distinctly like science fiction. Unsurprisingly science fiction texts themselves are the privileged locus for the articulation of this 'terminal identity', although that analysis bleeds into his theoretical approaches, with thinkers like Georges Bataille and Gilles Deleuze and Felix Guattari rather disarmingly described as writers of 'science fiction'.

A highly curtailed and circumscribed section of Ballard's oeuvre appears in Bukatman's account of this new reality, taking its lead, presumably, from Baudrillard's annexing of *Crash* as a paradigmatic text reflecting the science fictionalization of the real. Ballard's name does indeed appear regularly in these hyperbolized accounts, but the functioning of that name is co-terminous with the strategies of a postmodernism more modestly claimed as a new poetic or mode of writing. Given the increasing amount of critical statements situating Ballard as postmodern, it might be tempting to speed to the assertion: J. G. Ballard is (a) postmodernist. Any analysis of such readings, however, witnesses the double movement of de- then re-inscription of the border between high and low, popular and serious. Ballard can only be claimed as postmodernist, in definitional terms, at the expense of violently reinvoking the boundary.

This is visible in Colin Greenland's *The Entropy Exhibition*, although this is a common gesture. For Greenland, the lavish praise of 'main-stream' writers like Graham Greene and Kingsley Amis 'guaranteed [Ballard's] reputation as a novelist emerging from the dubious under-growth of sf' (93). Discussing Ballard alongside Moorcock, Greenland stakes his claim: 'Each is neither wholly in nor out of the broad "field" of sf, or even the vague compass of the "New Wave". They come under that most awkward of provisional labels, "post-modernism" ' (194). However, and here is where the border is re-inscribed, their work still fails to receive 'serious' attention because their names continues to adhere to science fiction, shackled to a readership 'not in the least concerned with serious literary intentions' (204).

The assertion of Ballard as 'postmodernist' has been more rigorously pursued since Greenland, for definitional taxonomies of postmodern-ism have 'discovered' science fiction. In J. A. Sutherland's analysis, the group associated with *New Worlds* in the 1960s is fortunate to be historically co-existent with the emergence of writers—on the other side of the line—'who seem intimately and continuously involved with science fiction, or something analogous. Many of the modes of post-modernist fiction and the so-called "literature of exhaustion" have assimilated aspects of traditional science fiction' (162). Theresa Ebert similarly identifies a convergence: 'The result . . . of the changes in mainstream fiction, on the one hand, and in science fiction on the other—is the blurring of boundaries between these modes of writing which are on the edges of literary experimentation' (94). Her general claim about the blurring of boundaries, however, is negated when it comes to the specific. Samuel Delany's *Dhalgren* moves out of science fiction and appears in the mainstream, or nearly does: 'Delany's narratives in certain sections are *hardly distinguishable* from . . . post-modern innovative fiction' (my emphasis, 95). This near entry is recorded at the expense of shutting the gates behind him: Delany 'transcends the restricting didactic and entertainment functions of mimetic science fiction' (99).

Ebert's essay pinpoints an important and enduring mode of reading science fiction, which might be called *legitimation by transcendence*. The effect is to elevate the specific work out of the generic and into a category where 'conventional' literary values operate without disturb-ance from the popular. Yet in order to do this, it works by reaffirming the rest of science fiction as disreputable and illicit, exactly confirming a division of high and low which the general argument apparently repudiates. Such strategies do nothing to problematize the border between 'high' and 'low'; they take their individual, smuggle him or her through a *cordon sanitaire* and then use the traditional high culture criteria to legitimate the passage.

Brian McHale's discussion of science fiction and postmodernism is equally instructive, not least for the shift between *Postmodernist Fiction* (1987) and *Constructing Postmodernism* (1992). In the first of these, 'Science fiction . . . is to postmodernism what detective fiction was to modernism' (16). Defining postmodernism through a shift of dominant from (modernist) epistemology to (postmodernist) ontology, science fiction is deployed because it is the simplest expression of this shift. Science fiction is postmodernism's ' "noncanonized" or "low art" double, its sister-genre' (59). If the quotation marks around 'low art' signal a warning, he nevertheless comments: 'as a noncanonical, subliterary genre, science fiction has tended to lag behind canonized or mainstream literature in its adoption of new literary modes' (69). Science fiction is re-fitted to conform to the historical trajectory of the emergence of postmodernism, moving through realist (1930s), modernist (1960s) and postmodernist (1970s to the present) phases in accord with Jameson's historical periodizations, yet in a condensed and tardy way.

The border is (re)announced. Science fiction, even within a charitable postmodernism, remains disreputable, except for one name: J. G. Ballard. Ballard leads science fiction out of the 'subliterary' and into the mainstream. *The Atrocity Exhibition*, with its ontological concerns, is a 'postmodernist text based on science fiction topoi' (69). A quantum leap has apparently been made here, from Ballard's early science fiction aspiring to mainstream status, to now mainstream texts exploiting science fiction tropes. In one text, he has suddenly leaped zones, and begins a backward movement toward that same problematic convergence. Given that McHale insists on science fiction and postmodernism's 'parallel development, not mutual influence' (64) Ballard's feat is nothing short of extraordinary.

Constructing Postmodernism emphasizes from its title onwards a new accent on the 'constructedness' of any critical account: McHale now 'tells stories', multiple and often conflicting ones, about the postmodern. Signals of science fiction's re-tooled importance are indicated early on: 'SF, far from being marginal to contemporary "advanced" or "state-of-the-art" writing, may actually be paradigmatic of it' (12). This is in part due to the emergence of cyberpunk, taken as representative of 'aesthetic contemporaneity', presumably equating with the notion of a science fictionalized *Zeitgeist* proposed by Bukatman and others. Cyberpunk marks an accelerating two way exchange between a postmodernist fiction appropriating science fiction tropes, and a science fiction converging with the ontological insecurities of postmodernism. The 'feedback loop' closes, a flicker of difference, deriving from a carefully documented 'nonsynchronization between SF and advanced mainstream fiction' (228), remaining.

The current 'apex' of the importance of science fiction, however, is still propelled by a telos governed by mainstream criteria: the history presented still pushes science fiction through discrete phases from 'ghetto' to a ' "levelling up" of SF's stylistic norms to something approaching those of conservative mainstream fiction' (227) in the 1950s, to its 'high-modernist' phase in the 1960s, finishing with postmodernism in the present. This trajectory echoes Fred Pfeil's essay on science fiction, where the borrowed historical trajectory from emergent postmodernism is again evident. The 'modernist' explosion of the 1960s is necessary purely in order to stage science fiction's response to the 'epochal paradigm shift' of postmodernism. If science fiction finally (at last) becomes modernist, there is the inevitable sense of imposing a teleological and indeed *anthropological* history of popular culture.[1] Science fiction is backward in development but it must pass through this stage, because there is only one narrative of development imposed from the highest stage, retrospectively. This posits a hierarchy of stages in which the shamefaced popular can only belatedly arrive.

McHale's revised version of the place of science fiction still invokes a sense of generic instrumentalization, but he also makes one crucial comment that exposes the limits of an attempt to negotiate the SF/mainstream boundary through a 'poetics' of postmodernism: 'the sufficient conditions for SF's legitimation are to be found not in SF poetics, but in shifts in the literary institution that lie outside the scope of the present essay' (236). *The frame of judgment*, the shadow of its institutional mechanism, appears momentarily, only to be entirely effaced, pushed beyond the horizon. That very horizon, however, still evidently directs and enframes the work produced within it.

Various strategies of legitimation of the popular can thus be discerned: the transparency of simplistic surfaces revealing latent truths; the severing of the particular case, the individual transgression of genre through transcendence; the postmodernist denial and later rephrased inscription of boundaries. The divide itself is either re-affirmed, evaded or re-negotiated; the divide is even necessary given the apparent mutual exclusion of Ross' terms the popular and the legitimate. The former must always be abject before the law of the latter and must always argue its 'case' before the tribunal which determines the limits and conditions of what constitutes the zone of the legitimate. If it appears that this divide is always (ultimately) invoked, it could be argued that this deference of the popular to the legitimate performs, in a technical sense, what Lyotard constitutes as a 'wrong':

> This is what a wrong would be: a damage accompanied by the loss of means to prove that damage . . . to the privation constituted by the damage there is the added impossibility of bringing it to the knowledge of others, and in particular to the knowledge of a tribunal (*The Differend*, 5)

Since science fiction is infantilized, deprived of the right of speech in these external legitimations and forced to justify itself before a tribunal whose laws refuse the testimony of the popular unless it transcribes itself into legitimate criteria, it would seem that a wrong is indeed performed. What would be required, then, would be a shift of focus to the 'inside', to science fiction, and allow it to find its own rules, its own speech, its own legitimacy.

Internal Legitimations

Fredric Jameson's statement 'It would be a mistake to make the apologia for SF in terms of specifically "high" literary value' because 'SF is a sub-genre with a complex and interesting formal history of its own, and with its own dynamic, which is not that of high culture' ('Progress', 149) should stand at the head, here, in its insistence that the generic is not a catastrophe to be effaced, but something that should exactly motivate analysis. However, these internal legitimations frequently display that science fiction 'judges' itself in the name of the very law which wrongs it. Science fiction wrongs, wrongfoots, itself; it goes as far as demanding its own death sentence.

This is not, perhaps, surprising, given the fundamentally asymmetrical power relations between the 'inside' and the 'outside'. In traditional terms the production of the canon is effaced, its legitimacy is perceived as 'self-evident'. Science fiction, however, is anxiously self-aware of its inadequacy before the sole judge of the legitimate. It must perform its legitimation by distorting or denying itself, in terms of the range of judgments that exist before it even presents itself to the tribunal. The border is once more re-affirmed at the expense of its own status.

I can speak of the 'inside' and 'outside' of science fiction since it has self-nominated its marginality as a 'ghetto'. Rather than following the etymology and usual usage of 'ghetto' (an enclosed area where a minority is *required* to live) it is seen, internalizing guilt, as self-imposed segregation, a tragedy of its own misguided history. Science fiction also has a very specific term for the outside: the mainstream. The methods of legitimation invoked are devoted to finding entry (or re-entry) to this mainstream of literature. This mimics, although the polarities are reversed, the border between the popular and legitimate. Science fiction criticism is also peculiar in the sense that it is rarely 'outside' the site of where the texts are produced. Science fiction critics are either the writers themselves (splitting personalities, say, like James Blish's critical persona, William Atheling), 'fans', or academics who have a singular relationship to the 'ghetto'. Science fiction is, more so than most popular genres, a community, if a disunited one. Writers are 'protected' by a phalanx of fans and the zone is policed as well as 'promoted' in alien territory by its spokespersons. Its strong anti-intellectual vein (not in its contents, but as it 'presents' itself) is simultaneously aggressive in self-promotion, but defensive and symptomatic of deference. Nevertheless those venturing from the 'outside' who reveal the slightest fallibility (a misplaced date, ignorance of certain 'central' texts &c.) are rebuked and abusively accompanied to the border where they are ejected. A badge of membership, of the right to speak, must be worn. When Kingsley Amis states at the opening of *New Maps of Hell* 'I am not that peculiarly irritating kind of person, the intellectual who takes a slumming holiday in order to "place" some "phenomenon" of "popular culture" ' (10), he marks his distance by narrating a kind of primal scene. Amis speaks of his seduction by the garish covers of an American science fiction pulp magazine when he was twelve years old. From this, science fiction is asserted as an 'addiction', 'mostly contracted in adolescence or not at all' (16). The desire for science fiction is initiated by (predominantly male) adolescence. It is, for Delany, 'a language learned early, by repeated exposure' (525). Such a scene is constantly repeated; it dramatizes the 'graduation', so to speak, of certain writers and critics from a teenage thrall. This compulsive reiteration of the primal scene of discovery is certainly a form of legitimation but it might also be said, perhaps too crudely, to be one of the key sources for legitimation. There seems to be an immense personal investment to justify and legalize what is taken to be some faintly illicit activity, a kind of arrested male adolescence, a childish foible, in an otherwise outwardly respectable demeanour.

This is evident in the defensiveness of Robert Conquest who insists on a kind of purity in this adolescent addiction, since aesthetic 'choice' can be ultimately reduced to the 'essentially primitive, basic nature of our views and tastes of literature' (94). The consonance of (the desire for) science fiction in adolescence and the perception of the popular as 'arrested adolescence' should be remarked as one of the sources of science fiction's anxiety.

Science fiction legitimates itself before the tribunal in three ways. Firstly, through the implementation of internal borders. Secondly, through a certain narrative of its (in/glorious) history, and finally through an appeal to the rigour of the scientific. The first two apply for citizenship within legitimate literature, whilst the last asserts a specialism, a specificity that either opposes the legitimate or else claims grounds of diminished responsibility. It should be said that these categories overlap in complex ways, and that the following delineation is somewhat artificial.

Science fiction critics often want to make grand claims for the genre. For Scholes and Rabkin, it 'create[s] a modern conscience for the human race' (vii); it fits, indeed supersedes, the great humanistic claims for literature as a whole. At the same time, however, and on the same page, they are equally aware that science fiction is constituted of 'trivial, ephemeral works of "popular" fiction which is barely literate, let alone literary'. Most of their subsequent work (and for much of science fiction criticism as a whole) is dedicated to affirming these two contradictory statements, by separating them out, divorcing them from each other as distinct and 'pure' sites within science fiction. An internal border is constituted whereby, on the one hand, the 'grand claim' is asserted and so entry to Literature can be gained, whilst on the other, science fiction can, in alliance with the categories of the legitimate, be condemned.

Scholes and Rabkin justify their own critical text on the basis that science fiction has ceased to be solely popular now that 'a sufficient number of works of genuine merit' have been written from within it (vii). The logic of legitimation through the implementation of internal borders can be stated thus: science fiction is a popular genre which yet contains within it a movement of profundity; in order to secure that 'serious' element, a mark, a line of division must be approved, by which the gutter of the popular is transcended. If, as Darko Suvin insists, 'The genre has to be evaluated proceeding from the heights down, applying the standards gained by the analysis of its masterpieces' ('Poetics', 71), and yet these very heights transcend the genre itself, such texts could be said to no longer belong to science fiction, because they have been elevated above their origin. Science-fiction-which-is-not is the apotheosis and judge of science fiction. This mimics precisely strategies found on the outside in, for example, Ebert's transcendent Delany.

This border can be imposed at key, significant sites. It can be superimposed on existing national borders: there is the great tradition in Europe of 'serious' science fiction in the names of Huxley and Orwell against the trashy popular entertainments of America. This national border is imposed by Brian Aldiss, whose chapter on the 1930s in *Billion Year Spree* fiction remarkably dismisses American science fiction *tout court* as 'tawdry . . . [and] illiterate' (209) to concentrate on the 'serious' Europeans. It is also imposed by Scholes and Rabkin whose Europe is 'emotionally powerful, intellectually demanding, and socially aware' and whose America is variously termed 'semi-educated', 'juvenile', 'overstated, self-approving and quite uncritical' (26, 35, 40, 51). Christopher Priest also consistently contrasts the European (British) 'individual voice' and the threat of its assimilation by the 'mass' culture of America ('British Science Fiction'). What is unusual to science fiction, however, is the very suppression of, in some senses, science fiction's country of 'origin', or certainly the site of its naming, which is of fundamental importance to the construction of a self-conscious genre. Huxley or Orwell can only be understood as science fiction given a detour through the site of the construction of its conventions, its limits, and mode of enunciation, i.e. America. That detour, however, would reveal how tenuous the claims on Huxley or Orwell as 'science fiction' would be.

The implementation of the internal border is usually enforced at the site of the definition. The science fiction 'community' of critics and writers is disunited on the basis of where 'real' or 'core' science fiction lies. This strategy involves isolating a central definition through which all other cases can be rejected or shifted to the edges as impure. These marginalia are, none too surprisingly, identical with precisely the elements that might mark the genre as popular; their displacement decontaminates it of the pulp and the illegitimate, leaving the 'core' works as the ground on which 'serious' claims are made.

Darko Suvin is the exemplar of this strategy. Science fiction is defined as the literature of cognitive estrangement, the elaboration of a radically discontinuous world from the 'author's empirical environment', which yet returns to confront that environment to foreground the artificiality of its 'natural' norms 'with a point of view or glance implying a new set of norms' ('Poetics', 60). This cognitive utility of science fiction is based on the rigour of applying scientific laws; such worlds must be *possible*. Suvin presents a definition that appeals to the specificity of 'hard' (scientifically rigorous) science fiction, a 'core' which is also asserted by Scholes in *Structural Fabulation*. The law of science, however, superimposes on the law of genre; this strict definition is the basis for a wholesale deportation of categories which surround, indeed interpenetrate inextricably, science fiction. For Suvin fantasy may estrange, but not in a cognitive way (it is the suspension of scientific laws). Thus 'SF retrogressing into fairy tale . . . is committing creative suicide' ('Poetics', 62); fantasy is intrinsically anti-cognitive, 'a sub-literature of mystification' ('Poetics', 63). What is truly astonishing in Suvin's system is the dismissal of virtually all, if not all, science fiction in itself. His essay 'Narrative Logic, Ideological Domination and the Range of SF: A Hypothesis' draws a fan-shaped diagram, in which the bottom point, the convergence of the range, is marked as the 'optimum' science fiction text. Above it, within the fan, are borderlines marking the 'good' and 'most' science fiction. This 'most' is dismissed as 'debilitating confectionary' and, he asserts, 'there is only one ideal optimum' (*Positions*, 70). This implies that there is only one way to write a text that could 'fit' Suvin's definition, and since this is 'ideal' it would suggest that even the optimum has not yet attained the science fictional. Those falling short of this ideal are discussed under the titles 'banal', 'incoherent', 'dogmatic' and 'invalidated': 'all uses of SF as prophesy, futurology, program or anything else claiming ontological factuality for the SF image-clusters, are obscurantist and reactionary at the deepest level' (*Positions*, 71).

Suvin's final and deathly proscriptions result from the desperate desire to speak in the name of the legitimate. Suvin's critical logic prescribes the first death of science fiction; the borderline of legitimacy constricts so far as to annihilate it. The optimum that is 'saved' has very little to do with science fiction and is more directed at external utility.

Suvin, at one point, insists on the *intrinsically* subversive nature of the 'popular', which might suggest that he would have to embrace precisely the pulp elements of the genre he is trying to expel. His answer, however, is that science fiction was only subversive before 1910. After that date, it was appropriated by bourgeois ideology (*Positions*, 10). This bizarre marking of a date as an absolute border introduces narratives of science fiction's history, the second mode of internal legitimation.

The history, in these terms, serves two functions: that of embedding science fiction in the mainstream (the historical erasure of the boundary), and of, once again, serving to eliminate the illicit site of the naming of science fiction (America). This narrative, which has a certain hegemony, can be summarized in the following way: once there was an

Edenic time when science fiction swam with the mainstream and was inseparable from it; then came the Americans who walled it up and issued a proclamation of martial law. This is the self-imposition of the ghetto, the 'forty years' (rather than days) in the wilderness as Judith Merril sees it (54). This narrative ends prophetically: there will come a time when the walls will be demolished, when science fiction will rejoin the mainstream and cease its disreputable existence. The signs are already apparent: the New Wave is to be welcomed, by certain elements, as the death of generic science fiction. This desire, on the inside, meets that of postmodernism on the outside.

Historical legitimations can in fact begin in prehistory; science fiction is merely a modernized version of the 'innately' human need for 'mythology' by which to orientate experience. The near *biological* need for science fiction is asserted by Scholes, who argues that the desire for narrative, once satisfied by myth, can now only be provided by popular forms, given the decadence and abandonment of narrative by the mainstream. This explains why normally respectable readers 'resort secretly and guiltily to lesser forms for that narrative fix they cannot do without' ('The Roots of Science Fiction', 53). This is the most extreme form of trying to dethrone the mainstream by reversing the polarity. The more properly historical mode, however, attempts to *embed and entwine* science fiction into the mainstream. Legitimation comes from appropriating, say, Swift, Thomas More, Lucian, even the Bible, in I. O. Evans' view, as science fictional forms; history saves the illegitimate child by attempting to uncover 'true' parentage. What is strange about this is that science fiction does not have its origins established. Rather, what is offered is a fantasy of non-origin. Science fiction doesn't 'begin' anywhere as such and the disreputable generic can be displaced to become a bit-part in a larger historical unfolding.

The suppression involved is that of a name: that of Hugo Gernsback. I am not suggesting that the origin of science fiction lies with Gernsback, but his originating of the site and the name of generic science fiction, in publishing *Amazing* from 1926, is crucial. Gernsback is ritually vilified: for Aldiss, Gernsback was 'one of the worst disasters ever to hit the science fiction field' (*Billion Year Spree*, 63); for Blish, he is solely responsible for its ghettoization (118); for Clareson, he initiated the abandonment of literature 'to propagandize for technology' (20); for Merril, the forty years in the wilderness begins in 1926. What follows is a movement either backwards to predate a baleful influence, or forward to celebrate his supersession. The attempt at erasure, however, cannot ignore Gernsback's initial elaboration of the conditions on which the genre has to be defined. His editorial policy was 'to publish only such stories that have their basis in scientific laws as we know them, or the logical deduction of new laws from what we know' (cited Ross, 'Getting out of the Gernsback Continuum', 419). This installed the modes of scientific rigour and extrapolation. His insistence that such fictions 'are always instructive. They supply knowledge . . . in a very palatable form' (cited Nicholls, *The Encyclopaedia of Science Fiction*, 159) developed legitimation through the educative role and Gernsback also initiated the 'grand claim' for its significance: 'Posterity will point to them [the science fiction story] as having blazed a new trail, not only in literature and fiction, but progress as well' (cited Ross, 'Getting out of the Gernsback Continuum', 415). Further, *Amazing* was instrumental in constructing a community through reader participation. Whether or not this sodality is seen as negative, science fiction as a genre can only be understood with reference to where its conventions and limits were inscribed: the American pulp magazines.

It might seem to be the most naive science fiction historiography to mark Gernsback as the initiator: naming, however, is different from origin. Gernsback did not appear *sui generis*. There are more cogently argued 'histories' of (properly) proto-science fiction. Aldiss has set something of a minimal source limit by nominating Mary Shelley's *Frankenstein*: the plot is initiated by extrapolated scientific possibilities; its text concerns the limits of scientific ethics and humanism. This choice is symptomatic, however, of the impure origins of science fiction, for almost every subsequent critic who has referred to this source has had to distinguish it from the horror genre. The notion that science fiction and horror could intermix is not countenanced.

The constitution of the site of the specific science fiction magazine in the 1920s was a product of some forty years of socio-cultural re-alignments around the 'literary'. H. G. Wells has been cited as both the progenitor of generic science fiction and the last instance of a 'SF' text being accepted into an undifferentiated field of Literature before the ghettoization effected by Gernsback. This is inaccurate: the latter decades of the 19th century were the crucial phase of the development of the categories of the 'high' and 'low' as they now operate institutionally. This is an incredibly complex moment in the construction of cultural value in, as Peter Keating observes, a publishing field that had explosively expanded into a bewildering diversity. The 'popular' or 'low' was not simply the demonized Other, the defining negative, of an emergent Modernism; moral panics over the links between penny dreadfuls and working class criminality had developed in the 1870s (see Bristow). If Thomas Wright had divided the high from the low in 1881, and 20 years later *The Times Literary Supplement* was set up to distinguish the 'better authors' from the 'rubbish heap of incompetence' (cited Keating, 76), it should not be forgotten that there was an equally belligerent assertion of the moral superiority of the re-vivified 'Romance'. Largely in the pages of *The Contemporary Review*, Andrew Lang, Rider Haggard and others, attacked the effete etiolation of the modern 'serious' novel and argued for the 'muscular romance'. Against the diseased interiority of the 'analytic novel', the romance 'deliberately reverted to the simpler instead of more complicated kind of novel', and, in an inversion that prefigures Scholes's attempt to displace the mainstream, Saintsbury also argued that 'romance is of its nature eternal and preliminary to the novel. The novel is of its nature transitory and parasitic on the romance' (415–16). Literary histories tend to emphasize this late Victorian phase as the construction of the Modernist 'art-work' in opposition to the now degraded 'low' (the thesis, as earlier seen, of Andreas Huyssen's *After the Great Divide*). But it was also, just as significantly, the moment in which the sites (increasingly low priced, increasingly specialized magazines), terminology, and the very forms and genres of the modern concept of popular literature were founded.

Two things require clarification about this in relation to science fiction. Firstly, it cannot be said that texts could be nominated as 'science fiction' within an undifferentiated 'mainstream'; the very spaces in which stories found publication were products of a rapidly fragmenting concept of fiction, quickly becoming figured in terms of 'high' and 'low'. Wells' anxiety to depart from being identified solely with the 'scientific romance' and his later deference to Henry James mark his awareness of the emerging equation between the popular and the degenerate. Secondly, the very use of the term science fiction for texts like Wells' is already a retrospective extraction of texts out of a mass of romances. Cross-fertilizations between juvenile adventure stories, imperialist narratives, Gothic revivalism, and the supernatural, as well as pseudo-scientific adventures deriving either from simple technological advance or sociological inflections of Darwin have been traced by Patrick Brantlinger and Judith Wilt. A text like *Jekyll and Hyde* could be said to be premised on a scientific 'novum', but it is equally overdetermined by Gothic, melodramatic and imperialist elements; this is no less the case for Wells. Even if this was the moment in which modern popular genres gradually emerged (in the sense of specialist sites, formulated conventions, formulated plots, and reader coteries), science fiction was a relatively late development in relation to the detective genre, the spy novel, or even the Western. As Andrew Ross has argued in his essay on Gernsback, even the pulp term 'science fiction' had to fight for predominance amongst other pulp magazines publishing what were variously termed as pseudo-scientific stories, weird science, off-trail, fantascience fiction. *Weird Tales*, the magazine that published the fantasy and horror of H. P. Lovecraft, appeared in 1923. Many pulp houses also published detective fiction alongside science fiction, sometimes with the same editor, Anthony Boucher being one example. What has to be stated is the *fundamental impurity*, the multiple origins that eventually arrived at the hegemonic notion of science fiction.

This uncomfortable impure origin does nothing, however, to calm the anxieties for legitimation, nor can it, since the demands for legitimacy appeal to an external authority. The fantasy of non-origin persists, and it meets its complement in the future with the fantasy of non-being. Explicit proposals, even demands, for the death of science fiction, from within science fiction, are commonplace. This is the ecstatic promise of transubstantiation back into the mainstream where the fantasy of non-origin had situated it before the interregnum of the generic. The most enthusiastic of these statements come from the proponents of the New Wave. Histories speak of the increasing 'sophis-tication' of the interregnum. The explosion of the New Wave is the detonation of science fiction itself. Aldiss senses a 'rapproachement' [sic] with the mainstream, the return 'from the ghetto of Retarded Boyhood' and asserts 'Science fiction per se does not exist' (*Billion Year Spree*, 257, 306, 307). Scholes and Rabkin end their history with the problematic 'place' of Ballard and Vonnegut: 'A writer like Vonnegut forces us to consider the impending disappearance of the category upon which a book like this depends . . . science fiction will not exist' (98–99). Judith Merril seeks legitimation for a 'valid' literature of science fiction, but, in deference to the border, realizes 'that as it achieves that validity, it ceases to be "science fiction" and becomes simply con-temporary literature instead' (54). Finally, the introductions to Harlan Ellison's *Dangerous Visions* evokes two deaths: that of the Golden Age being superseded by science itself, and that of the New Wave, which 'has been found, has been turned good by the mainstream, and is now in the process of being assimilated . . . Science Fiction is dead' (xxii).

It seems initially bizarre that a genre so concerned in the 1950s and 1960s with global disaster, invasion and supersession by alien forces should seem to will mass generic death. This fantasy of non-being, however, accords with the erasure of the border between the legitimate and the popular. It now becomes evident why certain science fiction critics have embraced postmodernism's apparently borderless field—it ends the wilderness years 'outside' the literary.

Death also haunts the third mode of legitimation, that attempted through scientific rigour. This mode is attached to the 'core' of the genre. What is specific about this mode, however, is its adversarial relation to the legitimate. Since it claims to be at the 'cutting edge' of science, it is dismissive of the mainstream. Robert Heinlein's definition of science fiction as 'realistic speculation about possible future events, based solidly on adequate knowledge of the real world, past and present, and on a thorough understanding of the nature and significance of the scientific method', allows him 'rigorous' future projection, one prediction of which is the disappearance of 'the cult of the phony in art . . . So-called "modern art" will be discussed only by psychiatrists' ('Introduction', 22, 17). Contemporary literature is 'sick', written by 'neurotics . . . sex maniacs . . . the degraded, the psychotic' ('Science Fiction', 42). This adversarial disrespect is nevertheless a defensively aggressive response to illegitimacy. Surprisingly, especially for someone like Parrinder, who declares him anti-scientific, J. G. Ballard can be found to make similar statements on science fiction's centrality. In his 'manifesto', 'Which Way to Inner Space?' Ballard declared: 'only science fiction is fully equipped to become the literature of tomorrow, and . . . is the only medium with an adequate vocabulary of ideas and situations' (118). Seven years later, Ballard will still be declaring 'far from being an unimportant minor off-shoot, science fiction in fact represents the main literary tradition of the 20th century' ('Salvador Dali', 27). This combines with the view that the mainstream 'social novel' has become entirely exhausted. Already this should begin to mark Ballard off from the usual perception of the 'New Wave'; at his most extreme, he declared: 'Fiction is a branch of neurology' ('Notes from Nowhere', 149)—a kind of re-statement of the scientific. Ballard, however, makes an absolutely crucial point in interview: 'The science one's writing about is the science that comes out of the TV tube, the mass magazines, the labels on oral contraceptive wallets, whatever . . . [T]he novelist . . . doesn't have to know the blood pressure of the young woman who's getting excited by her lover' (Barber, 'Sci-Fi Seer', 28). This is made clearer when he insists 'most of the confusions about the position of science fiction in the literary frame of things would be avoided if it were called by a more accurate title—"Popular science fiction" ' (Barber, 'Sci-Fi Seer', 28). Ballard accedes to the crucial point that this is *popular(ized) science* fiction.

The legitimation by science continually fails to meet its own allegedly rigorous demands. If Heinlein places a border between science fiction and fantasy by declaring that fantasy is 'any story based on violation of a scientific fact, such as space ship stories which ignore ballistics' ('Science Fiction', 19), his point that time travel stories are legitimate because 'we know almost nothing about the nature of time' is exceedingly weak. The depressing litany of rejections and exclusions of certain texts because their science 'doesn't work' insists on a purity that, by the very standards of the science it invokes to judge, fails. What has to be insisted on is the *mediation* of science, reflections on its imaginative potentialities, without the hierarchical gradation from plausible to implausible.

The 'history' of science fiction is marked, not by science at the 'cutting edge', but by mediations and meditations on the scientific. Any analyst of H. G. Wells' scientific romances has to admit that the 'scientific' mechanism of the time machine, for example, is merely a fictional device, surrounded by impressionistic technical details. What is significant is the fictional meditation on the implications of Darwinism wedded to contemporaneous political concerns. The editorial policies of Gernsback or Campbell claimed the 'cutting edge', installing scientific advisors to vet and legitimate its fiction, but its adherence to a positivistic, technological science was scientifically anachronistic even if politically current; Andrew Ross has analysed its belief in the inherent link of technology to progress in relation to futurism and other contemporary movements. In the 1920s and 1930s science fiction was not 'up to date' with developments in quantum mechanics—with the work of Einstein or Heisenberg—except insofar as 'relativity' and 'uncertainty' could be translated into time travel, parallel universes or faster-than-light speeds. Science fiction remained within positivism and adopted 'a populist principle that science could be explained and understood by everyone, and that its name would not be associated with exclusive rhetorical idioms or with obfuscatory accounts of the object world by overcredited experts' (Ross, 'Gernsback Continuum', 420). It thus adopted the political belief that the (social) engineer could end socio-political crises.

There is a brief hiatus in the late 1930s and early 1940s, where science fiction and the scientific community did enter into a complex interrelationship, specifically around the atom bomb projects. Heinlein was a naval engineer involved in military research; he disclaims any prophetic edge to his work, because he was in contact with the scientists themselves, and thus knew in advance the direction of research. The apotheosis of this mode of legitimation came with Cleve Cartmill's story in *Astounding*, 'Deadline'. The descriptions of the nuclear bomb were so close to the Manhattan project that the FBI raided *Astounding*'s offices. The frequent appearance of this anecdote indicates its utility for claiming the scientific accuracy and importance of science fiction. This may be so, but it also marks a death. Cartmill's fiction was overtaken within a year, it survives only as an anecdote, not as a read text. There is a sense, in the insistence on scientific rigour, that science fiction is fighting a shelf-life. L. Sprague de Camp states: 'one danger threatening science fiction is that the progress of science itself answers so many questions raised by science fiction, thereby removing one idea after another' (128–29). Accuracy itself contains the threat of death; to be too accurate is to risk erasure.

In its extremity the scientific legitimation aims to sidestep the claims of the mainstream on the ownership of the 'proper' text: 'Even if every work were on the lowest literary level . . . the form would still retain much of its significance—for that significance . . . lies more in its attitudes [the scientific method], in its intention, than in the perfection of its detail' (Bretnor, 287). And yet this strategy may destroy the very playfulness with scientific and technological notions in which science fiction engages. In Lyotard's terms the scientific statement is a denotative, an assertion with a truth-claim on a real referent. Its conditions of acceptance are that it must be open to repetition by others, and that the language of the statement is judged relevant and acceptable to 'scientific' discourse by the consensual community (the tribunal) of experts. A 'good', winning move in the game is the fulfilment of these conditions, the establishment, in terms of the law of the institutional frame, of proof. Science is, on first glance, a 'pure' game in that the conditions of proof can only be established through denotatives. If the legitimation of science fiction emphasizes science, such denotative proofs are invoked. As fiction, however, this claim is problematic; invoking the 'agonistics' of language games, Lyotard says: 'This does not necessarily mean that one plays in order to win. A move can be made for the sheer pleasure of its invention: what else is involved in that labour of language harassment undertaken by popular speech and by literature?' (*The Postmodern Condition*, 10). Literature 'mixes' pure games, and so must inevitably transgress, when placed in the scientific legitimation, denotative proof.

Perhaps too much aggression attends this presentation of the three modes for legitimating science fiction. However, the concern is with strategies that, for a popular genre, insistently work to negate the fact of genre. Whilst the isolated masterpiece escapes its constraints, generic definitions and historical narratives of its emergence are equally driven by the need to efface or displace the catastrophe of the popular. The issue of genre, bizarrely, is precisely that which is not addressed, or at least not without distortion. And to define the genre by an appeal to scientific rigour in fact results in its annihilation as literature. Internal strategies thus mirror the more overt anxieties of external legitimations. Again, this may emphasize the asymmetrical power between the popular and the legitimate; it may also reflect the relative poverty of available theorizations of the reading of genre work.

Reading Genre

Tzvetan Todorov suggests that a suspicion of genre emerged with the Romantics, such that critics 'write either about literature in general or about a single work, and it is a tacit convention that to classify several works in a genre is to devalue them' ('Typology', 158). Equally, the understanding of genre as constituting a static, prescriptive (or proscriptive) set of rules can only induce frustration about empirical aberrations or an irresolvable hermeneutic circle as to the priority of rule or text, text or rule.

Todorov's re-vitalization of genre theory, however, indicates perfectly the problems of generating accounts of the specificity of popular genre. Although structuralist, Todorov's account is aware of the dangers of static taxonomies; indeed, generic structure serves exactly to be transgressed. As he states in *The Fantastic* a text is granted entry into Literature 'only insofar as it produces a change in our previous notion' of literary conventions (6). That which serves to ground this transgressive value is popular literature:

> As a rule, the literary masterpiece does not enter into any genre, save perhaps its own; but the masterpiece of popular literature is precisely the book which best fits its genre . . . If we had properly described the genres of popular literature, there would no longer be an occasion to speak of its masterpieces. They are one and the same thing; the best novel will be the one about which there is nothing to say ('Typology', 159).

That this formulation can only produce an ahistorical generic model of exact repetition is evident. Static taxonomies will always remain problematic; genre as *process*, embodied not in texts but in reading protocols, seems more promising, and this is where the most interesting work is being done. And yet, deriving as it does from reader response theories, a similar encoding of the popular text as the impoverished object against which to measure Literature is again a consistent move. For Wolfgang Iser, a phenomenology of reading constructs a 'virtual' text in the negotiated space between the physical book and the unfolding experience of actualizing the book through the temporality of reading. Each sentence propels the readerly projection of expectations and pre-intentions about potential textual trajectories. This fluid and dynamic process is yet bounded by what Jauss terms a 'horizon of expectation' against which texts exist in tension. This is a useful model for the reading of genre. However, 'high' literary value is immediately attached to texts which consistently refuse and transform readerly pre-intentions: any *confirmative* effect is marked as a 'defect in a literary text' (214). Once again, a conception of the generic text as an exact repetition of its horizon is confirmed: these are texts which aim at 'deliberately excluding anything that might disturb the illusion once established, and these are texts that we generally do not classify as literary. Women's magazines and the brasher forms of detective story might be cited as examples' (219).

There does not seem much evidence of connecting to the experience of reading popular genre—it would seem, for instance, that the furious activity of projection, transformation and frustration of expectation perfectly embodies the reading of detective fiction, which gains its very dynamism from this process. However, the argument is not to legitimate the popular by erasing or moving the boundary; reading protocols *are* distinct between 'popular' and 'legitimate' fictions. The question rather concerns how a reader response theory, allegedly working to uncover the presuppositions which conceal the experience of reading yet works within unexamined institutional markers which map onto the very terms 'high' and 'low'.

The issue of this ingrained evaluation can, perhaps, be simply sidestepped: if, as Steve Neale suggests, genres are 'specific systems of expectation and hypothesis', which means that they 'always exist *in excess* of a corpus of works' (46, 51), this can open into an analysis of popular genre which avoids the pitfalls of structural fixity or evaluative condemnation. Certainly the most positive work on science fiction takes this direction. Samuel Delany's criticism, for instance, has been clearly influenced by the work of reader-response: like Stanley Fish, his technique is to read a 'science fictional' sentence for the generation of its expectations and pre-intentions, particularly as it departs from a 'realist' orientation. It is precisely generic context that renders meaningful a phrase like 'The door dilated' or extends the connotative range of 'Her world exploded'. In that sense Delany terms science fiction a 'sub-language of the greater language it is written in', a *learned* protocol of reading, gained only by 'repeated exposure' (525). Damien Broderick also theorizes the denigration of science fiction as an embarrassing sub-culture precisely because its 'learned code' requires training in generic protocols that a new reader or non-science fiction reader simply cannot process. Littered with 'novums' and neo-logisms, initial opacity of texts alienates through an operation that Delany describes as 'tak[ing] recognizable syntagms and substitut[ing] in them, here and there, signifiers from a till then wholly unexpected paradigm' (cited Broderick, 35). Such syntagms, sentences, texts, are incomprehensible without an orientation that derives from competency in the generic 'mega-text', which Broderick describes thus: 'built up over fifty years, even a century, . . . the sf mega-text works by embedding each new work . . . in an even vaster web of interpenetrating semantic and tropic givens or vectors' (59).

These formulations move to a lucid account in which science fiction genre writing foregrounds intertextual collective conventions, which can accommodate new and transformative texts, whilst recognizing it as a 'communal narrative form' with a 'concomitant de-emphasis on "fine writing" ' (Broderick, 156). 'Bad' texts, deploying a singular standard of literary value, can nevertheless be 'good' in terms of its skill in manipulating the mega-text.

It is important to emphasize, however, that the conception of genre as reading process must not focus exclusively on a kind of primary encounter between reader and text. Reading processes remain enframed by cultural regimes that exert influence with varying degrees of pressure. Iser's rather shady conception of 'expectation' is filled out by Stanley Fish's overdetermined linguistic, literary and historical frameworks. 'Interpretive communities' direct and constitute value-laden reading. Foregrounding the constructedness of genre is vital, but this does not lead to the ease of Adena Rosmarin's position that 'once genre is defined as pragmatic rather than neutral . . . then there are precisely as many genres as we need, genres whose conceptual shape is precisely determined by that need' (23). External forces inevitably dictate both the limits and values ascribed to generic writing, which a purely internally generated model of genre cannot control.

Equally, the 'science fiction reading protocol' should not be conceived outside of a recognition of the fundamental impurity of genre. Broderick adds late, and only parenthetically, the qualification that science fiction is read 'by a readership alert, as well, to the overlaid codes and connotations of authorized "literature" ' (100). Science fiction, that is, is read in tension between enframed protocols, which is to assert once again that the border between high and low, serious and popular, is not to be erased or side-stepped, but made the exact focus of attention in their productivity and how they are implicated in the construction of value. There is nothing inherent in the border between the mainstream and science fiction that installs a necessary distribution of respective praise and denigration. Yet, as has been portrayed throughout, the effects of that equation are consistently evident, often in the border's very effacement. This is where Ballard's texts become so useful, and so problematic.[2]

J. G. Ballard and the Generic Law

The imperative behind these analyses of legitimation has been to display how the very identity of science fiction as a genre is caught up in a history of enframing ascriptions of value, directed by an anxiety that attends the generic. In moving towards a reading of Ballard, however, exposing legitimating mechanisms, foregrounding their logics, is not intended as a neutralization of their efficacity, a kind of exorcism through lengthy incantation. Rather, all the processes of legitimation I have discussed in this chapter are precisely *crystallized* by Ballard, for his work plays on the border, along its normally effaced edge, and forms something like a metacommentary on his 'place' in the genre.

Ballard's name has frequently been cited in the modes of legitimation I have examined: as the one who transcends the 'popular', announcing science fiction's entry into the mainstream (whether as belated 'modernist' or timely 'postmodernist'); as the emergent 'sophisticate' in a form that can finally claim legitimacy on the basis of his name; as the claimant of science fiction's supersession of the mainstream. Siting Ballard is difficult, for the more his work is considered central to the genre and its history, the more it appears to be placed 'outside' it. The constant slippage that attends the reception of his work is often 'managed' by a narrative of two Ballards: one who began within the field of science fiction, the other being one who then departed from its confines. The first can be fitted into the teleological history of the genre, his early short stories exploiting the contemporaneous 'mega-text' of 1950s science fiction, grouped in definable types: elegiac space race narratives (modelled on Ray Bradbury), the psychological horror story (modelled on Robert Bloch), satires on media technologies and advertising (modelled on Pohl and Kornbluth), the world catastrophe (modelled on Wyndham). Intimations of departure are signalled by Ballard's role as 'The Voice' (as Moorcock famously announced) of the New Wave. Precisely when Ballard 'left' science fiction is subject to debate: where McHale proposes *The Atrocity Exhibition*, Randall Stevenson suggests the lush fantasy of *The Unlimited Dream Company*, whilst many have read *Empire of the Sun* as the roman-à-clef which, as 'non'-science fiction, turns round and 'autobiographically' decodes the traumatic source for the displaced 'aberrations' of all the science fiction texts that preceded it. Just as importantly, in terms of legitimation, this second Ballard reviews in 'quality' newspapers, from *The Guardian* to *The Daily Telegraph*, becomes the Booker Prize nominee and Guardian Fiction Prize winner (both in 1984), and remains an important television and radio pundit. In these sites, at least, Ballard is freed from the embarrassment of generic science fiction.

This narrative of 'departure' from science fiction should be suspected, not least in Ballard's divergence from other announcements associated with the New Wave. In 1977 Michael Moorcock contemptuously dismissed science fiction as a closed order, incestuous and syphilitic. Its readers had savaged his attempt to 'elevate' it, and the only response was to leave. In 1976 Barry Malzberg, in 'Rage, Pain, Alienation and Other Aspects of the Writing of S-F', also announced his retirement from a genre he had only entered because of the Jewish publishing conspiracy that had deprived him of entry to the mainstream. A few months later, Harlan Ellison also attacked the constraints on his writing imposed by science fiction readers.[3] Ballard, however, published in 1976 his most overtly thematic science fiction collection for ten years (*Low-Flying Aircraft*) and from as early as 1970 had blamed the failure of the New Wave on the *New Worlds* magazine *leaving* the genre of science fiction (Goddard). Ballard's own positioning seems to revoke the possibility of inserting a simple moment of departure, either here or later. Clearly, also, this attempt to render his work intelligible merely conforms to the peculiar logic of legitimating science fiction by imposing a border to ring-fence and defend that which is allegedly *no longer* 'science fiction'.

Nevertheless, it would be false to deny a strange oscillatory effect in the reading and critical reception of Ballard's work, or to feel the force of the question that anxiously announced itself on the cover of the magazine Delap's *FθSF Review* in May 1977, 'J. G. Ballard: Where Does He Fit?'. For it is evident that the science fiction coterie has always been as discomforted by Ballard's perverse renderings of science fiction topoi as those who would defend them. Never having won any of the major science fiction prizes, Ballard's frequent placing in the mainstream could be portrayed not so much as transcendence of the generic as expulsion from it. But then the 'mainstream' critical industry has always been somewhat embarrassed in dealing with Ballard's texts outside the frame of 'science fiction'. In a strange effect, Ballard is situated within the science fiction/mainstream binary only as he is projected onto the other side of the bar, effectuating a constant displacement. If displacement, for the psychoanalysts Laplanche and Pontalis, 'permits the objectivation, localization and containment of anxiety' (123), the effect here is one of de-localization, de-containment; Ballard is always projected into the other frame from the one being mobilized. But my final argument is that Ballard's texts provoke this anxiety and the attempt to (de)contain it exactly because they open and expose the binaristic logic of the border which would distribute texts on one or the other side of the line: science fiction/ mainstream, popular/serious, low/high. They do this because they sit on the very edge where the frame is supposed to be effaced—they *expose the generic law.*

I stage this reading of Ballard's work on two of Derrida's essays on Blanchot and the question of genre: 'The Law of Genre' and 'Living On: Borderlines'. Derrida's concept of genre is perhaps more 'classical' than the one employed here (he certainly doesn't have popular genre in mind), but if, as Derrida says, 'Each "text" is a machine with multiple reading heads for other texts' ('Living On', 107) then Ballard can read and extend Derrida, just as Derrida reads Ballard.

Derrida argues in 'The Law of Genre' that the conditions of the law, which lay down its purity, also contain at the same time the condition of the impossibility of the law. If the law of genre is purity, the law of the law of genre is impurity. In the history of genre, in the history of how genre has been used to classify texts, the historicity of genre itself has been occluded. The very indicators of genre cannot be classed, are not generic. Membership of a genre is signalled by a code or trait, 'the identifiable recurrence of a common trait by which one recognizes, or should recognize, a membership in a class' ('Law of Genre', 210–11).

Genre, the classing of classes, is an apparently 'external' marking and adjudging of the 'place' of a text in a given class, but this mark will always be re-marked, re-stated, in literary texts; it re-marks on its own generic class. This is not (simply or solely) a case of a moment of self-referentiality but the condition of the literary. In this sense, then, a text must always belong to a genre, and so signals itself, but the very trait that is re-marked does not itself belong to the genre: the 'supplementary and distinctive trait, a mark of belonging or inclusion, does not properly pertain to any genre or class' ('Law of Genre', 212). This mark and re-mark at once closes the genre (marks its purity) but since it does not itself belong keeps the genre open (impure).

This ambivalent re-mark is found in two of Blanchot's fictions: *La Folie du Jour* and *L'Arrêt de Mort*. In the first case, Derrida plays on the status of the 'subtitle', initially printed as 'Un Récit?' and subsequently as 'Un Récit'. Is its genre definable or precisely that which is in question? The récit (account) the text forms is concerned with the impossibility of being able to give an account of events to, significantly, the police. The police demand an account, at the end of the text, which the narrator cannot answer, but this failure to answer begins with the opening lines of *La Folie du Jour* itself. Is this an account of the failure to account or that account itself? This impossibility of knowing where the text begins or ends is a structure Derrida terms 'double chiasmic invagination'; the opening top edge of the text crosses over the bottom end to form a chiasmus. The police invoke the law of genre but in applying that very law the narrator discovers the law of the law of genre—its impurity, impossibility. Invagination thus signals, for genre, the opening of a fold or pocket in genre that draws the outside in and the inside out. Derrida insists, however, that this is not the erasure of borders but foregrounds the need 'to work out the theoretical and practical system of those margins, these borders' ('Living On', 84).

Ballard's texts exactly provoke the kinds of questions Derrida asks: 'What are we doing when, to practice a "genre", we quote a genre, represent it, stage it, expose its generic law, analyse it practically? Are we still practicing the genre? Does the "work" still belong to the genre it re-cites?' ('Living On', 86). If Ballard's texts can be read as writing the genre and the law of genre simultaneously, what are their status in relation to that genre? In effect, Ballard's texts continuously and obsessively re-mark on the law of the science fiction genre, on genre in general, and in doing so open the border to the strange effects of *invagination*, of purity and impurity, of the chiasmic crossing of inside and outside. If subsequent chapters will pursue this effect of being-between, Ballard's oeuvre (but what, then, would that be?) can be initially opened by focusing on four remarkable border effects.

The first is what appears to be a relatively 'straightforward' self-referential moment. 'The Venus Hunters' performs the 'classic' science fiction scenario of sightings of visitors from outer space (even if it teasingly refuses the climactic contact). The sceptical astrophysicist Andrew Ward is progressively seduced by the claims of Kandinski that Venusians are visiting Earth. At the opening of the story, Ward is sitting at a bar which:

> was also used as a small science fiction exchange library. A couple of metal book-stands stood outside the cafe door, where a soberly dressed middle-aged man, obviously hiding behind his upturned collar, worked his way quickly through the rows of paperbacks. At another table a young man with an intent, serious face was reading a magazine. His high cerebretonic forehead was marked across the temple by a ridge of pink tissue, which Ward wryly decided was a lobotomy scar. (*The Venus Hunters*, 86)

This is in fact a complex moment of self-reference, for if it signals the text as science fiction (it belongs), its representation of science fiction 'fans' as either aware of their illegality or else lobotomized young men tries to announce, in that very moment of self-reference that it does not belong to that community. And yet the story tells of a sceptical Ward being seduced by the 'science fictional'; he comes to belong (and so is expelled from his job by the authorities). Since 'alien' contact is denied representation, is left undecided, there is no way of judging where readers should place their belonging. In its self-referentiality, Ballard's story reveals how performing the law of genre troubles it.

The second re-mark goes to the heart of why Ballard's name so often appears in the legitimation of science fiction through a narrative of transcendence above the 'merely' generic. For certain of Ballard's texts employ this very story. Ballard's early texts were considered perverse inversions of science fiction topoi, attacked for their pessimism and nihilism. Central figures, in the face of catastrophe, refused the heroics of humanistic triumph over disaster (managed, contained or averted by a technology subservient to human ends), and appeared to will their own deaths: Kerans turns south into the sun (*The Drowned World*) and Ransom returns to the forest (*The Crystal World*), in expectation of certain death. But these 'deaths' have been consistently re-figured by subsequent critics like Warren Wagar and Gregory Stephenson as movements towards fulfillment, the transcendence of death-in-life for life-in-death. No wonder, for this is the exact re-marking of science fiction's dream of self-transcendence. Powers, in 'The Voices of Time', with narcoma that is progressively occluding his consciousness, chooses to irradiate himself and dissolve into the entropic temporality pulsed from the distant quasars: 'he felt his body gradually dissolving, its physical dimensions melting into a vast continuum of the current, which bore him out into the centre of the great channel, sweeping him onward, beyond hope but at last at rest' (*The Voices of Time*, 39–40). This imagery is close to the fantasy of non-being, of transcendence and dissolution into the mainstream that I analysed earlier. One could read the text's evocative description of the terminal lapse into narcoma as the death throes of generic science fiction and this final vision as the ecstatic release, the abandonment of generic boundaries. Science fiction 'returns' to the undifferentiated 'stream' of Literature, unbounded by the ghetto. In fact, these stories do no less than *expose the death-drive of science fiction*, if the death-drive is recalled as that 'instinct . . . to restore an earlier state of things' ('Beyond the Pleasure Principle', 308)—the ghetto now figuring as an intolerable blockage to energy which is seeking absolute discharge, the return to zero, the 'death' of genre as transcendent return. Gregory Stephenson's religiose reading of Ballard's oeuvre may universalize the appeal of Ballard's texts ('we all possess . . . the capacity for transcendence, the ability to disengage ourselves from this plane of being' [110]), but it is more the case that these texts re-mark the very specific desire of science fiction to kill itself into 'life' by escaping the body of the generic. The dream of not belonging to genre paradoxically anchors the texts to the genre.

The third re-mark concerns the very 'mega-textual' conception of the genre of science fiction. Tom Shippey, in a statement that parallels that of Damien Broderick, warns that 'Science fiction shows a strong conventional quality which makes its signs and symbols interpretable only through familiarity . . . It is this conventional quality which makes literary criticism difficult, and foredooms to failure the search for isolated fictional pearls' (108). How, then, to 'isolate' the Ballard texts that allegedly 'transcend' science fiction when his work contains all the elaborate patterns of repetition, modulation, intersection, overlapping and 'plagiarism' that are defining of genre? No text exists here that is not always already revised or re-modulated: where to begin on the obsessive reiteration of triangulated relationships between narrator, woman, and 'rogue' pilot—'Cage of Sand', 'The Dead Astronaut', 'Myths of the Near Future', 'Memories of the Space Age', *The Kindness of*

Women? How to master the repetitions of proper names between and across texts—Maitland, Marquand, Melville; Traven, Tallis, Talbot, Travis; Helen, Judith and Coma? How to map and spatialize the reiterated geographies of desert non-spaces and resonantly over-determined iconic sites like Cocoa Beach, Cape Kennedy, Dealey Plaza? How to negotiate the complex system of self-citation between texts and titles, titles and texts? Do the stories 'Concentration City', 'Venus Smiles' or 'The Sixty Minute Zoom' remain readable in themselves outside their re-circulation as paragraph sub-headings in *The Atrocity Exhibition* (112, 35, 24)? Are the 'autobiographies' outside this series of obsessive repetitions, de-crypting their compulsive return, or are they themselves part of the series? What to do with a text like *Vermilion Sands*, which contains a structural repetition of the same story which is itself about repetition compulsion? And how to master this whole oeuvre when even the proper name of the author no longer sustains its authority over and outside the series? For even the name 'Ballard' appears in the corpus of texts, in *Crash*. Such dizzying cross-references and reinscriptions remark Ballard's oeuvre *as* genre.

This is not simply involution, however, but invagination, which fractures the line of the border marking the 'purity' of genre, the inside from the outside. The fourth and final re-mark concerns nothing less than the border itself, the explicit thematization of its effects. Rather than an indivisible line, border zones multiply and proliferate. In *The Unlimited Dream Company* Blake's repeated attempts to escape Shepperton opens a space at the edge which fluctuates bizarrely: 'Although I was walking at a steady pace across the uneven soil, I was no longer drawing any closer to the bridge . . . If anything, this distance between us seemed to enlarge. At the same time, Shepperton receded behind me, and I found myself standing in an immense field' (38). This pocket or fold (uncannily termed 'evagination' in *The Drowned World* [124]) works the same effect in *Empire of the Sun*. With a central narrator educated in the surreal colonial 'bubble' of the International Settlement, Jamie is obsessed with trying to demarcate the boundaries of war—its beginning, its end, its re-beginning—and finds himself consistently on the wrong side of the borders established across Shanghai. Like the earlier story 'The Dead Time', much of the novel unfolds in the curious space between the end of the war and the 'beginning' of peace, a place of transgression even between life and death. *Concrete Island* concerns a similar hetero-topography, where, caught in the very marginal non-space between routes, the traffic island becomes inexhaustibly dense in meaning. Once Maitland abandons his attempts to escape the island imperceptibly begins to expand at the very moment of his decision. This paradox is also explored in 'The Enormous Room'. The narrator here impulsively declares an exile to the 'prison' of his suburban home. Surviving only on the food which remains at the moment of his decision, the spaces of the house begin to exponentially expand. Eventually he is reduced to lying in the kitchen to avoid losing himself in the infinite space of the hall. Repeated again in 'Report on an Unidentified Space Station', the spatial logic of these texts offers a logic of 'imprisonment' which actually constitutes a form of radical freedom (something that Sartre notes of Genet's *Our Lady of the Flowers*). This could be read as a persistent denial of the possibility of transcendence, a kind of arrest at the very border limit of the generic, exposing the indivisible line between the inside and the outside as a fiction. Re-marking that border limit, the law of genre, opens the impurity, the in-folding of inside and outside, that is the law of the law of genre.

To 'place' Ballard, then, to find a protocol of reading for his unsettling and a-topic writing, is to insist on a siting at the very edge of genre. Ballard must be read *generically* as science fiction, for any to attempt to shunt his works into 'legitimate' literature effaces the very border that is so persistently foregrounded and problematized in his texts. At the same time, however, so faithful is the tracking of the logic of genre that Ballard *exposes* the generic law in its impurity, its necessary contiguity with its own 'outside'. But what pre-given protocol could read this divided corpus, one which troubles the logics of an indivisible boundary between popular and serious, high and low? Derrida concludes his essay on Blanchot in the following way:

> No law of (normal) reading can guarantee its legitimacy. By normal reading I mean every reading that insures knowledge transmittable in its own language, in a language, in a school or academy, knowledge constructed and insured in institutional constructions, in accordance with laws made so as to resist (precisely because they are weaker) the ambiguous threats with which the *arret de mort* troubles so many conceptual oppositions, boundaries, borders ('Living On', 171).

It is not a case of simply transposing Ballard's work into the laws which legitimate the legitimate. Nor is it a case of either celebrating or dismissing his work as simply science fiction. The apparent difficulty of placing his work is the difficulty of an exposed institutional law, the difficulty that Ballard must be divided between the popular and the legitimate. My initial argument has, I hope, revealed that it is difficult but necessary to think of these 'two' Ballards as co-terminous. If this begins to sound like a grand claim I am making for Ballard it should also be recalled of Blanchot's *La Folie du Jour* that the narrator there *engenders* the law, the representatives of the law, engenders them 'in giving them insight into what regards them and what should not regard them' ('Law of Genre', 224). The law and the *necessity* of borders is precisely what is revealed.

This (non)place, this weird hiatus or (non)site, is the angle between two walls. It requires a Janus-faced process of reading, at once inside and outside the science fictional, forever tripping over the stubborn insistence of border demarcations. If this can begin to open a reading of Ballard's extraordinary texts, the imperative is to avoid the 'catastrophe' narrative of genre. Very well. I shall reverse the genitive and move from the catastrophe of genre to the genre of catastrophe.

CHAPTER TWO

J. G. Ballard and the Genre of Catastrophe

Ballard's first four novels insert themselves, as a series within a series, into a distinctly British sub-genre of science fiction: the catastrophe novel. Best represented by John Wyndham's *The Day of the Triffids* (1951) and *The Kraken Wakes* (1953), John Christopher's *The Death of Grass* (1956) and Charles Eric Maine's *Thirst* (1958), these texts mark an intensification of a catastrophe narrative that haunts British popular fiction from the late nineteenth century, from Richard Jefferies' *After London* (1885), through H. G. Wells' paradigmatic *The War of the Worlds* (1898), to Conan Doyle's *The Poison Belt* (1913).

The mega-textual apparatus of the genre insists on a rigorous distribution of 'iconic' scenes, plot and narrativization. The 'pleasures' of recognition begin with an identification with the always already surviving narrator amidst genocidal carnage: the disaster (whatever It is) quickly assumes global proportions, offering the spectacle of cities in panic and decay. The 'veneer' of civilization and the fragility of the social order is stripped away. The genre, in other words, is propelled by a pseudo-scientific conception of 'degeneration' and the narrative moves towards the threat of remainderless destruction, the possibility that even narrative itself may not survive, before a re-generative solution is found, either inexplicably or through the machinations of an elite scientific cadre. This is a dilatory genre, then: it opens the fantasy space of violence and aggression, before closing the social once more into a re-vitalized order of technico-scientific rationality.

The paradoxical optimism of the genre (its mass destructions are in some ways 'hygienic' reorganizations of the social) and the security of its identifications render it 'safe'; Brian Aldiss has given an influential portrait of the genre as 'the cosy catastrophe', whose 'essence is that the hero should have a pretty good time (a girl, free suites at the Savoy, automobiles for the taking) while everybody else is dying off' (*Billion Year Spree*, 294). Aldiss further historicizes the genre's intensification as integral to the 1950s; despite the pleasures of destruction, he suggests, 'the catastrophe novel presupposes that one starts from some kind of established order' (296) and more importantly returns to it, its destructiveness yet bounded (even constituted) by rigid the social orders of the period.

It is both this security and the sense that its closures re-affirm the humanistic control of science that perhaps accounts for the violence of reaction to Ballard's perceived perversion of its formulated narratives. Being Ballard's first novelistic exercises, they secured the antagonistic relation with which his work exists in relation to the corpus of science fiction. Although *The Wind From Nowhere* (1962) is a conventional generic exercise (written in two weeks to fund the shift to professional writing), tracking the rise and fall of destructive force on the fabric of the social, the subsequent three novels (*The Drowned World* [1962], *The Drought* [1965] and *The Crystal World* [1966]) were initially received as a mocking refusal of scientific optimism or even logic. Exploiting generic recognitions, they abandon both the concern with representing the path of the catastrophe (and any plausible scientific reason for its arrival) and any thought of a circular return to a reinvented social world. They take place *between catastrophes*, in the space after the initial catastrophe and the 'catastrophe' which follows: death. It is not solely the lack of science as a rational system to contain and possibly master the catastrophe, then, but fundamental notions of human behaviour which are seen to be under attack. The displacement of scientific endeavour as the impetus of narrative is elided with the condemnation of the 'almost pathological helplessness' (Blish, 127) of Ballard's characters. In this catastrophe, Algis Budrys thundered, 'you are under absolutely no obligation to do anything about it but sit and worship it' (128). One authoritative science fiction reference work signals Ballard's inversion of the genre thus:

> Contrary to most treatments of the theme, the four books are not centred on the frightful destructiveness of the cataclysm but on its awesome beauty . . . (and) on the perverse desires, mad ambitions, and suicidal manias of aberrant personalities now free to fulfil fatal aspirations devoid of any rational motivation (Barlow, 32).

Such condemnation is curious, however, given the very perversity of the genre of catastrophe itself, its 'cosy' sadism. It might be suspected that the virulence of response to Ballard's work is not a result of deviation from the genre so much as an exposure of the seam of its fantasy. Ballard's in-version displaces the manifest pleasures of identification to reveal its latency—a genre, it might be said, finding perverse enjoyment in the assertion of the instincts of aggressivity and self-destruction which Freud saw as the constant underside of the increasing restraint of 'Civilization'.[1] Moving from a competent performance of the genre in *The Wind From Nowhere*, the serial novels that follow constitute psychological commentaries on the very motivation of the repetitive representation of catastrophe.

Ballard's texts both constitute their own interpretations of the genre and positively insist on further hermeneutic inquiry. The culminating 'deaths' of *The Drowned World* and *The Crystal World* have invoked an intense critical industry that oscillates between taking the deaths literally, as unveiling at last the secret death drive of the genre, or as metaphorical acts of transcendence of the bodily, the material, and (in a logic already familiar) the generic.

Inside or outside, performance or commentary, the act of reading the novels institutes the necessity of thinking about interpretations the catastrophe calls forth. For if the catastrophe is currently theorized as that irruptive and unrepresentable event, which blocks mimesis, narrative and historiographical containment,[2] the repetition of the catastrophe in a popular genre should not be policed through the impossible demand for literal representation, or condemned for its troubling pleasures. Rather, these repetitions should be comprehended as being *called forth* by the 'hole' blasted in signification by the catastrophe. These narratives can only be displacements, only 'allegories', written in the gap between the unrepresentable event and the urge to master its trauma in ceaselessly reiterated narratives. Curiously, however many times the destruction of London or New York is lovingly detailed, this is never the catastrophe itself, but its allegorical displacement: Susan Sontag's 'The Imagination of Disaster' attempts multiple readings of the genre to capture hermeneutically the 'deeper' significance of these 'literal' disaster narratives. In a crucial way, Ballard's refusal to represent the catastrophe, focusing only on the psychological effects of its aftermath, 'purifies' the hermeneutic inducements the genre offers to pursue the final determination of absented catastrophic meaning.[3] The following readings of Ballard's catastrophe novels are generated self-consciously in the tension between readability and unreadability caused by their suspensiveness between catastrophes.

Ballard's texts in this proposal strip away the props that would determine a reading of the genre simply in terms of its 'cosy' liberations, secure identifications, or as texts which should be measured by impossible demands of a 'literal' (or even scientifically plausible) representation of the disaster[4]. They do not leave the genre for that reason, however. It becomes important to track the critical attempts to close the anxious space of undetermined meaning in Ballard's series of novels, for these are consistently held to initiate a reading which will support the entire oeuvre, a singular 'project' announced and reiterated through a disclosure of how the catastrophic functions in these early texts. In short, the catastrophe may either begin a sequence of proliferating death-driven perversities, or demand a re-figuration of 'death' as metaphoric transcendence. Whilst the latter has established an orthodoxy, the first is the place to begin. In an article which condemns the entirety of Ballard's work as 'advocating a life style quite likely to involve the sudden death of yourself or those you love', Peter Nicholls yet clearly reads Ballard's catastrophe novels within a context of British history. In asking 'Who knows what masochistic streak in the British character has brought about this obsessively repeated theme' (Nicholls, 'Jerry Cornelius', 26) of catastrophe, his immediate, though unexplored answer, is end of empire. This initiates the first attempt to close on the undetermined allegorical root of the catastrophe.

The Imperial Sub-text

'I'm expecting the end of the world today, Austin.'
'Yes, sir. What time, sir?'
'I can't say. Before evening.'
'Very good, sir'. (Conan Doyle, 205)

Conan Doyle's parodic exchange between Challenger and his butler, as if the catastrophe were an unreliable guest with no sense of punctuality, encapsulates the peculiarly 'English' response to the disaster, the bizarre discrepancy between the consequences of global destruction and the inadequacy of response. This recalls the scene of Phyllis and Watson in *The Kraken Wakes,* surrounded by rising waters and proposing a toast to honour T. S. Eliot, a poet who *could* have found adequate response in extremity (222). These moments of self-parody co-exist, however, with random violence, mass death and rape deployed strategically as the signifier of ultimate barbarism. For Fredric Jameson, it is Ballard who exposes the allegorical ground of the genre:

Let the Wagnerian and Spenglerian world-dissolutions of J. G. Ballard stand as exemplary illustrations of the ways in which a dying class—in this case the cancelled future of a vanished

> colonial and imperial destiny—seeks to intoxicate itself with
> images of death that range from the destruction of the world by
> fire, water and ice to lengthening sleep or the berserk orgies of
> high-rise buildings or superhighways reverting to barbarism.
> ('Progress', 152)

Ballard's exemplarity de-codes the genre of catastrophe by his writing
of its latent fantasy text: this is the first situating and grounding of the
genre in the allegory of the destruction of empire. Is such a hermeneutic reading plausible?

The historical coincidence of decolonization and the production of
science fiction catastrophe texts in the 1950s is marked. The period
between 1945 and 1951 saw the reduction of imperial subjects from
475 million to 70 million, and the 1950s continued with a series of
violent and unceremonious colonial withdrawals from Palestine in
1948 to the repression and systematic killing in Kenya. The 1956 Suez
crisis is usually presented in historiographic narratives as Britain's 'last
imperial adventure', with both Eden and Gaitskell still affirming the
anachronistic belief in 'the moral aim of preserving civilized standards
wherever Britain had once exercised responsibility' (Bogdanor, 118).
Britain's belief in its status as an independent power was humiliatingly
curtailed by the unlikely alliance of American and Russian condemnation, and the immediate result was the 1957 defence review
which effectively surrendered control to America. Decolonization,
although presented by Kenneth Morgan in largely humanitarian
terms, merely reflected the progressive shift of power to America: 'one
of the external stimulants towards decolonization was the impatience
of US and multi-national corporations with the restrictive trade practices imposed by colonial power' (Sinfield, 125). This process was
coupled with reverse migrations of Africans and Caribbeans to the
colonial centre, the liberal narrative of tolerance shattered by the 1958
Notting Hill riots and subsequently progressively restrictive immi-
gration laws.

From this rudimentary historical data, is it possible to propose it as
the allegorical ground of the catastrophe? There are, of course, overt
deployments of this context: Margot Bennett's *The Long Way Back*
(1954) has African explorers reversing the anthropological gaze by
visiting a post-holocaust Britain, now collapsed into barbarism. The
'waves' of destruction, the first signs of the catastrophe, always seem to
begin obscurely in the Far East and move inexorably towards England
(the 'death of grass', in John Christopher's novel of the same name, is a

result of a virus unleashed 'due as much as anything to the kind of failure in thoroughness that might be expected of Asiatics' [39]). Indeed, this potential ground is re-inforced by the equal concentration of catastrophe narratives in the 1880s and 1890s. Here, Hobsbawm argues, the first structural crises of imperialist overextension were felt, resulting in the contemporaneous transformation of the signifiers of Empire into domestic public spectacles which worked to solidify a concept of the nation within a state threatened by internal dissension. Rider Haggard's fantasy of the African terrain as that space where the decline of England into effeminacy could be reversed and re-masculinized was translated directly into terms of genre, with the 'unnatural' knowledge of women the Naturalists were held to possess replaced by the rigorous and muscular adventure (see 'About Fiction'). Haggard was also producing elegies for the destruction of rural England as the source of ideal nation and manhood which establishes a clear relation between the frontiers of Empire and the fragility of the centre— frequently the 'target' of the de rigeur sequence of destruction in the catastrophe genre. Certainly, Wells' *The War of the Worlds* offers early legitimation to reading it as a fantasy-nightmare of reverse colonization.

It is M. P. Shiel's *The Purple Cloud* that is the most overt of these fin-de-siècle catastrophes. Shiel (author also of *The Yellow Peril*) produces endless descriptions of bodies frozen in panic as they move West before the advancing cloud; when Adam arrives at Dover 'I . . . could not believe that I was in England, for all were dark-skinned people' (86), and he finally realizes 'the empires of civilization have crumbled like sand-castles to an encumbrance of anarchies' (92). The visit to his home town in Yorkshire to find his home invaded by foreigners finally de-rails his identity: 'I am hardly any longer a Western, "modern" mind, but a primitive, Eastern one' (139–40). Cross-dressed in a riotous confusion of different national clothes he proceeds across the world annihilating cities; it is only when he discovers his 'Eve' that a certain civilizing 'Westernness' returns.

There is a specificity, or at least Alan Sinfield argues, to the 1950s imperial crisis. The duplicitous liberal narratives that could serve to legitimate colonialism as humanitarian were destroyed by the advent of violent anti-imperial nationalist struggles. This had such an effect that 'imperialist ideology was readjusted to produce a myth of "human nature" ': it is savage' (Sinfield, 140). Sinfield's primary examples of this in the cultural sphere are William Golding and Graham Greene: Golding's *The Lord of the Flies* is read as the paradigmatic case of the civilized 'veneer' hiding an essential savagery; Greene exploits exotic landscape as the objective correlative of moral crisis and innate sin. This readjustment to universal savagery is 'the final desperate throw of a humiliated and exhausted European humanism' (Sinfield, 141).

Sinfield's narrative is painfully simplified (the emergence of 'universal savagery' can hardly be said to emerge in the 1950s), but it does begin to elaborate more of a ground for those uncomfortable elements that were ignored in the delineation of the 'cosy catastrophe'. Aldiss' dismissal of John Wyndham's texts as being 'totally devoid of ideas' misses, as Rowland Wymer has shown, the strain of vicious social Darwinism that challenges the otherwise cosy liberalism, with Bocker (in *The Kraken Wakes*) and Zellaby (in *The Midwich Cuckoos*) insisting on the necessary violent defence of the genus from invaders. Liberal ethics are replaced by the biological imperative—or would be if only science were heeded. The uncomfortable dissection of the incapacity of liberalism and parliamentary democracy, made by one of the children in *The Midwich Cuckoos* (197–201), echoes the proposals of the dissolution of impotent democracy for the autocratic rule of the scientific élite enacted in J. J. Connington's *Nordenholdt's Million* or desired in Fred Hoyle's *The Black Cloud*. The sudden regression of human nature constitutes the main subject of Maine's *Thirst* and Christopher's *The Death of Grass*. Wade, the central figure of *Thirst* is constantly portrayed as irresolute and convention bound; he must learn the 'General Adaptation Syndrome': 'In a crisis people behave differently—they revert to some fundamental level. It has to do with survival . . . The intellect tends to become paralysed. Their behaviour is dominated by the survival drive' (27). *The Death of Grass* is more elegiac, with its nostalgia for an England of 'broad avenues celestially lit' and its 'policemen—custodians, without anger or malice, of a law that stretched to the end of the earth' (112). The dream of England is inextricably linked to the exercise of imperial rule, a dream which dwindles as the characters move, ironically towards a rural retreat, through rape, murder and eventual fratricide.

Given the (more or less) explicit allegorical grounding of the imperial sub-text, how do these texts function for it, why is the catastrophe obsessively reproduced? Does the fantasy of extremity encode a call to arms, as in Zellaby and Bocker's biological (racial and imperial) imperative? Does the imperium require catastrophe to revitalize? And is this, as Jameson suggests, what Ballard's texts *manifest*, what makes them at once central to the genre (the unveiling of its 'secret') and marginal to it (in the very enunciation of its masochistic fantasy)?

A scanning of the surface of Ballard's catastrophe novels lends a certain plausibility to this grounding: between the Cameroon setting of *The Crystal World* (which recalls Graham Greene's *A Burnt-Out Case*, although subverting this 'heart of darkness' into a forest of crystalline efflorescence) and the tropicalized London of *The Drowned World* (deploying the fantasy of 'reverse colonization' in landscape, and the effect of 'primitivization' that that landscape induces), *The Drought* seems to occupy *terra nulla*, the indifferently drawn desert(ed) topos of colonial space, devoid of history. But Jameson's interpretation does not draw its explanatory power from any literal tracing; rather it comes from the energetic leap between mysterious surface and grounding depth in an act that Katherine Hayles has termed the double hermeneutic of suspicion and revelation (Hayles, 174). Jameson interprets the interval, and it is the very distance between text and sub-text that paradoxically ensures Ballard's exposure of the fantasies that motor the genre.

That interval, however, doubles the interval in which Ballard's narratives take place—in the time after the catastrophe. Indeed, *The Drowned World*, *The Drought* and *The Crystal World* are trajectories of being-between, spacings between the unprecedented global catastrophe and the equally unrepresented catastrophic 'deaths' to which their endings point. This is important to emphasize, for the notion of 'interval' in Homi Bhabha's work is that lag between the event and its narration, which is open to disruptive reinscriptions and re-narrations, and exactly concerning colonial history.

If the security of the imperial sub-text can close the enigmatic gaps that constitute the space of the novels, the interval continually re-opens. For Ballard, contra Jameson, is hardly 'exemplary' of a 'dying class'. Accepting, for the moment, Ballard's insistence that 'the drowned world' of London is a translation of the abandoned Chinese paddy-fields of his youth, then the 'evaginations' of the lagoons in London may be seen to repeat the curious enclave the Shanghai's International Settlement, the 'pocket' (and contemptuous gift of the Chinese) in which Ballard spent his childhood. What is crucial, and Ballard states this in response to an explicit question about an imperial sub-text to his work, is that the zone of the Settlement was an overwhelmingly *American* one; his conception of England was as much a fantasy, subject to deflation, as any migrant to the old colonial centre (and this is presumably why Ballard rejected the topography of the English catastrophe genre: 'The rural landscape of the meadow didn't mean anything to me . . . That's why the SF of John Wyndham, Christopher and so forth I can't take. Too many rolling meadows' [Goddard and Pringle, 32]). If the catastrophe novels are about the dissolution of empire, he states, then it is an American one, and of its ideology as bearer of the Future—it is 'the end of technology' (32), as confirmed by the later, satirically-inflected catastrophe novel, *Hello America*. The enclave of the Settlement existed as a disjunct temporal zone projecting, as it were, a future dissolution not simply of a colonial but also, potentially, a neo-colonial economy. In this narrative it is possible to propose a strange loop of time where memories of the past, as already future, maroon the present as an *interval between catastrophes*. Which is to say that the temporalities of Ballard's catastrophe novels, as kinds of oblique translations, could be as much *post*-colonial narratives as colonial ones.[5] The time after time of these post-catastrophe texts, the interval which they portray, is a zone which sustains multiple and even contradictory readings. They must do so, for the unrepresentable catastrophe will always induce multiple callings to potential narratives of explanation.

This is not simply to deny the operation of an imperial sub-text, but to resist its singular determination of the catastrophe, its rush to offer the final determination. The enigmatic lag between catastrophes 'demands a commentary, a cause'. But, as Lyotard writes of a similar space between traumatic event and its subsequent narration, the search for a cause 'is mistaken, for the beginning is part of the plot, and so is the wish for a beginning and the wish to have done with the beginning' ('Anamnesis of the Visible', 229). What traverses the space between catastrophes is open, ambivalent, multiple: Ballard may manifest the latent aggressivity of the genre of catastrophe, but that 'exemplification', by the impure law of genre, may also make the texts exceed it by its very faithfulness to the law. And so, the propulsion towards death, the 'perverse desires, mad ambitions, and suicidal manias' of the texts can be read as literal drives, but they can also be re-functioned as 'metaphorical' instances in which death figures as a mode of transcendence.

This, in fact, has been the second phase of interpretations of Ballard's catastrophe novels; they are seen not as perverse movements towards death, but as symbolically encoded journeys towards transcendence of a certain mode of living. The global catastrophe opens the space of a progress towards the catastrophe *after* catastrophe: the apocalypse. This approach will allow a detailed reading of the texts.

From Catastrophe to Apokalupsis

It was in interview, in 1976, that Ballard offered his correction of the nihilistic reading of his novels: 'I don't see my fiction as disaster-oriented . . . they're . . . stories of psychic fulfilment. The geophysical changes which take place in *The Drought, The Drowned World* and *The Crystal World* are all positive and good changes . . . The changes lead us to our real psychological goals, so they are not disaster stories at all . . . Really, I'm trying to show a new kind of logic emerging, and this is to be embraced, or at least held in regard' (Goddard and Pringle, [40]) The 'perverse' argument, then, is an inverted logic, a subversion of the generic narrative in which the movement is not away from the catastrophe, with heroic accounts of survival and triumph, but *towards* it: in *The Drowned World*, Kerans abandons the research team heading North from the tropical heat, and turns South, into the sun, to his death; in *The Drought*, Ransom refuses to continue the dreary routine of surviving on the receding shores, and returns to the heart of the desert; in *The Crystal World*, Sanders returns to the crystallizing forest to be transfigured in death.

The catastrophes which bracket the texts are thus profoundly different entities: the first, the disaster (*disastro*: unlucky star) propels us towards the second, *apokalupsis* in the etymological sense of disclosure, uncovering, lifting the veil on the hidden. Derrida's investigation of the meanings of apocalypse pursues its unveiling in terms of 'the sex or whatever might be hidden, a secret thing, the thing to be dissembled, a thing that is neither shown nor said, signified perhaps but that cannot or *must* not first be delivered up to self-evidence' and emphasizes that 'nowhere [in Greek] does the word *apocalypse* have the sense it finally takes on . . . of fearsome catastrophe' (Derrida, 'Of an Apocalyptic Tone', 4).

The elements of the revised reading of Ballard's 'apocalyptic' novels can be quickly assembled. For Gregory Stephenson, the entire oeuvre of Ballard's work is concerned with 'transcendence', in terms of 'exceeding, escaping the limits of the material world, time and space, the body, the senses and the ordinary ego-consciousness' and far from being nihilistic, the texts are 'an affirmation of the highest humanistic and metaphysical ideal: the repossession for man of authentic and absolute being' ('Ontological Eden', 38). This would seem to place Stephenson's reading in an existential register, but in fact his argument is distinctly Jungian: the narratives, 'psychic journeys', are a process of healing self-divided protagonists, each of whom 'comes to recognize the apocalyptic potential of the particular disaster he is faced with, who perceives it as a metaphor for his own and the general human psychic state, as an interior landscape exteriorized, as the fulfillment of an unconscious human desire, and so accepts it, co-operates with it, assists it' (41).

Warren Wagar largely concurs with this reading: Ballard effects a 'transvaluation', a reversal of poles, from the negative 'literal' catastrophe, to the positive 'metaphorical' utopias of the disaster sequence. Again, there is a synthesis of theoretical terms, with Ballard as both existentially transcendent ('self-overcoming in perilous confrontation with the world'[56]), and as offering a kind of mythico-psychological transcendence, interpreted in an overtly Christian framework, the crystallized forest being 'a vision of the City of God'(55).

Peter Brigg also posits that Ballard's texts are an inversion of the traditional narrative of the genre, to be understood on a psychological level, proposing not submission to death but 'an acceptance of the path to psychic wholeness' (*J. G. Ballard*, 46). Brigg, however, introduces another 'thetic' level in discussing *The Drought*. He states: 'The desert wastes and the detritus of civilization do not cohere in an important statement on, say, ecological stupidity, but are simply there, outside of the characters' emotional fields . . . Ransom, and . . . the other characters, are left with their private selves against a blank and meaningless landscape' (*J. G. Ballard*, 51). This alters, even negates, the notion of 'an inner landscape exteriorized' in a statement which is virtually identical with Camus' conception of 'the Absurd'.

There are, in these commentaries, at least four competing frames of reference for reading the catastrophe: the Jungian process of annealing a self-divided subjectivity; a specifically religious meaning of Apocalypse as redemption; an existential process of moving from alienated being toward a transcendent apprehension of Being; and a Camusian conception of an absurd universe. Apparent in all these readings is also the perhaps most 'self-evident' frame: the Freudian typography of subjectivity. The landscapes of the novels are those of the unconscious, a scenography of the 'secret' desires of and for the catastrophe. No wonder the initial response from the science fiction community was antipathetic: dubious human sciences replace the hard edge of Science, and the place of the 'explanation' of the catastrophe was, in Norman Spinrad's words, 'mumbo-jumbo in hard science terms and made sense only on a metaphysical and metaphorical level' (Spinrad, 184).

It may seem pedantic to question these accounts, not least because they are substantially right. They take their cue from the profuse textual evidence of such allegorizing intent. The accounts double, in effect, the textual traces of the explanatory frames from within the novels, which contain 'thetic' proposals offering up the 'larger' significance of their own narratives. To repeat this in the work of criticism obviously need not be redundant: it is what Derrida terms the 'doubling commentary': 'This moment of doubling commentary should no doubt have its place in a critical reading . . . Without this recognition and this respect, critical production would risk developing in any direction and authorize itself to say almost anything' (*Of Grammatology*, 158). My concern to interrogate this dominant interpretation of Ballard, however, derives from Derrida's immediate qualification: 'But this indispensable guardrail has always only protected, it has never *opened*, a reading' (158). If Ballard's texts are opened into the frameworks of Jungian, existentialist and Freudian theory, differential emphases can begin to be discerned.

At the moment, the dominant critical approach to Ballard, generated from these inversions of the catastrophe genre, narrate 'transcendence' by homogenizing complex frames of reference (psychoanalysis, analytic psychology, existentialism) into an unrigorous mish-mash of mystical religiosity, which is then—and this is the major concern—offered as *the* interpretation which would unlock the entire chain of Ballard's oeuvre. Whilst its maddening repetitions might encourage such a move it is my contention that, even from within the tightly grouped catastrophe series, important modulations, even profound differences, emerge to question any account that would wrap up the series (the entire series of Ballard's work) within a singular frame. The desire for the single explanation is, once again, impelled by the enigmatic space between catastrophes—but that interval, between event and enunciation, is exactly what precipitates multiple traversals of its space.

'Inner Space'

Perhaps the best place to begin to fracture the homogenization of these overdetermined frames is by analysing the term 'inner space'. In his first editorial for *New Worlds*, 'Which Way to Inner Space?', Ballard explicitly opposed this terrain to that occupied by (traditional) science fiction: outer space. The term, however, accrues more resonance than the simply oppositional. The minimal consensus on 'inner space' is that Ballard's landscapes 'externalize a crisis in the consciousness of the main character in terms of a disaster in his environment' (Ryan, 45); Ballard attempts 'to identify things . . . as external representations of the inner map of the contemporary psyche' (Brigg, *J. G. Ballard*, 12). The landscapes of disaster, then, are projections of psychic space; it was fatal ever to take these catastrophes literally. It is a short leap to suggest that if the landscape is the topography of the psychic apparatus externalized, the figures that occupy it are emblems of the 'psychic journey' the hero undertakes. Hence—with a confusion of Freudian and Jungian topographies—Pringle reads off characters as representatives of the superego, ego and id, with women as anima figures and other 'doubles' representing the Self. Kerans/Ransom/Sanders must negotiate through these figures to achieve 'a state of grace, or integration with the universe; they wish to find themselves and create a whole' (*Earth is the only Alien Planet*, 49). The fiction of inner space, in this formulation, is an intensely solipsistic one, the enactment of a solitary journey through the psyche. This reading may also, incidentally, ascribe to the 'conservatism of the unconscious' the problematic representations of race and gender in the novels.

The Encyclopaedia of Science Fiction gives the coinage of the term 'inner space' to Ballard in 1962, but the term's history is more complex than this simple ascription suggests. In the more emphatically Jungian sense 'inner space' is found in J. B. Priestley's 1953 article 'They Come From Inner Space'. Priestley sees science fiction as a set of contemporary myths, deploying the familiar equation of the popular and the unconscious (and anticipating, incidentally, Jung's own book, *Flying Saucers*, published in 1959). These myths are to be read as the 'characteristic dreams of our age, and are psychologically far more important than our own rational accounts of ourselves. They take the lid off. They allow us to glimpse what is boiling down below . . . The Unconscious is protesting against the cheap conceit and false optimism of the conscious mind'(712). Priestley concludes his article by stating: 'We are in fact warning ourselves that society, like a rocket ship bound for some distant nightmare planet, is hurrying at full speed in the wrong direction; and that dangerously over-extraverted, we are refusing to deal justly with the unconscious side of our minds'(714).

This statement might be compared with the following: 'We are far more out of touch with even the nearest approaches of inner space than we now are with the reaches of outer space. We respect the voyager, the explorer, the climber, the space man. It makes more sense to me as a valid project—indeed, as a desperately urgently required project for our time, to explore the inner space and time of our consciousness'.

Ballard's 'Which Way to Inner Space?' argues that contemporary space flights only confirm what the 'space operas' unintentionally proved: outer space is banal. And yet the above quotation does not come from Ballard's editorial, but from R. D. Laing's *The Politics of Experience*; the consonance of the two is remarkable. For Laing, inner space is inaccessible to the existents of alienated everyday being, and can only be uncovered by the schizophrenic inner journey which Laing, despite occasional disclaimers, celebrates as a revelatory state, more 'true' than 'our collusive madness . . . we call sanity' (*Politics*, 62). Ballard's insane characters—perhaps more explicitly so in early stories like 'The Overloaded Man' (in which a progressive bracketing of external reality leads to suicide as the ultimate act of freedom) or 'The Gioconda of the Twilight Noon' (where Maitland deliberately blinds himself to protect his rich internal visions from dispersal)—are more difficult to contain within the holistic Jungian version of 'inner space' than the more disclosive state of schizophrenic as shaman, celebrated by Laing.

The frames of reference begin to proliferate: Jane Dunlop's *Exploring Inner Space*, published in 1961, was a discussion of experience under the influence of LSD; Colin Greenland notes William Burroughs' use of the term at the 1962 Writers Conference in Edinburgh, although he was in fact quoting Alexander Trocchi's phrase 'astronauts of inner space' as designating that dispersed Elect who would induce his programme of cultural revolution (as promoted in *The Invisible Insurrection of a Million Minds*). The resonances of 'inner space' move across a highly diverse set of contexts; Robert Hewison, in his history of the 1960s, in fact uses the term as the (ultimately debilitating) orientation of the whole counter-culture in general.

Hence, simply accepting the 'solipsistic' version of 'inner space'—as the externalization of the unconscious—is oversimplified (and if the existential frame for the novels is to be taken seriously, as it should, such projective inner space can only be the most banal subjectivism: Heidegger critiques the notion of a projective 'inner sphere' in *Being and Time* [87]). Ballard's polemics and manifestos in *New Worlds* called for a science fiction of the present and in many ways his texts are echo boxes of contemporaneous thought, less of hard science than of anthropology, philosophy, psychology, media theory and so on. Ballard's catastrophe novels are inextricably intertwined with the intensification of eschatological thought contained in that much contested denotation of epoch: the Sixties.

Ballard himself conceives 'inner space' as an antonym to an exhausted strand of science fiction, and demands that 'science fiction should turn its back on space, on interstellar travel, extra-terrestrial life-forms, galactic wars and the overlap of these ideas' ('Which way to Inner Space?', 117). The demand is to pursue an equivalent experimentation to that of cinema and painting, the 'creation of new states of mind, new levels of awareness, constructing fresh symbols and languages where the old cease to be valid' (117). It is only in the final paragraph that Ballard refers explicitly to the unconscious, through a discussion of Dali. This manifesto was written at the same time as *The Drowned World*. In 1966, his 'Notes From Nowhere' also repeats Dali's imperative: 'After Freud's explorations within the psyche it is now the outer world of reality which will have to be quantified and eroticized' (149), but this comes after the elaboration of an imaginative space where public events, immediate environment and 'the inner world of the psyche' combine: 'Where those planes intersect, images are born' (149). With this notion of 'intersection', the solipsistic projection of the unconscious is denied as the sole source for the constitution of landscape. Rather it is the angles between, in the shifting conjunctions of the public, somatic and psychic, where Ballard places the landscape of his fiction.

'Notes From Nowhere' is directed towards the elaboration of the aesthetic for the 'condensed novels' of *The Atrocity Exhibition*, and indeed the essay explicitly bids 'farewell' to 'jewelled alligators, white hotels, hallucinatory forests' (150)—the landscape of *The Crystal World* just completed. My point is that 'inner space' cannot finally be determined under a single definition, and extended across the work: its particular inflections and revisions have to be attended to according to the dominant 'thetic' frame which the specific text deploys. Landscape as 'unconscious' is a reading that is most supported by *The Drowned World* and *The Crystal World* and I will deal with these first.

Inside and Outside the 'Jungian' Catastrophe:
The Drowned World, The Crystal World

If Ballard is 'unacceptable' to science fiction, then Jung has always been 'unacceptable' to more dominantly Freudian conception of the unconscious. Phyllis Grosskurth, Samuel Weber and others have analysed how Freud's attempts to assert his authority over the interpretation and institution of psychoanalysis involved a constant need to negate 'deviations', especially that of Jung who, before the 1913 split, had been marked by Freud as the figure on which to transfer authority.

When Edward Glover published *Freud or Jung?* in 1950 it was in response a perceived shift of popularity away from Freud to Jung. The public, he felt, 'regard Jung as a great mystic who is also a great liberator and Freud as the purveyor of a diseased psychology' (18). Indeed, Jung's contrast of Freud's imposition of interpretation with his own emphasis on analysand as self-analyst seemed superficially more appealing in its holistic agential approach, for 'the healing processes to grow out of the patient's own personality' (Jung, 58).

Despite this apparently holistic approach, Jung problematically concentrates on the phylogenetic as opposed to the ontogenetic ('race' memory as a key determinant of the individual psyche), and his freewheeling use of alleged anthropological insights through analysis of 'primitive cultures' links to his search for transcultural patterns of myth. It is this phylogenetic emphasis that is exploited in *The Drowned World*. For Jung, fundamentally opposed to Freud, the division of the conscious and the unconscious is one of the 'curses' of modern man, an accident rather than structural; there is a fantasy of holistic origin, the undivided Self. The Modern division of the conscious and unconscious is explicitly seen in terms of catastrophe, for a suppression of the unconscious means its return in distorted forms: 'Our times have demonstrated what it means for the gates of the underworld to be opened. Things whose enormity nobody would have imagined . . . have appeared and turned our world upside down'. 'Slowly, but inevitably', Jung says, 'we are courting disaster' (193).

Ballard's 'The Reptile Enclosure' (in *The Terminal Beach*) narrates something like this catastrophe. It belongs to a sequence of stories in which the launching of satellites is seen to be an increasingly unsustainable transgression of the 'proper' space of humanity, and results in catastrophic effects on the consciousness. Roger Pelham sits above a densely crowded beach with the intellectual's disdain of the passivity of the mass, bent on worshipping the sun and the Echo XXII, which will complete the media canopy of communication satellites. Through the noise and packed bodies, Pelham insistently attempts to explain to his wife Sherrington's theory that the launch will activate 'innate releasing mechanisms . . . inherited reflexes' (109) in unforeseen ways. Although Sherrington is a physiologist, Pelham provides a more 'psychological' explanation:

> I think the psychological role of the beach is more interesting. The tide-line is a particularly significant area, a penumbral zone that is both of the sea and above it, forever half-immersed in the

> great time-womb. If you accept the sea as an image of the
> unconscious, then this beachward urge might be seen as an
> attempt from the existential role of ordinary life and return to
> the universal time-sea—(111)

His wife cuts in and 'look[s] away wearily', tired perhaps of this
awkwardly unassimilated 'thetic' speech. However, the launch indeed
sets off a kind of compulsive repetition of the trauma that caused the
extinction of Cro-Magnon man, and the entire beach populace
advance, lemming-like, into the sea. The story is an example of the
over-laying of a 'commentary' on a fairly familiar science fiction 'plot',
the text providing a reading of its own genre, one obsessed with
theorizing the psyche beyond ontogeny, with 'the biological, prehis-
toric, and unconscious development of the mind in archaic man, whose
psyche was still close to that of the animal' (Jung, 64).

Ballard has been explicit about the Jungian frame for *The Drowned
World*: 'I wanted to look at our racial memory, our whole biological
inheritance, the fact that we're all several hundred million years old,
as old as the biological kingdoms in our spines, in our brains, in our
cellular structure; our very identities reflect untold numbers of
decisions made to adapt us to changes in our environment, decisions
lying behind us in the past like some enormous largely forgotten
journey' (Henessy, 62). It is Kerans' fellow researcher Bodkin who
repeats this 'metabiological fantasy' in his new science of Neuronics.
The moment of 'hard' scientific explanation is brief and perfunctory—
solar storms cause heat-rise, the massive expansion of tropical rainfor-
est mutate by excessive radiation and the melting of the polar ice caps
flooding much of Europe—and this catastrophe is displaced by the one
that follows it; the return to Triassic landscape provokes 'triggers' of
regression and devolution, figured as a literal descent down 'spinal'
consciousness. The lagoons that transfigure London are marked as a
'zone of transit' between states of consciousness, between, as Bodkin
terms it, the final movement from the thoracic to lumbar vertebrae
(43). The crisis is whether to continue the military project of mapping
the landscape before moving North, or whether to accept the 'new
logic' and head South.

Ballard's disaster novels all contain 'heroes' teetering on the brink of
acceptance; this is the central drive of plot. There is an obsessive
concern with ambiguous motive, both of their own and others' actions,
as if aware that the transformation of landscape marks the termination
of rationally motivated instrumental consciousness, and offers signs of

a re-nascent 'collective unconscious'. The central figures themselves are 'zones of transit' between an often overly signalled oppositional set of characters. Thus, in *The Drowned World*, Hardman (whose rapid devolution and escape to the South prefigures Kerans'), Beatrice and Bodkin are seen to possess the 'key' to the ultimate significance of the enigma of the catastrophe, whilst Riggs, the military commander, and Strangman are figures, in different ways, of a now superseded 'rational' defiance of the inevitable apocalyptic transfiguration. As 'archeopsychic time' runs backwards, Riggs obsessively resets municipal clocks running to protect the ordered advance of clock time; the sympathies are evidently with a return to an almost Bergsonian conception of durée—the continuous, unfragmented, 'natural' movement of temporality. At one point, Kerans dreams Riggs 'dressed as William Tell, striding about in a huge Dalinian landscape, planting immense dripping sundials like daggers in the fused sand'(61). The explicit surrealist reference recalls Dali's use of the figure of William Tell as the Oedipal father threatening castration, here imposing the law of the Father's temporality.

The transposition of Dali's iconographic references indicates Ballard's peculiarly effective strategy of further undermining 'intentionality' of instrumental consciousness through what could be called 'intertextual landscape'. The actions of the characters are not only increasingly directed by the psychological significance of landscape, but through the haunting sense of echoes of other geographies, other maps and plots. Like *The Drought*, where the text is framed by Tanguy's painting 'Jours de Lenteur', *The Drowned World* has the frame of Delvaux and Ernst's 'phantasmagoric forests' (29). When Strangman arrives, it is evident that he wishes to direct the action according to an allegorical painting, and the action fades in and out of its frame in uncertain ways. These frames of control are left undeterminable, haunting, as if it were possible that Ballard's texts are generated as 'commentaries' or re-narrations of other, only half-discerned, texts. The echoes of Conradian exotic locales of subtle corruption are strong, but again cannot be pinpointed; *The Crystal World*'s adoption of the multi-symbolic site of the leper colony from Greene's *A Burnt-Out Case* has the same effect. It is *The Drought* which most effectively exploits these echoes and half-echoes; within the painting's frame, Lomax is at once Prospero and Lear, Quilter Caliban and Miranda Lomax a hideous deformation of Shakespeare's Miranda. Ransom has explicit parallels to the Ancient Mariner, while Jonas, the leader of the fishermen, rants his apocalyptic vision like a latter-day Captain Ahab. It is as though a 'neutral' landscape were a container of an over-determined con-catenation of significances of a singular Catastrophe that yet remains inaccessible, only to be glimpsed through narratives of other narratives, without finality or ground; for these echoes are all precisely of texts which themselves confront a catastrophe that cannot be contained. Landscape erodes intentionality or self-determined motivation; the response of the characters is to play other characters who may provide the key, the revelation.

In Jungian terms, these ghostly texts behind the text would be termed 'archetypes', and indeed Kerans explicitly refers to this: 'His unconscious was rapidly becoming a well-stocked pantheon of tutelary phobias and obsessions, homing onto his already over-burdened psyche like lost telepaths. Sooner or later the archetypes would become restive and start fighting each other, anima against persona, ego against id' (90). This intimation of larger psychic roles comes immediately before Kerans' first experience of the apocalyptic dream of a huge engulfing sun, throbbing with a 'primal' heart-beat. He has now accessed the 'corporate nightmare', the 'collective' dream which gener-ates Bodkin's thesis and 'explains' Beatrice's languorous distraction. The thin strip of 'intentional' consciousness is being eroded by the progressive collusion of internal and external landscape. This is the landscape of those catastrophic 'signs' of history: 'Hiroshima and Auschwitz, Golgotha and Gomorrah' (72). With this revelation the decision is made: to escape Riggs' 'military' temporality and accept the catastrophe. At this point, however, Strangman arrives.

How seriously are we to take this thesis of devolution beyond individual pre/history, ordered and directed by the Collective Unconscious? How acceptable is both Ballard's access to Jung's proble-matic anthropology, and his peculiar fictive cross-fertilization of it with 'neurology'? When the overtly thetic does appear within the literary text it produces a strange disjunctive effect, a disconcerting moment of self-consciousness in the reader, of being jarred out of the fragility of the fictive, of exposing the conditions, the rules and limits of its discursive regime. This disjunctive clash unsettles both registers; if it produces an awkwardness for the fictive (and Ballard's prose is no doubt 'awkward'), the thetic also loses its logical certainty, its frame of rigorous argument. When asked in interview explicitly about his 'use' of the Collective Unconscious, Ballard replied: 'I accept the collective unconscious—I don't think it's a mystic entity, I think it's simply that whenever an individual is conceived, a whole set of operating instructions, a set of guidebooks are meshed together like cards being shuffled' (Revell, 45). There is a sense that the super-abundance of 'thetic' registers in the texts have significance in the sense of their aesthetic conjuncture at that moment, the pleasing symmetry of a dealt hand. If Jung is deployed as a form of structuration at this moment, and I do not deny it holds truth-effects in *The Drowned World*, this is replaced by the almost complete constitution of the self through media networks in *The Atrocity Exhibition*. Indeed, in a review written at the time of the completion of *The Atrocity Exhibition*, 'Alphabets of Unreason', Ballard compared Desmond Morris' 'anthropological' analysis of contemporary culture to Hitlerian ideology in its dangerous 'biological interpretations of history' (26), which would suggest that either that the framework of *The Drowned World* has been rejected, or that it merely held strategic value as a metacommentary in the process of its writing.

More than this, however, Strangman's role in *The Drowned World*, beyond that of a possibly Jungian shadow or threatening 'double' to Kerans, seems to be to register the awkwardness and uncertainty of the thesis proposed by the text: Strangman *finds it funny*: 'Strangman seemed unable to take the explanation seriously, swinging abruptly from amusement at their naivety to sharp suspicion' (90). He determines to call Bodkin's thesis 'the Total Beach Syndrome' (89); a moment of dry wit at portentousness. The whole passage of Kerans' dive into the Planetarium is undermined by Strangman's ironic commentary on its corny and thunderingly obvious 'return to the womb' symbolism. When Strangman warns Kerans: 'don't try to reach the unconscious . . . remember it doesn't go down that far'(102), he is in fact obscurely citing the farcical appearance of Dali at a London press-conference, dressed in a diving-suit.

The Strangman episode is also structurally crucial, bearing in mind Ballard's relation to the genre of catastrophe as a whole. The landscape of *The Drowned World* has been, up to this point, horizontal, with an emphasis on the langorous heat and glaring reflections from the flat surfaces of the lagoons. 'Action' has been minimal, and largely cerebral. When Strangman drains the lagoon, however, there is a sudden explosion of random violence, the return to those 'expected' scenes of urban destruction. The 'evagination' (124) that the draining effects opens up a fold or pocket that is inside/outside the generic set. So, the draining of the lagoon 'returns' to the scenarios of the genre at the same time as marking a distance from it. If the preternaturally white, skeletal Strangman (echoing a figure from within the frame of Delvaux's painting) leads to a marauding group of black looters, this is a 'negative' of the 'London scenes' in J. J. Connington's *Nordenholt's Million* where even aristocratic white women follow Herne the Hunter, the 'nigger leader', through orgiastic rites. The figure of Strangman is thus complexly overdetermined: a Jungian Shadow to Kerans; the deranged inversion of Riggs' rationalistic refusal to accept the 'new logic'; the harbinger of a momentary return, an invaginated pocket in the genre of catastrophe; and, finally, the figure that may ironize the entire 'thetic' proposal of devolution and regression, upsetting that very 'return' to the genre's central concerns.

Kerans' escape from Strangman begins the journey South. The final revelation lies beyond the last pages of the book, his 'emergence into the brighter day of the interior, archeopsychic sun' (144), but the *physicality* of that death is beyond doubt when he discovers the blinded Hardman, eyes destroyed by cancerous growths.

There is one figure I have not yet considered, who is crucial not least for the audacious name she is given: Beatrice. David Pringle argues that all of Ballard's women characters can be essentially condensed into a single figure: the 'lamia', the siren. They are desirous yet threatening, however much the landscape of the disaster is a post-sexual one. The figure of 'Woman', however, is crucial to the revelatory apocalypse. In 'Of an apocalyptic tone recently adopted in philosophy', Derrida sets in motion the sexual resonances of the apocalypse. This analysis intertwines with Kant's attack on 'mystagogues' who believe they have bypassed reason for an intuitive revelation of 'the truth', figured as raising the veil of Isis. The 'debate' Derrida follows is between those who have had an apocalyptic revelation, lifted the veil of the goddess to uncover the 'secret', and Kant, who sees this 'derangement' of reason as castrating philosophy. Philosophy must expel Isis, 'murderess of Osiris all of whose pieces she later recovers, except for the phallus' ('Of An Apocalyptic Tone', 19). The Apocalypse, in this reading, is indissociable from a (metaphorical) castration of reason by the feminine element, holding the secret 'behind the veil'.

Beatrice hovers on the edges of *The Drowned World*; it is she who owns the frame, the paintings of the 'phantasmagoric forest', that may act as a key to unlock significances. Kerans' early indecisiveness only becomes solidified in her presence. Beatrice is, of course, Dante's guide through Paradise, the symbol of divine revelation, although, for Kerans, there is another potentially more threatening form of revelation. At one point he sees Beatrice transformed into Pandora, 'with her killing mouth and witch's box of desires and frustrations, unpredictably opening and shutting the lid' (30). Woman as guide may also become Woman as embodiment of death drive.

It is Beatrice's enigmatic speeches and languor that marks her as one of the first to have access to the Collective Dream. The only relation between her and Kerans is in the intersections of the collective unconscious. If she guides the way, only Kerans leaves for the South, abandoning her at the lagoon. The question is whether Beatrice figures as a symbolic access to the Jungian meaning of the apocalypse, leading the way to revelation. For might not the irresolvable enigma of Beatrice, of the feminine as catastrophe and apocalypse, not so much 'point the way' as merely call forth narratives to contain her mystery, without ever 'lifting the veil'? Is the allegorical ground of the Ballardian apocalypse ever reached? Is the catastrophe plumbed, or does it retain its 'secret'? This can be examined further by turning to *The Crystal World*, where the 'secret' of the forest multiplies, not least in with the presence of two feminine figures, Serena and Suzanne.

Ballard's central figures have been consistently criticized for their 'pathological helplessness', their paralysis of action. This, however, might be compared to the conditions required to inaugurate the process of individuation, 'when the ego gets rid of all purposive and wishful claims and tries to get to a deeper, more basic form of existence' (Jung, 163). If *The Drowned World* concentrated on phylogenetic elements, *The Crystal World* follows that more intensely personal journey of individuation towards a repossession of the self. Like the demand of the catastrophe, this is figured as a 'call' from the Self to the ego to begin the journey, often in threatening anticipatory dreams of disaster. The chapter on individuation in *Man and His Symbols* explicitly calls for a turning towards the darkness, to embrace it.

The Crystal World also contains and constitutes its own 'commentary'. Here, the catastrophe, rather than residing in the distant past in *The Drowned World*, is entered at its beginning, marking in landscape the psychological entry to the process of individuation. Hence the ruling opposition of dark/light and the choice of crystal, a key Jungian symbol of the completed Self, holding as much importance in Jung's iconography as the mandala.

The Crystal World is highly effective in maintaining the enigma of the meaning(s) of the catastrophe. It is suspended through elliptical and at times nonsensical dialogue; through the elusiveness of officials at Port Matarre; through the misreading of documents (crucially Sanders cannot decide whether Suzanne's letter about the 'jewelled forests' is literal, or just a surfeit of metaphor); through the redundancy and incomprehensibility of the 'scientific' explanation. This, fatally for science fiction critics, entertains the possibility of parody. The explanation 'leaks' across several sections, until it is finally determined in a letter to Paul Derain halfway through the book, bracketed by the text having to 'cite' an extraneous document. The scientific thesis, supposedly the most rigorous and logical, is in fact the most precarious and 'aesthetic' explanation, and presumably Derain will have as much difficulty discovering the dividing line between the literal and metaphorical as Sanders did of Suzanne's missive.

Sanders' immediate response to his first view of the crystallizing forest makes the locus of significance plain:

> For some reason he felt less concerned to find a so-called scientific explanation for the phenomenon he had just seen. The beauty of the spectacle had turned the keys of memory, and a thousand memories of childhood, forgotten for nearly forty years, filled his mind, recalling the paradisal world when everything was illuminated by that prismatic light described so exactly by Wordsworth in his recollections of childhood. (69)

The forest marks, like the lagoons of *The Drowned World*, the erasure of a determinable line between literal landscape and its 'metaphorical' resonances. The crystallizing virus in the forest seems to attack reference itself. Again, Louise Peret misunderstands the now missing Anderson's reference about a 'forest of jewels': ' ". . . it was meant as a joke you know". She gestured in the air. "A figure of speech?" "Exactly" '(31).

Sanders is ostensibly on a mission to resolve his affair with Suzanne Clair (the French, of course, for 'light'; Suzanne will 'shed light' on the catastrophe, as with Beatrice), but is distracted by a series of successive enigmas. Arriving at Port Matarre, 'motives' unresolved, Sanders is drawn into a brief liaison with Louise Peret, Suzanne's uncanny opposite, eyes veiled by huge sunglasses. Both need access to the restricted area of the forest, seemingly bleeding light from Matarre. The light/dark oppositions are encoded from the opening paragraph's description of the landscape, and have their counterparts in the white-suited Ventress and the cassocked priest Balthus, each with rival claims on the forest. As Louise notes, they have also arrived at the Equinox, the exact splitting of light and dark, again a moment of crisis and decision: 'At least you can choose . . . Nothing is blurred or grey now' (37). Sanders concurs: 'At these moments of balance any act was possible' (38). These significant oppositions and doublings proliferate with Sanders, Max and Suzanne repeating the Ventress, Thorensen and Serena triangle.

Sanders interprets these structural oppositions for Louise (135). The Jungian frame could be implemented here, given the complementarity of opposites. Since the forest is a zone effectively 'out of time' (exiting the zone Sanders sees the crystallized face of his watch dissolve and the hands begin to move again [119]), Sanders argues it is the only place where a union of these opposites can be affected.

Sanders is still, in his discovery of Radek's half-crystallized body, tied to a more literal understanding, horrified at the physicality of this death-in-crystal. He still takes Ventress' cryptic comments as jokes, figures of speech. The 'meaning' offered by the catastrophe, as in *The Drowned World*, involves the figure of Woman, but here it is uncertain as to which possesses the key. Louise is soon abandoned outside the affected zone. Sanders finds himself entangled in an incomprehensible and violent vendetta between Ventress and Thorensen, until the central 'secret' of the forest, Serena, Ventress' dying wife, is discovered. This passage appears to be the culmination of much of the bizarre action, the source of Ventress' drive to penetrate the forest, and yet it is peculiarly flat and anti-climactic; there is no revelation.

It is Suzanne in fact who begins to affect a resolution. Suzanne's introduction has something of the stylized entry of the *femme fatale* of *film noir*; her features will 'shed light' but 'Suzanne still remained hidden in the shadows . . . The faintly quizzical smile that had hovered about her mouth since his arrival was still there, almost beckoning him' (126). The smile is transformed in the light into a rictus of leprosy; she has the beginnings of a 'leonine mask'. The unveiling (Suzanne is last seen escaping, trailing 'her dark gown like an immense veil' [143]) is, paradoxically, the *addition* of a mask. The psychological investment Sanders has suspected in his work with lepers is revealed and related in complex ways to the proliferating virus at work in the forest. This is the point at which Sanders begins to operate a 'metaphorical' understanding with a logic that might, on a literal level, be unsustainable. The hosts of shadowy lepers drawn to Mont Royal stand in for the psychic disfigurements that the forest will anneal. In Balthus' translation of this meaning: 'here everything is transfigured and illuminated, joined together in the last marriage of space and time' (162). Sanders' last message, before returning finally to the forest to that state beyond life and death is: 'However apostate we may be in this world, there perforce we become apostles of the prismatic sun' (169).

There have been suggestions that the bizarre images of the crystalliz-ing forest derive from hallucinogenic drugs, deployed as treatment by

R. D. Laing as a strategy of annealing 'the divided self', with much the same affirmative rhetoric evident at the close of *The Crystal World*. Laing in fact writes more sympathetically of Jung's therapeutic technique than the supposedly penetrative techniques of Freud, although this is more a response to the institutionalization of Freud in 'ego-psychology', and its 'killing' insistence on ego normativity. Jung's conception of the psychic apparatus is indeed more 'affirmative' than Freud's, and the appeal of Jung's holism intersects with other key elements of counter-cultural thinking. Without any apparent theorization of the bar of repression between conscious and individual unconscious, and without any sense of the foundational necessity of the unconscious for the formation of subjectivity, the process of individuation is simply the manifesting of the individual unconscious, directed by the Collective Unconscious, in a union which arrives at the (re)possession of the Self, the completely self-knowing, self-intending apocalyptic consciousness. It is easy to see the connection of this, in inadequate shorthand, to the process of 'tuning in', establishing a relation to the alienated inner self as that 'true self' suppressed by Western culture that so dominated the thought of the Sixties' 'regime of truth'. *The Crystal World* can thus be inserted into a matrix of historical productivity. It also finds re-confirmation in the 'doubling commentary' of the interpretation of the disaster novels as shifting catastrophe to *apokalupsis* as revelation and unveiling. 'The external world corresponds perfectly to internal meaning', and Ballard's central characters 'realiz(e) that they are now in a world that frees them to fulfill their inner natures' (Brigg, 'Time out of Mind', 43–44). The passage of death is simply re-birth, narratives of *fulfillment in transcendence*, vaulting too the walls of the generic ghetto.

Whilst there may be unsettling elements to *The Drowned World* and *The Crystal World*—Strangman's parodic relation to the text's own thetic register; the sense that those theses exist internally as provisional narratives called forth by the interval of the catastrophic; the continuing withdrawal of the feminine, as bearer of the revelation, from access to 'readability'—this impulsion towards transcendence is indeed the central dynamic of the texts. But it is exactly a being-*towards*. Given a rigorous understanding of existentialism, rather than an unsatisfactory elision of it with Jungian holism, the central panel of this triptych, *The Drought*, can be seen to resist the language of completion, unification, and the final achievement, in Stephenson's words, of 'the repossession for man of an authentic and absolute being' ('Ontological Eden', 38).

The 'Existential' Catastrophe:
The Drought

It is important to separate 'existential' philosophy from a certain style, which became recognizable in the 1950s and 1960s. Its popularized conception was evoked from a number of freely interpreted key words: choice, freedom, angst, death, absurdity. David E. Cooper summarizes this version as a philosophy for a post-war Europe, the 'signs' of 'Auschwitz' and 'Hiroshima' rendering impossible belief in political ideology. This results in the individual's 'return to his "inner self"' . . . to live in whatever ways he feels are true to that self'. The 'hero' of this narrative lives 'totally free from the constraints of discredited traditions and commits himself unreservedly to the demands of his inner, authentic being' (12). Cooper sets out to correct this misconception, but it cannot be denied that this misreading generated powerful meaning effects in the 1960s; Ballard's texts too are read within this misrecognized existentialism. They may have even been written inside the 'cod' existentialism that floated through the Sixties, but my intent now is to demonstrate how *The Drought* might support a rigorous existential reading if we step, in Derrida's words, beyond 'the guardrail' and attempt to open it out towards existentialism.[6]

The frames for Ballard's disaster novels that I have been analysing here are not simply separable; they overlap, are overdetermined. R. D. Laing, of course, was proposing an *existential* psychiatry. Laing turns to existentialism because, for him, it offers a 'science of persons' rather than separating disease from person. 'Disease' was to be seen not as an external invader, but as an expression of a Self from a phenomenological 'take' on reality which must be condemned by the hegemonic version of reality as 'insane'. Laing's holistic Self uses existential terms: '. . . we cannot give an adequate account of the existential splits unless we can begin from the concept of a unitary whole, and no such concept exists, nor can any such concept be expressed within the current language system of psychiatry or psychoanalysis' (*The Divided Self*, 19). This self is seen as the final, authentic ground of the subject, even though existential philosophy is more concerned with the 'unthinkable' relation between existence and its inaccessible ground: Being. This relation has been, in Heidegger's terms, 'forgotten', and his philosophy devotes itself to the problematic spatiality between beings and Being. Everyday subjects can never fully elaborate the conditions of their existence, the 'gift' from Being in terms of self-knowledge. The Self, that is, is exceeded by an unknowable Being, the 'I' defined to the extent that it has *lost* Being (Heidegger, 152). Laing's Self is thus a simplification, one which seeps into the reading of the Ballardian apocalypse.

Perhaps the most obvious connection of existentialism to Ballard's work is Camus' theorization of absurdity. Ballard, it is said, is the exemplar of 'absurdist' science fiction, a term often applied to the New Wave. This was probably communicated via the brief ascendancy 'Absurdist drama' of in the late 1950s; as Sinfield notes, Camus was at this time imported to English intellectual networks and elevated to the status of a countercultural hero. The terminology of existentialism and Camus are evident in the doubling commentaries on Ballard: the catastrophe after the catastrophe is the search for authentic being in the 'ontological garden of Eden' (a phrase from 'The Terminal Beach') and this reading is extended over Ballard's oeuvre.

Like Ballard, Camus' texts offer searingly vivid portraits of landscape and seem largely concerned with the relation of the central figure to that landscape rather than the affectless relations between humans. Mersault's achievement of 'a happy death' (in the posthumous text of the same name) is crucially related to the 'proper' setting. *The Outsider* effectively evokes the heavy heat and blinding light of the beach where morality and logic seem suspended. Similarly, in introducing The *Myth of Sisyphus*, Camus uses the metaphor of landscape; although it is a book concentrating on suicide it is 'a lucid invitation to live and to create, in the very midst of the desert' (*Myth*, 7). The purpose of absurd reasoning, he argues later, is to take logic to its very limits and 'to stay there . . . insofar as that is possible, and to examine closely the odd vegetation of those distant regions' (Myth, 17).

It is not simply the 'desert' setting of *The Drought* that insists on this consonance. The relation to the landscape has a significant difference of emphasis from the other two novels analysed. Brigg's description is worth repeating: 'The desert wastes and the detritus of civilization . . . are simply there, outside the characters' emotional fields . . . [they] are left with their private selves against a blank and meaningless landscape' (*J. G. Ballard*, 51). This is evidently not the case with *The Drowned World* and *The Crystal World*. Further, the landscape cannot easily be accorded to the 'inner space' of Ransom. The opening paragraph of the novel offers an audacious description of Quilter, the 'idiot son' with hydro-cephalic head, staring down at the draining river, suggesting a clear relation. Everyone, to survive, has 'water on the brain', but is this landscape Quilter's rather than Ransom's fantasy? Each character struggles to impose their own psychic investment that would open the landscape to a specific apocalyptic understanding. Johnstone states: 'There are too many people now living out their own failures, that's the secret appeal of this drought' (29). This suggests at least competing 'inner spaces'—but more than that begins to interrogate the whole subjectivist logic from which the notion of 'inner space' derives.

But there is a further and 'catastrophic' difference between *The Drought* and the other two novels: there is no 'literal' death at the conclusion of *The Drought*, only the coming of rain. This arrival in fact dissolves the whole notion of the Absurd itself. The 'absurd', as Camus defines it, is a tension: it appears out of the incommensurability of the human desire for rational explanation and unity and the 'unreasonable silence of the world' (*Myth*, 31–32). The 'solution' of suicide to this impossibility of meaning and knowledge is rejected as dissolving this essential tension. The fact that Ransom does not enter a state of 'death' would seem to concur with this, but the coming of rain works as a cipher of apocalyptic revelation. Curiously, this marks Ballard as more 'properly' existential than Camus; Cooper remarks that in no way can Camus be considered as central to existentialism, because his relation of being to the world is one that insists on the *maintenance* of alienation, not its overcoming.

The landscape of *The Drought* is one of a phenomenological reduction. With the evacuation of Mount Royal effected, the initial catastrophe long passed, Ransom stays behind in an arid landscape with which he profoundly identifies. There is a complex description of the river (13) as losing its 'forward flow', like the procession of linear time; what matters now, in the movement of temporality, are the 'random and disconti- nuous' eddies, multivallic intervals that traverse the space between catastrophe and apocalypse. The perverse decision to remain in a landscape that liberates from inauthenticity is, in existential terms, an ethical and indeed necessary choice.

However, this 'choice' to act in 'freedom' is contested. The trajectory toward disclosing Being-as-a-whole, in its ownmost possession, is in fundamental tension with the necessity of defining Being as *Dasein*, Being-*in-the-world*, Being-*with*, or Being-*with-Others*. In *The Drought*, Ransom's desire to disclose ownmost Being through environment is threatened by rival actions of Others in competition for the meaning of the desert—Johnstone's religious Apocalypse, Jonas' cult of fishermen, Lomax's hidden motives and sources of survival. All this may be contained by Quilter's head or else by the frame of Tanguy's painting, 'Jours de Lenteur', which is a constant reference. The first section of the text is a neutral landscape, a 'terminal zone' of reduction; the second section, at the shoreline, is even more overtly existential. The journey to the South is necessitated by the impending facticity of death (what Heidegger would call the merely empirical fact of 'demise', which has nothing to do with and in fact *conceals* an existential understanding of 'death'); unlike the voluntary journeys undertaken by Kerans and Sanders, this is 'pointlessly following a vestigial instinct that no longer had any real meaning for him' (92). The initial arrival at the beach, obliterated by the endless ranks of cars and people, is the descent into *Das Man*, the 'they' of inauthentic life lived according to compromised being-for-others. Here, the beach is a 'zone of nothingness that waited for them to dissolve and deliquesce like the crystals dried by the sun' (119). The relation to landscape is now reversed, an imposition of a singular meaning, the drudgery of survival, and 'the erosion of all time and space beyond the flaccid sand and draining beaches, numbed Ransom's mind' (126–27).

On the apparently 'suicidal' return journey to Mount Royal, however, Ransom looks forward to being 'merged and resolved in the soft dust of the drained bed' (112); is this desire any different from the immolation of the beach? For Ransom, the distinction is between the inauthenticity of redundant structures of the beach and the apocalyptic 'death' at Mount Royal, moving 'forward into zones of time future where the unresolved residues of the past world appear smooth and rounded, muffled by the detritus of time, like images in a clouded mirror' (152). In Camusian terms, equally, the decision to return to Mount Royal is away from the false 'solution' to absurd existence offered by the narrow parameters of survival; it would seem to accord with that imperative to live 'in the very midst of the desert'.

The resolution comes, however, with the 'gift' of rain. The apocalypse comes; but what is It? Ransom 'had at last completed his journey across the margins of the inner landscape he had carried in his mind for so many years' (188)—but what is the meaning of this circular journey, this return to zero? The figures of Woman, here, are not as significant or central: Catherine Austen remains, in every sense, impenetrable; Miranda's sources of survival are obscure; and Ransom's wife Judith is at one point seen trying to disguise a presentiment of catastrophe in her face with a fold of hair, the veil drawn *back over* (37). In Heideggerian terms, this return to the heart of the desert makes sense as a turning towards an 'authentic' relation to Death—precisely a Being-*towards*. It is not, or never can be, a completion, or full arrival at the possession of ownmost Being, for Being 'eludes in principle any possibility of being grasped at all' (*Being and Time*, 280). This is exactly the point where an existential account of *The Drought* departs from the 'doubling commentary' that has interpreted the texts as transcendence fulfilled.

It is easy to see where this misunderstanding arises. Heidegger writes: 'The Self of everyday Dasein is the they-Self (*Das Man-selbst*), which we distinguish from the *authentic Self*. . . As they-self, the particular Dasein has been dispersed into the "they", and must first find itself', which it does by 'a clearing away of concealments and obscurities' (167). Is not Ransom's turning away from the atavistic social structures of the beach, and his circling back to Mount Royal a disclosive clearing away? And yet the refusal of Ransom's death is exactly in accord with the maintenance of an approach *towards* Death which defines a 'proper' existential stance. Being is defined as Being-ahead-of-itself, a reaching across the space *between* Being-in-the-world and Being-as-a-whole: to complete or fulfill this movement towards death would in fact annihilate the possibility of unveiling Dasein *at all*. Paradoxically, then, when the trilogy of Ballard's catastrophe novels is collapsed into a narrative of an embraced death-as-Transcendence, arguing the achievement of that apocalyptic Death does not unveil anything, but promises only nullity. It turns the novels back into accounts of the perverse and nihilistic desire for death. The Self cannot be 'whole', for Being contains a 'not-yet', which 'has the character of something *towards which* Dasein comports itself' (*Being and Time*, 293).

The rain, the 'answer' of rain, has of course to be read metaphorically. What can it disclose? As something of the 'environment', it cannot be of Being itself; if anything it can only set to task the thought of the unthought of Being. But if there is a shift to the philosophy of Karl Jaspers, some kind of answer becomes available.

In *The Drought* there is a repetition of this phrase: 'the shadows of the dead trees formed brittle ciphers on the slopes' (17); 'the wind had turned, and carried the plumes toward the north, the collapsing ciphers leaning against the sky' (75); 'the brittle trees along the banks, ciphers suspended in the warm air' (81); 'a metal windmill, its rusty vanes held like a cipher above the empty wasters' (143). It is a question, it seems, of reading the ciphers.

'The Reading of Ciphers' is the final part of Karl Jaspers' *Metaphysics*. It concerns the meaning of transcendence and its 'catastrophic' inaccessibility. Transcendence can only be 'read', without producing any cognitive knowledge of it, through 'ciphers', in which the Transcendent appears in 'veiled but palpable form' (cited Samay, 172). Jaspers concentrates on the relation between Being and existence, like Heidegger; Being is the 'gift' to existence, and existence can only come about through the Being which existence is not. The concern with existence thus extends beyond the empirical or intentional consciousness, which cannot ultimately be self-knowing and self-intending, since it depends on the 'gift' of an absolutely unknowable other. Nothing can be known of the Transcendent but Jaspers offers the cipher as a 'glimpse of Being'. These are sudden, brief flashes in which a greater totality is intimated. These glimpses can be translated into communicable forms in myths and legends, which are themselves translated into speculative language—philosophy. Philosophy works to recover the original impetus, pin down and name the Transcendent in its essence. The process is circular, beginning with the glimpse of Being, its translation and re-translation to speculative thought which goes beyond the cipher to achieve the determination of Being.

Jaspers, however, absolutely refuses any moment of 'deeper' knowledge or truth in this process; the cipher which begins it simply is, and nothing can be added or subtracted from it, there can only be an endless process of translation and re-translation which gets no nearer to determining the Transcendent. The philosopher simply 'reads the original cipher-script by writing a new one: he conceives Transcendence in analogy to his palpably and logically present and mundane existence' (117). As such, metaphysics has no claim to any knowledge of the Transcendent. There can be no end to translation, the 'cipher' shifts 'from language to language'(120).

The cipher is at once impenetrable and fragile. It stands in for nothing but itself. It remains uninterpretable. Any object can become a 'cipher' (Jaspers gives the example of landscapes (126)), but it is only a momentary glimpse. The landscape of The Drought is full of ciphers, incomprehensible languages. Not only the 'dead trees' (17) or 'brittle trees' (81) are ciphers, but there are other codes: the smoke rising from torched cities is variously described as 'like the calligraphic signals of a primitive desert folk'(25), as 'drifting away like the fragments of an enormous collapsing message'(38), or again, as 'calligraphic patterns'(150). Jonas' fishermen draw strange symbols in the sand; the haunting catastrophe texts that indeterminately structure the novel turn characters into 'ciphers' of a larger plot.

What can be taken from Jaspers' delineation of the cipher, however, is the non-determinability of such signs, the inaccessible meaning of the Transcendent. The Catastrophe, and the apocalypse that follows it, is only a translation and re-translation; the catastrophe itself remains hidden. Though Ransom moves through this landscape, it is uncertain whether he is even witness to these ciphers. The coming of rain, that moment of apparent redemption, may still only be a new cipher-script, coming no nearer to the 'truth' of the catastrophe.

This incidence of codes, forms of writing, manifesting themselves 'unreadably' within the landscape, also occurs in 'The Terminal Beach'. Many of the frames of the catastrophe are overdetermined here. The immediate point of departure is the nuclear context; for Paul Brians' literalist reading of the disaster, this is more 'thoughtful' than Ballard's other disasters, 'an attempt to reconcile his [Traven's] personal guilt with that of the culture of which he is a product, expiating in advance the guilt of destroying the human race in a thermonuclear war' (2). Traven is at one point compared to Eatherley, the 'mad' pilot of the Enola Gay, emblem of national guilt. For the reading of Ballard's landscapes as projections of a solipsistic consciousness, the island of Eniwetok is the primary example; Traven refers to it as a 'state of mind' (136), devoid of all non-human elements, a purely 'constructed' zone that constitutes a catastrophic 'sign' of history. It is likened to 'an Auschwitz of the soul' (136), and public guilt constantly crosses and re-crosses with private meanings: the phantasms of the dead wife and child and the 'philosophical' discussion with the dead Japanese pilot Yasuda. Finally, in the existentialist frame, Traven's quest is directed by the being-towards-death that the Bomb imposes: he explains to Osborne that '[f]or me the hydrogen bomb was the symbol of absolute freedom. I feel it's given me the right—the obligation, even—to do anything I want' (147). Traven's discussion with Yasuda also centres on the search for the 'ontological Garden of Eden' (153), a place of the absolute reduction to simple essence, complete certainty. This may recall R. D. Laing's assertion that schizophrenia (for Traven is plainly 'insane' by Osborne's standards) is an increasingly 'epochal' condition due to 'ontological insecurity'.

In a sense, then, 'The Terminal Beach' offers in condensed form all the potential narratives of catastrophe, but it also effectively isolates the very problem of reading Ballard and of reading for the final determination. 'The Terminal Beach' was the first of Ballard's 'condensed novels', the stripping down of narrative into sharply defined units of imagistic prose. The text appears in brief, titled 'blocks' of prose. In order to construct a 'logical sequence', the blocks have to be rearranged into some kind of linear temporal sequence. Traven, of course, is trapped within the hundreds of testing blocks on Eniwetok, himself trying to uncover their meaning. The reading process doubles Traven's reading. And yet the landscape is 'covered by strange ciphers' (134): 'the tall palm trees leaned into the dim air like the symbols of a cryptic alphabet' (134); the light pouring through the slits of a bunker 'studded the west wall like runic ideograms. Variations on these ciphers decorated the walls of the other bunkers, the unique signature of the island' (139); the apertures are again described as 'the tutelary symbols of a futuristic myth' (140), and the blocks 'like the cutting faces of a gigantic die-plate' (141). Abandoned medical charts of chromosome mutation offer another unreadable language (144). There seems only one impenetrable advance between the opening and closing blocks of prose; if the palm trees are 'symbols' and 'ciphers' of an alphabet, the ending repeats this with a minor difference: 'The line of palms hung in the sunlight, only his motion varying the shifting ciphers of their criss-crossing trunks' (154). The secret of this motion on the ciphers, however, is again unwitnessed, the glimpse of the Transcendent offered, but denied. Brittle ciphers track a path in the interval between the catastrophe and its apocalyptic disclosure, but any meaning offered is merely a translation or re-translation of the impenetrable signs.

Conclusion: *Beyond . . .*

In concluding, I wish to return to the very first formulation of the catastrophe I proposed. The catastrophe is irruptive out of temporality, and yet demands, calls forth, a narrative. Critical interpretation is itself a narrative called forth by the narratives of catastrophe, a desire to pin down and name the sub-textual movements of the disaster. I have analysed the many potential narratives which seek to render the peculiar interval of the Ballardian apocalypse in explicable terms, a process which begins to resemble Jaspers on the Transcendent, the endless translation and re-translation, tracking the cipher from language to language which cannot contain it.

Is this the final statement that can be made of the genre of catastrophe? Would it be impudent to propose another, final frame that might return to the question of genre and repetition?

If the genre of catastrophe retains its 'unacceptable' status, and if Ballard's texts themselves are unacceptable to it, what better than to propose a relation to Freud's most 'unacceptable' text, *Beyond the Pleasure Principle*, with its aberrant, speculative foray into myth, philosophy and 'telling stories' (Weber), its 'shocking lack of logic' (Laplanche, 122). *Beyond* is that text, catastrophic for the institution of psychoanalysis, which must be managed and contained, isolated; like the action of the death drive the text famously introduces, its tension must be reduced to zero.

Once again, it is a text that produces uncanny resonances with Ballard's work. A term that I have hitherto loosely used, repetition compulsion, marks Ballard's obsessive repetition of plots, characters, place-names and geographies with a drivenness. Further, as Nicholls and others so insistently note, these plots tend towards death or mutilation, the inexplicable and apparent pleasure at the unpleasurable. There is also another crucial resonance. In the most 'speculative' chapter of *Beyond*, Freud elaborates the function of the death drive. If the pleasure principle is concerned to reduce tensions in the psychic apparatus, to bind up excess or 'unbound' energy which causes disturbance, this is in opposition to the death drive which aims for absolute discharge of energy, the reduction of energy in the system to zero. It is a desire to 'restore an earlier state of things' (*Beyond*, 305), to return the organism to the state of the inorganic, the dead. This death must be the system's ownmost, 'proper', internal death, it cannot invite or entertain an external imposition of non-being. As such, if 'the aim of all life is death' (*Beyond*, 311), it cannot ignore or evade external stimuli and must constantly adjust to it; death is the aim, but the 'proper' death must evade that threatened externally. What 'life' constitutes is detour, a constant series of adjustments, a passage *between two deaths*, two zeros.

Jaspers' notion of the cipher has an evident etymology: according to the *Oxford English Dictionary* it means 'a secret or disguised manner of writing, whether by characters arbitrarily invented . . . or by an aribtrary use of letters or characters in other than their ordinary sense . . . intelligible only to those possessing a key'. The root of cipher, however, is given as 'the arithmetical symbol of zero or nought', from the Sanskrit meaning 'empty'. Could the ciphers which litter Ballard's landscapes merely draw a zero? Could the Jungian mandala, that symbol of wholeness and completeness that Powers builds in concrete in 'The Voices of Time'—could its plenitude of suggested meaning actually be empty? It should be recalled that Traven journeys to Eniwetok because the zone between wars, between deaths, pushes towards the 'psychic zero' (137). Yasuda also interprets Traven's quest as the search for 'the white leviathan, zero' (153). The crystallizing process in *The Crystal World* is projected as eventually encompassing the entire universe, reducing it to the 'ultimate macrocosmic zero' (85).This could be multiplied further: to get over his breakdown, Larsen, in 'Zone of Terror', is sent to the desert for its 'hypotensive virtues, its equivalence to the psychic zero' (*The Disaster Area*, 123)—

landscapes are sought out for this status of approaching zero, death. And what of 'Now: Zero' which proposes the very act of inscribing the story as affecting the death of its reader, or 'Time of Passage', which details a personal history in reverse, beginning with death and ending with the return to the womb, to zero, to non-existence, 'an earlier state of things'. Could it be that all these signs in Ballard's texts mean 'nothing', or rather mean nothing *finally*, initiating only the translations and re-translations of narratives called forth?

Beyond is intriguing because it contains and refutes those narratives that would seek to expose the final ground of the catastrophe. The first evidence for the death drive is the compulsion to repeat in the psychoanalytic session and in the repetitive rituals of certain forms of neurosis. 'Traumatic neurosis' provides the problem, for this evidently repeats unpleasure, the active seeking of unpleasure which transgresses the pleasure principle's operation to maintain a level of minimum excitation by repeated discharge.

Freud offers a number of explanations for this process which would remain under the dominance of the pleasure principle. Trauma is occasioned by fright, an unexpected breach of external stimuli through the protective filters and screens. One explanation of the compulsion to repeat the trauma is a retrospective action of developing a preparedness, the construction of an anxiety that would have contained the stimuli that had breached the screen. Another, relating to Freud's famous example of the child's fort/da game, is that this is a response to the passivity of abandonment which the game transforms into an active attempt at mastery.

The genre of catastrophe, in the traditional reading of 'popular' culture, is the expression of a national unconsciousness, the site of collective anxieties. The repetitiveness of the genre is a token of the importance of that anxiety. In Freudian terms the bizarre temporality of the catastrophe genre projects the disaster as having already happened, but it returns it to the present, retroactively, to construct an anxiety that would have 'dealt' with the catastrophe. Again, the passivity, the insignificance of the individual in relation to the global disaster, is turned into active narratives of survival. This could account for the 'anomaly' of disaster fiction's popularity. But there is pleasure here, manifest pleasure; could this be explained by Freud's suggestion that unpleasure for one element may be pleasure for another or that there is pleasure in 'revenge', destructiveness?

However, Freud rejects these explanations, he must posit 'the operation of tendencies beyond the pleasure principle, that is, of tendencies more primitive than it and independent of it' (*Beyond*, 287). It is here that speculation enters. For Laplanche this is nothing more than a complete transgression of the designated 'zone' of psychoanalysis; it leaves the psychic order, and enters the biological sciences, the 'vital order'. In prompting these primary, primitive instincts of life and death Freud is himself forced to confess that he has had to fall back on 'figurative language' (*Beyond*, 334). If *Beyond* is attempting to reach bottom, gain the final ground, all that is discovered there are figures, metaphors—that 'beyond' remains hidden. As for his reflections on the origin of life and sexuality, the forces escaping the original state of death, Freud turns to myth, the story from *The Symposium* of the double humans split in two by Zeus, seeking solace of their former unity in the sexual act. As Weber shows, this 'story' has no authority in *The Symposium*; Aristophanes is concerned he will be ridiculed and tries to detract what he has said. Further, the text of *The Symposium* is itself a report, second-hand, an attempted reconstruction of a previous conversation. The origin of repetition is itself a repetition.

The repetition of repetition: this is the structure I accord to the operation of Ballard's texts and their repetition of the genre of catastrophe. It is a repetition that resists easy conclusions or claims of transcendence fulfilled. This is not to deny the pull of a narrative that would expose, contain and finally explain the catastrophe—witness these frames—the imperial, the Jungian, the existential (in Camusian, Heideggerian, and Jaspersian versions), the Freudian. And yet the space between the initial catastrophe and the apocalyptic conclusion can only be intimated, and these frames only a chain called forth by the catastrophe itself.

My intention in presenting this overdetermined set of frames ought to made clear: what impels this labour of interpretation is the enigma of the interval, the peculiar space of the texts as *taking place between catastrophes*. If there is a lag between the catastrophic event and its narration and re-narration, then that lag opens the possibility of multiple and even incompatible ways of theorizing its space. 'Time-lag', to recall Homi Bhabha, 'is not a circulation of nullity, the endless slippage of the signifier' (*The Location of Culture*, 245). The theories of the catastrophe offered do not cancel each other out, or insist on provisionality and relativism, for each hold powerful truth-effects. Rather, this dance is led by the maddening space of Ballard's *being between*. I have demonstrated the many ways of passing through the catastrophe novels. The chance is now available to investigate further this strangely productive interstitial space in relation to Ballard's other novels.

CHAPTER THREE
The Atrocity Exhibition
and the Problematic of the
Avant-garde

I loathe the word 'literature'—J. G. Ballard (Goddard, 25)

horrible . . . pointless . . . boring—Paul Theroux (56)

How is one to approach this object, this text or texts? The fifteen sections that make up *The Atrocity Exhibition*[1] appeared singly, across a wide range of journals, both science fiction and non-science fiction; are these short stories, then, separable as such? James Blish sensed a design: 'pieces of a mosaic, the central subject of which is not yet visible . . . these fragments . . . are going somewhere, by the most unusual method of trying to surround it, or work into it from the edges of a frame' (127). The assumption here is that the sequence will coalesce. Blish's statement, that 'the plain, blunt fact is that we do not yet know what it is Ballard is talking about' (128) has echoed ever since. Ballard and subsequent commentators, have used the term 'condensed novels' for *Atrocity*. The compacted space of these micro-novels performs a self-consciously 'experimental' stripping-down of the 'social novel', declared 'dead' by the accompanying manifesto, 'Notes From Nowhere'. This strategy of condensation is to be taken seriously; to unpack the compacted space of this disquieting text or set of texts will require a counteracting expansiveness.

How to determine this new, condensed space? Contemporaneous statements by Ballard propose 'We're living inside an enormous novel' and that 'the function of the writer is no longer the addition of fiction to the world, but rather to seek its abstraction, to direct enquiry aimed at recovering elements of reality from this debauch of fiction' (Louit, 53). This breaches entirely the frame of the 'literary'. Even if this is rhetorical excess, there is still a sense in which *Atrocity*'s status is problematic: for Greenland, this text is 'a minimal overlay of narrative gestures on a mass of theory' (Greenland, 115). Is it possible to divide the literary and the theoretical, defend *Atrocity* as a novel centring on T----, with an appendix of scientific reports, those 'psychoanalytic' papers that conclude it? Or is it entirely a scientific report, written Doctor Nathan? Many have noted that the form of the text (or texts), with its brief paragraphs titled in bold type, parodies the structure of scientific papers. Where to insert the border? How to frame *Atrocity*?

This persistent recourse to the notion of a frame opens yet another approach. The densely allusionistic text frequently involves citations of artworks. Paragraph titles refer to 'The Exploding Madonna', 'The Persistence of Memory' (Dali, 16, 22), 'The Annunciation' (Magritte, 23), 'The Robing of the Bride' (Ernst, 39), 'The Bride Stripped Bare of Her Bachelors, Even' (Duchamp, 35). 'Chapter' titles also cite artworks, like 'The Great American Nude' (a series of works by Wesselman), or else allude to them, like 'The Summer Cannibals' (a shift of season from Dali's 'Autumn Cannibalism'). Ballard had already presented the co-ordinates of his work in relation to Surrealism in his essay 'The Coming of the Unconscious' by an invocation of the titles of key paintings (De Chirico's 'The Disquieting Muses', Magritte's 'The Annunciation', Ernst's 'The Eye of Silence'). In 1969 Ballard curated an exhibition of crashed cars at the New Arts Laboratory. Could *Atrocity* in some way become a bizarre exhibition catalogue, paragraphs as statements or evocations on their 'titles', a kind of narrativized set of 'commentary notes', where action takes place within a sequence of framed paintings? But then this simple relation of text to image was itself interrogated by 'the surrealist book': 'For the surrealists, the work to be illustrated does not constitute a model or even an antecedent. Text, drawing, or photograph plays . . . the role of an inner model that stimulates but never contains his imagination' (Hubert, 21). This implies a more complex model than indebtedness to the painterly, and if Ballard has been commonly described as a 'surrealist' writer, *Atrocity* is the place to determine the full effect of that paradoxical pictoriality.

Titles do not solely refer to artworks, however; 'Concentration City' (112), 'Venus Smiles' (35), 'The Sixty Minute Zoom' (24) refer to titles of other Ballard stories, and 'chapter' titles are elsewhere paragraph titles within other 'chapters'. With the 'hierarchy' of titles constantly shifting, this echoes those questions central to Derrida's interrogation of genre, literature and painting:

> What happens when one entitles a 'work of art'? What is the topos of the title? Does it take place (and where?) in relation to the work? On the edge? Over the edge? On the internal border?

In an over-board that is re-marked and re-applied, by invagination, within, between the presumed centre and the circumfer-
ence? (*The Truth in Painting*, 24)

These questions also arise when reading *Atrocity*, as titles reveal a
fundamental instability, a troubling lack of authority, making the edges
of the text difficult to discern.

If these concerns are opened by the form of *Atrocity*, it also becomes
difficult to offer a 'commentary' on it. As Noel King has remarked of
Don DeLillo's *White Noise*, 'any act of criticism would seem misplaced
. . . for seeming to be everywhere anticipated, pre-empted, forced into
an unsettling critical sphere between the welcome and the redundant'
(69). *Atrocity* is similar: the 'thetic' voice of Nathan's dogged exegeses
dominates; the props of character later disappear entirely in the
'scientific' reports. Further, in the recent American (re-)publication of
Atrocity by the Re/Search group, each page has a wide margin down
which Ballard, some twenty years later, has provided a commentary
and elucidation of obscure references. The space of the text was difficult
enough to determine, but the critic now also finds the margins
occupied. Another frame is breached; the scribbled explanatory notes
of the reader have already been written.

This indetermination, this difficulty of approach, may mark *Atrocity*'s
success; it is, it may be said, the quality of the avant-garde to de-
stabilize, burst the frame of the 'object' or 'artwork'. Parallels abound
here: of working (in Blish's phrase) on 'the edges of a frame' ('To set the
frame in itself in motion: to pry it loose from its mute invisibility and
free it for circulation; that too is the task of the avant-garde' (Mann,
100)); of breaching the autonomy of the literary by 'recovering
elements of reality', a technique familiar from the collage and the
ready-made; of using disgusting or obscene material precisely to shock
or make tremble delicate literary sensibilities. To call *Atrocity* an avant-
garde work, however, is to invoke the whole armature of the theory of
the avant-garde—of modernism and postmodernism, of the death (or
not) of the avant-garde, of the crucial place of the 1960s in the fortunes
of avant-garde practice. To de-compress the explosive violence of
Atrocity is to negotiate this territory, both to install Ballard in its lineage
and to find that the peculiar positionality of *Atrocity* (as both science
fiction and avant-garde) inserts an intolerable oscillation in the borders
that still patrol literary and artistic practice.

'Avant-Garde Science Fiction'?

Generational condemnation: Kingsley Amis, calling himself one of the first intellectuals to deal 'properly' with science fiction feels his control slipping. *Atrocity* indicates that 'Sf is dying, disappearing, changing into something else' ('ARRGH!' 6); Martin Amis concludes that Ballard in his experimental phase between *Atrocity* and *Crash* has failed: 'In sf Ballard had a tight framework for his unnerving ideas; out on the lunatic fringe, he can only flail and shout' (cited Pringle, *Bibliography*, 99). What is this 'something else' and where is this 'lunatic fringe'? The answer in the anonymous review in *The Times Literary Supplement* in 1973, is that with *Atrocity* and *Crash* Ballard 'earned the disparaging reputation of being the intellectual of avant-garde science fiction' (Anon, 1466).

It is worth pausing on this phrase 'avant-garde science fiction', for what could it mean? It might obviously serve to nominate the New Wave, science fiction's 'leading edge' in the 1960s to which Ballard became 'the Voice', in Moorcock's phrase. But is it the internal edge of a popular genre, or a breaching of the very boundaries of the generic? As an 'internal' avant-garde, this would appear to demolish the opposition set up so influentially by Clement Greenberg in 'Avant-garde and Kitsch'. Against the avant-garde's aim to 'maintain the high level of . . . art by both narrowing and raising it to the expression of an absolute' (crystallized by the move to the 'formal immanence' of Abstraction (5)), would not science fiction, in Greenberg's élitist terms, precisely embody the kitsch of mass culture—its formulaic, repetitive, vicarious and unreflective enjoyments? The Modernist conception of the avant-garde, as Andreas Huyssen has noted, is rigorously defined *against* the popular. 'Avant-garde science fiction', then, would be a problematic transposition of a strategy to a place where, strictly speaking, the avant-garde could not perform. But if it is merely internal, what to do with Ballard's evident debts in *Atrocity* to 'Modernist' devices derived from Surrealism, Cubism, and other movements?

'Avant-garde science fiction' could be read in another model: the vanguard breaching of the boundaries of artistic institutions as guarantors of taste. Contemporaneous with Ballard's experimental fictions, Leslie Fiedler had announced science fiction as the form in which writers were turning 'high art into vaudeville and burlesque' (478). This 'crossing the border' between high and low art, avant-garde and kitsch, however, is premised on the *destruction* of avant-garde strategies by a move to popular genres like science fiction 'at the furthest possible remove from art and avant-garde' (469). In this incipient moment of the emergence of the rhetoric of definitional postmodernism, science fiction might lose its ghettoized status but the whole force of Fiedler's essays is to render the phrase 'avant-garde science fiction' a nonsense. If paradoxically coupling a high art modifier to a low art genre, the announcement of Post-Modernist fiction is built on the grave of the very distinction which gives the phrase its force. *Atrocity* could not be avant-garde in this formulation either: it could, however, become an exemplary instance (as it is for Brian McHale) of postmodernist fiction.

The aggression shown by many science fiction critics towards the New Wave and *Atrocity* in particular works by shifting the meaning of 'avant-garde' once more. Peter Rønnov-Jessen, for instance, narrates the move of *New Worlds* from science fiction pulp magazine to avant-garde journal supported by the Arts Council as a story of eventual demise by progressive incorporation. Here, the avant-garde does not signal that which is in revolt against bourgeois taste or art institutions but is exactly equated with 'dominant culture'. In a reversal of value, the heroic marginality of the pulps guarantees subversive edge; Moorcock's *New Worlds*, by becoming avant-garde, wanted to insert itself into the mainstream tradition of 'Eng. Lit'. Extrapolating from this argument, *Atrocity* might appear to be a radical text, but is in fact the leading edge of a willed recuperation and neutralization of science fiction's subversiveness.

The above three paragraphs recapitulate, very precisely, the tangled web of theories of the avant-garde. The 'modernist' avant-garde defines itself in opposition to the popular; *Atrocity* could apparently find no place there, despite its substantial use of collage, found texts, shock and textual violence. Postmodernism, eliding high and low art, garners its politics from the abandonment of avant-garde strategies, which would seem to deny many of the devices deployed by Ballard. The concern of Rønnov-Jessen, whilst reversing values, yet retains the central issue of avant-gardism as defined by Susan Rubin Suleiman: how to avoid recuperation. It seems that a serious investigation of *Atrocity* cannot avoid a sustained engagement with the theory of the avant-garde, for *Atrocity* traverses its field in an insistent way. In doing so, in the 'impossible' simultaneity of its Modernist and Postmodernist, avant-garde and 'post'-avant-garde stances, it places itself, in a phrase that echoes constantly through the text, 'in the angle between two walls'.

Theories of the Avant-Garde

The theory of the avant-garde is a paradoxical and fraught discourse: to develop a systematized theory is virtually to admit to the avant-garde's failure to resist theorization; to offer a history of its practices is to reduce it to the 'art history' it sought to explode. To theorize it is to announce its death. It is also a contested discourse: its two main theorists—Bürger and Adorno—completely contradict each other on its definition, the one stressing 'sublation' of art and life, the other insisting on the autonomy of art.

Peter Bürger's *The Theory of the Avant-Garde* has been very influential. Bürger wishes to move beyond the implacable opposition of Adorno versus Luckàcs, (avant-garde as resolutely political and anti-bourgeois; avant-garde as a sign of bourgeois decadence). For Bürger, the avant-garde is not a left or right politics within art, but a politics opposed to the very notion of 'Art'. In this debate Kant is the key figure and Bürger unfolds a retroactive history of his influence. Kant is the first to determine aesthetics as an autonomous non-purposive sphere. For Bürger, this is co-terminous with the rise of the bourgeois state, and is double edged. Firstly, art is removed from the 'means-end rationality' of the productive economy (tied 'ideally' to use, but ultimately exchange); art stalls this process not in being its own end but by proceeding with an end in view that cannot be realized. Secondly, however, autonomy is gained with the very loss of integration into everyday praxis. If Art is measured by social function, it gains the ability to evade re-functioning by external factors (this, for Adorno, constitutes the power of its critique), but loses any effective social function.

It is Bürger's thesis that such autonomy did not become 'visible' as art's condition until autonomy became the very subject of art in aestheticism in the late nineteenth century. Further, the conditions of aestheticism only become clear once the avant-garde launches its attack. The central elements of Bürger's avant-garde can thus be established: at the apex of autonomy Art's institutional foundations are revealed and displayed as socially ineffective. The avant-garde is to be defined as seeking to destroy institutional inefficacy by three routes: problematizing the non-purposive by dissolving the distinction of art and life; by a 'radical negation' of institutional artistic production (determined by the signature, and the 'framable' work); and by attacking the passive bourgeois reception of artworks by insisting on strategies that provoke a participatory response, either by meanings that need to be 'completed' (collage, say) or by emphasizing 'democratic' methods (the ready-made, automatism). These three elements circulate through the majority of discussions of the avant-garde.

Adorno's conception of the avant-garde is very different; briefly, Art's negation can only be operable as it evades instrumental rationality (re-functioning for use) and so autonomy must be maintained. Any breach into social effectivity thus erases the avant-garde partition, since it risks its useless use being processed into instrumentality, swept into the relativism of the exchange economy. In Bürger's terms, this remains internal to the institutional parameters laid down for Art's field, but also offers an unequal equation: the avant-garde's explosion of the institutional frame does not re-absorb art into the everyday as it stands, since it aims to sublate both art and the means-end rationality that dominates the everyday into an entirely new, utopian relation.

Both agree, however, on the result of this project. Bürger initially indicates his position in a footnote, which names the avant-garde he adopts as models: Dada, Surrealism, the Russian and Italian Futurists (109). The very ability to 'name' them marks their reintegration into art history. Dada and Surrealism used 'shock', but these punctural effects were quickly repaired. Hence these attempts are termed the *historical avant-garde*, indicating their irrecuperable pastness. Bürger contends that subsequent attempts to revive avant-gardism can only mimic already pacified strategies: 'the demand that art be reintegrated in the praxis of life within the existing society can no longer be seriously made' (109) for 'the culture industry has brought about the false elimination of the distance between art and life' (50).

The culture industry is the 'spreading ooze' (in Dwight MacDonald's phrase) that is in the process of eroding the autonomy of the avant-garde in Adorno's terms: 'There are no longer any hiding places' (*The Culture Industry*, 103). The very uselessness of art has become appropriated within a vastly and uniformly expanding market, as a specific marker for use—'tolerated negativity' as cachet, symbolic value, traded on the art markets. Shock tactics and anti-institutional stances are resumed elsewhere: 'Advertising has absorbed surrealism and the champions of this movement have given their blessing to this commercialization of their own murderous attacks on culture' (*The Culture Industry*, 59). Negation becomes affirmative. If the high is brought low, the low, the mass, becomes the normalizing and neutralizing programme of affirmative culture.

These positions (as baldly stated) lead directly into well-established and polarized positions within postmodernism. For those who would equate autonomy and negativity solely within the position of the historical avant-garde, the postmodern turn is fatal: for Terry Eagleton 'The culture industry in its postmodernist phase has achieved what the avant-garde always wanted: the sublation of the difference between art and life'. Postmodernist culture is a 'sick joke', a 'sardonic commentary on the avant-garde work' in its blissful and uncritical merging with commodity culture (61). On the other side, the 'celebrants' of post-modernism tend to emphasize in their criticism of modernism not Bürger but Adorno, arguing that the maintenance of autonomy was a regressive withdrawal, a misfired 'shoring up' that itself constituted the divide between high and low. Others, with Bürger as support, but shifting his conclusion, contend that the modernist conception of negativity must not be lauded as an ahistorical fixed set of strategies; the avant-garde may be specifically modernist, but its 'death' does not negate negation. John Tagg warns of romanticizing the position of marginality and joins with Rosalind Krauss in attacking the mobilizing myth of the avant-garde: the marginal critique by the specific, unique, 'original' artist. 'In deconstructing the sister notion of origin and originality, postmodernism establishes a schism between itself and the domain of the avant-garde, looking back at it across a gulf that in turn establishes a historical divide' (Krauss, *The Originality of the Avant-garde*, 170).

Where to place the avant-gardism of *Atrocity* in these accounts? There seems to be nowhere, for if *Atrocity* 'rises' from a 'low' genre and so threatens to dissolve Adorno's theorization of the avant-garde, then placing it within the frame of postmodernism—which is in opposition, positively or negatively, to the avant-garde—doubly denies any linkage.

The terms of the above debate are crudely stated: they need to be problematized. The coherence of definitional postmodernism always seems to depend on a caricatured modernism, and this works, in one method, through a simplification of Adorno. Peter Osborne has usefully suggested that, at least for art theory, Adorno's position has been collapsed into the more monumentally fixed opposition of Clement Greenberg's 'Avant-garde and Kitsch', such that Adorno's autonomy is mistakenly read as pure formal immanence. There is thus the contention by certain art theorists that against this formal imma-nence, postmodernism re-introduces a 'politics of representation' (as if it could not be there in immanental, abstract forms). As Adorno's *Aesthetic Theory* indicates, the autonomy of modernism, whilst giving space for negation, is a space precisely given by bourgeois socio-economic organization, and is therefore always implicated in its structures. Autonomy is a goal of 'purity' that is never attained; the antagonisms of the everyday 're-appear in art in the guise of immanent problems' (8); in short, 'it becomes impossible to criticize the culture industry without criticizing art at the same time' (26). A much earlier essay, which adds to Adorno's famous statement on the 'torn halves' of high and low culture, suggests that the divide is not an immanent difference of form or evaluation, but is an artificial erection of 'wire fences', because without this segmentation 'the inhabitants could all too easily come to an understanding of the whole' (*The Culture Industry*, 31). For Adorno, then, the avant-garde and autonomy are never coincident, and the high and low are never 'purely' opposed.

Bürger has 'served' definitional postmodernism by failing to emphasize how far Adorno puts the avant-garde 'in play' rather than as an isolatable position. If Bürger attempts to shift the definition of the avant-garde away from 'pure' negation to emphasizing the breach of art as institution, he nevertheless concludes that the project of the sublation of art and life can never succeed within bourgeois society, and so the only strategy left is precisely that initially criticized in Adorno: negation by the autonomous work. For postmodernism, a double death is announced: the first two routes of avant-garde strategy are blocked, for if sublation fails, the retreat to autonomy is already blocked by Adorno himself: 'There are no longer any places to hide'.

It is interesting that Bürger criticizes the neo-avant-garde for precisely the strategy that earlier he had posited as the third route, reception. Warhol, as exemplar of neo-avant-gardism, is dangerously ambivalent, for his work 'contains resistance to the commodity society only for the person who wants to see it there' (53); it is a 'manifestation that is void of sense and that permits the positing of any meaning whatsoever' (61). This disturbance of the passive reception of works is deemed not enough; Warhol's work entertains a fatal complicity with commodification. However, it is precisely *ambivalence*, the indeterminability of affirmation or negation, that is central to positive or negative evaluations of postmodernist art. Despite 'pure' negation being questioned by the collapse of modernism's 'self-constituted' divide from the 'mass', it is negation that remains the measure of critical art. Linda Hutcheon, for example, initially supports the 'democratizing' aspects of postmodernism in its critique of élitist Modernist practices, but she still requires a distinction between 'critical' postmodernism and its merely 'kitsch' imitation. Once she sets up a mutual interference of postmodernism and feminism, the former's 'complicitous critique' is too ambivalent to support a 'distinct, unambiguous' feminist politics

(*The Politics of Postmodernism*, 141). Ambivalence, from the view of negation, cannot register a politics.

I have consistently proposed that Ballard's work effects an oscillation. *Atrocity* intensifies this in its uncertain status between the art historical categories just elaborated. Ballard's own statements oscillate between compartments. His view that 'I consider I left the [science fiction] genre completely with *The Atrocity Exhibition*, but I don't have any substitute terminology for what I write' (Louit, 51) is flatly contradicted elsewhere. Ballard criticized *New Worlds* for moving 'outside' science fiction in specific terms. He praised the 'conventional' editor of *New Worlds*, Ted Carnell, as far more radical than Moorcock: 'Moorcock in fact was following what were wholly traditional and conventional lines—the avant-garde in short; experimental and exploratory writing of a kind long since established in the early years of the 20th Century' ('A Personal View', 10–11). Testing boundaries within science fiction is more radical than avant-gardism (in this he evidently agrees with Rønnov-Jessen). This, however, needs further qualification. Ballard has recently viewed his career as departing from science fiction in 1966: 'But labels stick . . . one must break down these damned categories' (interview with Pringle 1987, 14).

The publishing history of *Atrocity* is also confusing in this regard. Doubleday, the American pulp fiction house almost published it before its director decided to withdraw it before the first print run had been distributed, as it was considered obscene and libellous. *Atrocity* was then picked up, re-titled as *Love and Napalm: Export USA*, and given the avant-garde cachet of a William Burroughs introduction in a Grove Press edition, the avant-garde publishers who translated and distributed work by William Burroughs, Georges Bataille and the Marquis de Sade. Bizarrely, then, pulp pulped becomes in effect 'high art'.

The specific case of the 'chapter', 'Why I Want to Fuck Ronald Reagan', further indicates this circulation. 'Plan for the assassination of Jacqueline Kennedy' had provoked questions in the Houses of Parliament (and an anxious reassertion of British respect for the Kennedys by Randolph Churchill), but the Reagan piece, unpublishable except in pamphlet form in the strangely titled *Ronald Reagan: Magazine for Poetry*, had one of its stockists, the Unicorn Bookshop in Brighton, successfully prosecuted for obscenity. Ballard's book was only one piece of evidence alongside works by Bataille and Burroughs. Despite the successful defence of Selby's *Last Exit to Brooklyn*, through similar 'high art' grounds that famously allowed the publication of *Lady Chatterley's Lover*, one suspects that 'Why I Want to Fuck Ronald Reagan', as a 'chapter' of a book entitled *The Atrocity Exhibition,* escaped prosecution was because, in Britain, it was published within the confines of science fiction. Obscene pamphlet and non-obscene 'chapter', the piece also re-appeared in non-art guise at the 1980 Republican Convention as an official 'Survey' document, distributed to delegates as an analysis of Reagan's potential. Vale and Juno report that 'some ex-Situationists were responsible for this black humour critique' (88). This text displays a remarkable mobility, and this intrusion, however briefly disruptive, is consonant with avant-garde surrealist and situationist strategies of subversion.

Atrocity still effectuated 'shock' therefore. This is not enough to cite it within the problematic of the avant-garde, however, even though Bürger ultimately tends to reduce avant-gardism to this one effect, and the non-repeatable nature of shock to its recuperation and failure. 'Shock' is not enough, period. Bürger's intention is to set in motion historicized aesthetic categories, to move away from the ahistorical (as he perceives it) 'completed' aesthetics of the avant-garde in Adorno. It is strange, however, that this historicization effectively stops, as Hal Foster has noted, on consigning the historical avant-garde to failure. All theories of aesthetics are historical, he states. Very well: Bürger's 'Post-script' to a Second Edition states that, despite criticism, the book has remained unchanged because 'it reflects a historical constellation of problems that emerged after the events of May 1968 and the failure of the student movement in the early seventies' (95). It is necessary to historicize Bürger's historicization of the avant-garde; it is as if, just as the avant-garde only revealed retroactively the institution of art, so 'May 68' reveals, retroactively, the failure of the avant-garde. Narratives of avant-gardist failure only begin to appear decades after their initial disruptive effects; it is as much these narratives as the events they narrate that are historically significant. Bürger's *The Theory of the Avant-Garde* appeared in Germany in 1974, which places it two years after Peter Wollen's suggestion that the dissolution of the Situationist International in 1972 constitutes the terminal point of the twentieth century avant-garde. 'May 1968' and its failure reveal, for Bürger, the end of avant-gardism, which is then displaced back in time.

In these terms, the time in which the sections of *Atrocity* were written (1966–9) could still fall within the moment of the avant-garde *as long as* the avant-garde is not considered as a completed, historical set of strategies, but as a mobile and constantly self-transforming set of tactics. The monolithic opposition of modernist avant-garde and postmodernist neo-avant-garde is far too straightforward. *Atrocity* is nothing if not a sustained and reflexive investigation of the complex of negation, affirmation and oscillation that constituted countercultural avant-gardism in the 1960s.

The perception of the time was that the counterculture was an avant-garde sublation of art and life. The aim of the milieu was 'to ignore all boundaries and conventions, and as far as possible to escape the imposed definitions of material reality by exploring inner space' (Hewison, 86). The counterculture was premised on the belief that the economics of post-scarcity has arrived. Complicit and co-terminous with economic boom, the problematic of production was deemed solved. This is the premise both of Marcuse's *One Dimensional Man* and *An Essay on Liberation*, as well as other equally influential texts, like McLuhan's *Understanding Media*. Marcuse, in the *Essay*, is careful to signal only signs of 'hope', but this is nevertheless only the first indication of a genuine liberation: 'the space, both physical and mental, for building a realm of freedom, which is not that of the present: liberation also from the liberties of the post-exploitative order'— *de*-sublimation in effect. With the arrival of post-scarcity, vital needs, the basis for authentic, non-alienated Man, have to be revised. Marcuse sees this imaginative reconfiguration of vital needs in 'The New Sensibility' of the new historical subjects: blacks in the American ghettos and the student rebellion. Since the proletariat have been integrated into advanced industrialism, revolutionary consciousness shifts to these new subjects. This avant-garde cadre cannot proceed through any organized party, however, but through 'surrealistic forms of protest' (30). Surrealism, in fact, is the constant measure of the counterculture. Breaking the Kantian boundaries of Art to re-situate the 'sensual power' of the imagination as a productive force is a shared goal. Marcuse argued that the first anti-art fell within form, and thus remained within recuperable categories of Art. The new avant-garde desublimates form: 'The new object of art is not yet "given", but the familiar object has become impossible, false' (38). 'Today's rebels' step entirely beyond Kantian, the 'orderly, harmonizing forms' (46) that re-captured the first anti-art attempts.

It is vital to note firstly that the perception here is both of a shift in the site and an *intensification* of negation, and that secondly this is powered by new subjects, 'groups which have thus far remained outside the entire realm of higher culture' (46). Although Marcuse rather problematically cites black music as exemplary of this (natural rhythm as subversive), he begins to indicate that Sixties avant-gardism is no longer to be located in the extremities of 'high culture'. Rather it is a set of mobile strategies that move through the high and low as well as between groups. *Atrocity* as 'avant-garde' here becomes less the flat contradiction that it first appeared—and indeed the whole project of *New Worlds* begins to make sense in what becomes a punctual (if unsustainable) moment, where a science fiction journal could begin to contribute to the *nouveau roman* (Brian Aldiss' *Report on Probability A*), publish Thomas Pynchon's 'Entropy', undertake collaborative writing projects (like the multi-authored Jerry Cornelius stories), and cite avant-garde writers and film-makers like William Burroughs and Chris Marker as exemplary of new forms.

At the time of the composition of *Atrocity*, state 'liberalization' co-existed with a counter-reaction: homosexuality was legalized, but convictions increased; the 'servants' could now read *Lady Chatterley's Lover*, but controls intensified on 'obscene' publications. Stuart Hall has latterly tempered the 'transgressiveness' of the counterculture. Hall terms it 'profoundly adaptive to the system's productive base' (65) largely necessitated by shifts in production away from a 'conserving' work ethic towards a 'repetitive cycle of consumption' (64). A 'caesura' within formations, Hall thus accounts for oscillating forms of the counterculture: incorporable elements are the 'planned permissive-ness' of alternative 'life-styles' ; oppositional elements, remain never wholly recuperable (gay and feminist politics, terrorism).

Internally disaffiliated, forming into a diffuse milieu, the strategy operated by 'pushing contradictory tendencies in the culture to extremes . . . subvert[ing] them, but from the inside, and by a negation' (Hall, 62) Negation still operates here, but across and between an oscillation of incorporation/opposition. Combining both Marcuse's contemporaneous account with Hall's narrative, an extension of avant-gardism is being posited here. The accounts of both the modernist avant-garde and postmodernism are united by an intolerance of ambi-valence. Oscillation, however, in Hall's account marks the very milieu of the counterculture. What if indeterminability, lack of fixity, could form a 'politics'? If 'pure' states of affirmation and negation are rendered inoperable through the capitalist penetration of the 'cultural' sphere, the strategy of playing on the edge between affirmation and negation troubles simple accounts of the 'political' spaces of art.

Atrocity is a 'punctual' text, of its moment. If it has been seen as both modernist (Pfeil) and postmodernist (McHale), it is not a question of deciding one or the other, but of marking its oscillation. This can be discerned very exactly. In what follows I unpick the density of *Atrocity* by analysing its extension—in strategy, reference and device—of

Surrealism and Pop Art, two distinct moments in the problematic of the avant-garde.

The Atrocity Exhibition as Avant-Garde Composition

Traven/Talbot/Tallis/Trabert/Travis/Talbert/Travers—the figure I shall call 'the T-cell'[2]—appears in disjunctive guises: as both lecturer and patient at a psychiatric institution, a former H-bomb pilot, as well as signifier of 'Christ's return'. In the opening sections of *Atrocity* the T-cell is searching for a 'modulus', a measure, a mode of explanation, that would both re-fix his name and identity as well as serve to de-code the densely overdetermined landscapes in which he appears. The landscapes of the text are synaesthetic, as it were, capable of absolute translation from one level to another, different meanings collapsing into nodal points of simultaneity. This is the primary content of Nathan's didactic theorizing, that 'for him [the T-cell] all junctions, whether of our own soft biologies or the hard geometries of these walls and ceilings, are equivalent to one another'(56).

If Nathan is analysing his fellow doctor or patient ('Mrs Travis, I'm not sure if the question is valid any longer. These matters involve a relativity of a different kind' (12)—admirably Laingian), he is also offering a commentary on the central device of the text itself. Nathan re-cites the manifesto 'Notes From Nowhere', published in *New Worlds*. Its crucial premise is:

> Planes intersect: on one level, the world of public events, Cape Kennedy and Viet Nam mimetized on billboards. On another level, the immediate personal environment, the volumes of space enclosed by my opposed hands, the geometry of my own postures, the time-values contained in this room, the motion-space of highways, staircases, the angle between these walls. On a third level, the inner world of the psyche. Where these planes intersect, images are born. With these co-ordinates, some kind of valid reality begins to assert itself ('Notes From Nowhere', 148)

This is a step-by-step statement of the central device of *Atrocity*. Practice, however, erases this progressive layering, and its density makes it difficult and lengthy to loosen the process of narrative. The effect is of a compacted simultaneity, a dense, 'unreadable' space, recalling the Cubist canvas ('Notes From Nowhere' comments: 'Cubism . . . had a greater destructive power than all the explosives discharged during World War I' [150]).

This overdetermined synaesthetic collapse of levels is signalled by two methods: the list and the associative chain. In 'You and Me and the Continuum', where the T-cell is so dispersed that even a relativized proper name cannot 'fix' him, evidence of his identity is collected in a set of photographs:

> **Kodachrome**. Captain Kirby, MI5, studied the prints. They showed: (1) a thick set man in an Air Force jacket, unshaven face half-hidden by the dented hat-peak; (2) a transverse section through the spinal level T-12; (3) a crayon self-portrait by David Feary, seven year-old schizophrenic at the Belmont Asylum, Sutton; (4) radio-spectra from the quasar CTA 102; (5) an antero-posterior radiograph of a skull, estimated capacity 1500cc; (6) spectroheliogram of the sun taken with the K line of calcium; (7) left and right hand-prints showing massive scarring between second and third metacarpal bones. To Doctor Nathan, he said, 'And all these make up one picture?' (83)

Apparently heterogeneous images are forced into a conjunction, playing on the tension between a chaotic range of reference and a strict logic of regimented order by numbered 'exhibits'. The condensed 'fusions' operate to elide different discursive regimes, as if co-habiting the same space were enough to spring connections: Ernst, after all, defined collage as 'the coupling of two realities, irreconcilable in appearance, upon a plane which apparently does not suit them' (cited Chipp, 427). Even the logic of the 'levels' chosen, however, is elusive, as the T-cell, for example, charts the transitions of the '(1) Spinal . . . (2) Media . . . (3) Contour . . . (4) Astral' which form a 'renascent geometry assembling in the musculature of the young woman, in their postures during intercourse, in the angles between the walls of the apartment' (24).

Alongside this 'random' listing is the process of an associative linkage of 'levels'. 'You: Coma: Marilyn Monroe' offers a complex drift between the undulating dunes, the female body, the 'damaged dome of the planetarium', the geometry of the apartment as 'a cubicular extrapolation of . . . the cheekbones of Marilyn Monroe' (42), and Karen Novotny as the 'modulus', the obscure switching centre for these translations. It is difficult to transcribe the peculiar effect of this drift, which operates on a macro-level, cumulatively, as well as at the micro-level:

The 'Soft' Death of Marilyn Monroe. Standing in front of him as she dressed, Karen Novotny's body seemed as smooth and annealed as these frozen planes [of the walls]. Yet a displacement of time would drain away the soft interstices, leaving walls like scraped clinkers. He remembered Ernst's 'Robing': Marilyn's pitted skin, breasts of carved pumice, volcanic thighs, a face of ash. The widowed bride of Vesuvius. (39)

There is a complex chain of associations here; their density indicates how difficult it is to 'unpick' *Atrocity*. Initially, there is a straight analogy between Novotny's body and the walls of the apartment. The second sentence ('Yet a displacement . . .') is incomprehensible without jumping to the first phrase of the third. 'The Robing of the Bride', the title of the opening paragraph of the 'chapter', is a disturbing double portrait by Max Ernst of the Bride and her attendants. She dresses in an enormous red gown before a mirror which reflects back an ossified image of herself. This is nowhere imaged in the text, but there is a transcription of Ernst's painting back into the T-cell's double vision of the white walls of the apartment as suddenly excoriated, reduced to 'scraped clinkers' by a 'displacement of time'. This analogical reference to Ernst thus explains the colon of the final sentence which posits an equivalence between the painting and Monroe as reduced 'to stone'— 'volcanic thighs' her sexuality, 'a face of ash' her death mask. This is complex enough, but the title of the paragraph also marks a citation of Dali's 'soft' images. One of Dali's devices, anamorphosis (an image or drawing distorted in such a way that it becomes recognizable only when viewed in a specified manner or through a special device), describes the process undertaken in the paragraph; a 'secret code' deciphers the logic of association.

The list and the associative chain recall a central element of Bürger's determination of the avant-garde 'work': collage. Opposed to organic form, a harmonized unity passively received, collage detaches fragments from their original contexts and re-contextualizes them. Bizarre juxtapositions demand a 'closing' response, the 'spacings' between fragments necessitating an explanation of their proximity: an active, allegorical interpretation, as Benjamin Buchloh suggests, is unavoidable ('Allegorical Procedures'). If Bürger draws heavily on the work of Walter Benjamin, Benjamin's theory of allegory is central for the logic at work in *Atrocity*. Scholem's view of Benjamin's allegory is that it works as 'an infinite network of meanings and correlatives in which everything can become a representation of everything else' (cited Buck-Morss, 236). This is the sense gained by the overdetermined, condensed spaces of *Atrocity*, where 'all junctions . . . are equivalent to one another' (56), endlessly transposing meanings in a synaesthetic promiscuity.

The T-cell's search for a 'modulus' is a search for an allegorical reading that would link the fragments into narrative. This is doubled by the reader's constant attempt to decode the compacted sentences of *Atrocity*. Just as 'The "Soft" Death of Marilyn Monroe' can have a logic uncovered, so Perry and Wilkie note that the list quoted above is not as random as it appears: the T-cell figures here as a returning Messiah, not in a singular embodiment, but as dispersed through evidential traces. So the 'scarring between second and third metacarpal bones' alludes to the crucifixion, just as 'radio-spectra from quasar CTA 102' refers to reports of the time that 'the emissions from the quasar provided evidence of an intelligence at work' (Perry and Wilkie, 'The Atrocity Exhibition', 181).

Yet, as in *The Drought*'s density of ciphers and untranslatable cryptic languages, *Atrocity*'s proliferation of connection between levels fails to uncover a final interpretation, and the T-cell's erasure in the closing sections of *Atrocity*, his dispersal into traces across numerous discourses, seems to signal failure to prevent promiscuous translatability. The compulsiveness of the production of allegorical narratives to 'explain' these posited patterns is thus unending—for the T-cell, for the reader.

The main device of collage is 'the insertion of reality fragments into the painting, i.e. the insertion of material left unchanged by the artist' (Bürger, 77). This accords with Ballard's view that *Atrocity* aims at 'recovering elements of reality'. The Re/Search edition also contains an 'Appendix' of other texts written at the same time as the other 'chapters': these are 'found texts' from cosmetic surgery manuals which replace proper names (Mae West, Princess Margaret) for the anonymity of 'the patient'. This Appendix, added after the appended mock-scientific reports, makes the bottom edge of the text even more difficult to mark, ending as it does in folds of citation, 'plugging in' to ever wider discursive frames.

The space of *Atrocity* can also be seen as Cubist. The condensed texts suppress the connectives which might establish narrative links. Each paragraph or block appears as if superimposed on previous blocks. In 'The University of Death' the space in which the 'events' are enacted is continuously re-inscribed; in painterly terms, the ground on which the figures are drawn is no longer fixed, the ground itself becomes a figure:

this is Cubism as Rosalind Krauss describes it ('In the Name of Picasso', *The Originality of the Avant-Garde*). Seemingly set at the edges of a city (the previous 'chapter' loosely references Eurydice in 'the suburbs of hell'), under abandoned motorway overpasses, the T-cell takes a helicopter flight (signifier of Vietnam) to the (Demilitarized) Zone, which nevertheless appears to be the same site. The Zone is also The Plaza, and the embankments and underpasses are clearly the fantasy-invested space of Dealey Plaza, the site of Kennedy's assassination. The Plaza is 'a modulus that could be multiplied into the landscape of his consciousness' (23), and the T-cell wishes 'to kill Kennedy again, but in a way that makes sense' (36). The space shifts again, however, as the topography of ridges and embankments becomes a crash-testing circuit.

This 'chapter' also contains the paragraph title 'The Persistence of Memory', a clear reference to one of Dali's most famous paintings. The paragraph appears, on one level, to be a simple description of the painting, but there is also a clear sense that the T-cell conceives himself as a figure within it, walking on its expansive beach, the infinitely receding ground that Dali repetitively used as a space on which bizarre figurations could be invoked. The space of 'The University of Death' is thus complexly overdetermined, a simultaneity of differently perceived perspectives which patently do not 'add up'; the space does not 'work', the gaps between fragmentary references constantly foreground themselves.

Although the suggestion is that this is a 'Cubist' strategy, it can only ever be a Cubism in quotation marks. It is a displaced, a citational avant-gardism. There is the strange effect of deploying, as one fragment, Dali's 'The Persistence of Memory', a painterly space that in its illusionistic quality is resolutely opposed to collage, yet is cited within collage. One avant-garde, Surrealistic illusionism, is cited within another. These two devices are combined in a citation whose quotation marks signal a difference from the historical avant-garde rather than a simple identity with it.

Ballard and Painterly/Paranoiac Surrealism

Ballard is frequently seen in terms of his 'visual' style, the evocative landscapes, the attention to ground far more than (human) figure. When Kingsley Amis worried that Ballard was escaping from Amis' definitional rights over the genre, the solution was to 'encourag[e]

Ballard to abandon writing for painting' ('ARRGH!' 6). The allusions in his work to Surrealist painting begin early: *The Drought* written 'within' Yves Tanguy's 'Jours de Lenteur'; *The Drowned World* invoking the 'metaphysical' spaces of de Chirico's vertiginous town squares, and where Strangman directs action according to his recovered Paul Delvaux painting.

And yet, as Ballard notes to Will Self, painting had a precarious position in Surrealism. Maurice Nadeau's *History of the Surrealist Movement* 'centres' the movement in political debates of the 1920s. Breton asserted the dissolution of art/life through Surrealism, but simultaneously defended its artistic autonomy from the Communist's demand that Surrealism be subsumed to its project. Nadeau considers the constitution of a 'surrealist aesthetic' in the 1930s as marking the failure of Surrealism as an avant-garde. The propulsive force of this failure, Nadeau intimates, is the dominance of Dali, and the rise of painterly surrealism.

Other narratives of Surrealism, however, suggest that the 1920s were prototypical moves, ineffective attempts at elaborating avant-garde strategies before it fully flowered in the 1930s. For Laurent Jenny, Dali's arrival saves the movement. Sarane Alexandrian makes Surrealism co-extensive with Breton's life (Surrealism died with him in 1966), but Whitney Chadwick, in 'recovering' the largely erased history of women involved in Surrealism, moves the centre of concern away from the (all-male) experiments and definitions of the 1920s to the late 1930s, where women artists established an internal distance from Breton's continuing attempts to control the movement. The 'centre' of Surrealism is difficult to determine, but the arrival Dali is crucial in all these narratives. This is all the more remarkable given that Dali was only a member for a brief time. His entry in 1930 was delayed over the shit-smeared figure in 'The Lugubrious Game' (a painting Breton's rival Bataille praised, nearly 'poaching' Dali from Surrealism). Praising Hitler as a 'surrealist innovator' in 1934, he was estranged by 1936 and expelled in 1939.

It does in fact possess a satisfying symmetry that Ballard should cite Dali as his major influence. Dali meets Ballard, as it were, at the edge of the high/low divide; Dali's sensationalism, avidity (Dali was anagrammatically christened Avida Dollars by the Surrealists on his expulsion), and above all *popularity*, have marginalized him from Surrealist accounts and this is mirrored—exactly in reverse—by the account of Ballard rising above popular ghetto origins and thus betraying science fiction. Carter Ratcliff is prepared to place Dali's 'perverse' play with the 'low' as far beyond that ever achieved by Pop Art: thrown out of the high, he entered into 'the lower depths—and that is precisely where he wanted to be, for it is in the limitless mudflats of consumerism, with no heaven of high art above, that his image-ingestion and regurgitation brings him the fullest degree of worldly power' (66). Strangely, Ballard, was requested to remove all references to Surrealism from the catastrophe novels because association with this movement might compromise his work.

Surrealist activity at first centred on dream and automatic writing and emphasized writing rather than painting. Breton rejected 'the stabilizing of dream images in the kind of still-life depiction known as *trompe-l'oeil*' (cited, Krauss, 'Photography in the Service of Surrealism', 20). However, when Naville pronounced 'Everyone knows there is no surrealist painting' (cited, Nadeau, 118), Breton removed him from the editorship of *La Revolution Surrealiste*, and set about finding a place for the painterly.

Dali's arrival re-invigorated the tortuous logic of 'automatism' and the conception of painting as a secondary form. Automatic writing attempted the fantasy of absolute, non-delayed identity with the expression of the unconscious. Dali moved from this expressivist model to the notion of the paranoid construction of art. In Dali's reading this was an active and always interpretive mode of perceiving the external world according to the subject's perverse desire. Paranoia, rather than purely internal, perceived the same everyday objects as everyone else, but according to a bizarre and perverse narrative establishing unforeseen connections. The advantages were clear: if automatism, little more than a realist fantasy trying to avoid representation, Dali's paranoiac-critical method made a virtue of its 'secondary' interpretive role. It moved from passivity to the 'active derealization' (Jenny, 110) of a shared environment.

Atrocity can be seen to deploy this Dali-esque device. Dali defined the paranoiac-critical method as 'the critical and systematic objectification of delirious associations and interpretations' (cited, Ades, 200), which operated according to double or multiple condensation in a single image. The most ambitious use of the device was 'The Endless Enigma', in which six readings of the same landscape could be discerned. This unstable oscillation condensed different meanings within the same object. There is a link here to the compression of landscapes analysed in *Atrocity*, and a certain similarity between Dali's very public performance of his obsessions and the T-cell's experimental re-enactments of atrocities.

For Dali, the paranoiac exploits the external world, imposing his obsessions and transforming reality itself. So, if paranoia already constitutes a form of interpretation itself, as Jenny suggests, the T-cell's search for a 'modulus' is disturbingly doubled in the act of reading the attempt to make *Atrocity* make sense. The disturbing thought here is Ballard's provocation that *Atrocity* is the distillation of 'reality' from a 'debauch' of fiction; what form of knowledge is this? The specificity, the peculiarity of paranoia is its masterly mimicry of reason, and Jacques Lacan (whose early work appeared alongside Dali's in *Minotaure*) confesses at the end of his essay 'On a Question Preliminary to any possible treatment of psychosis' that the psychoanalysts' knowledge cannot be separated from the paranoiac's, that the former's shares the same structure as the latter's. As Lacan notes: 'That such a psychosis may prove to be compatible with what is called good order is not in question, but neither does it authorize the psychiatrist, even if he is a psychoanalyst, to trust to his own compatibility with that order to the extent of believing that he is in possession of an adequate idea of the reality to which his patient appears to be unequal' (Lacan, 216). Remembering Nathan's inability to answer the question 'Was my husband a doctor or a patient?', this might further illuminate Perry and Wilkie's sardonic comment that Nathan constitutes the paranoid's ideal doctor: he agrees and shares the delusion.

Given the 'terminal irony' of Ballard's experimental work, his 'sanity' is often put in question. Peter Nicholls views Ballard as 'advocating a life style quite likely to involve the sudden death of yourself or those you love' (Nicholls, 31). If part of the device of *Atrocity* is indeed a taking up of Dali's methodology, paranoia-criticism's mimicry precisely rests on the confusion of sanity and madness. Breton and Eluard's *The Immaculate Conception* used parody to simulate madness: 'the authors hope to show that, given a state of poetic tension, the normal mind is capable of furnishing verbal material of the most profoundly paradoxical and eccentric nature, and it is possible for such a mind to harbour the main ideas of delirium without being permanently affected thereby' (Breton, 50–51). Parody distances, but what of paranoia?

The mimicry of mental states, the parody of paranoia's 'reasoning madness' also recalls Roger Caillois' beautifully Surrealistic analogy between animal camouflage and schizophrenia, first published in *Minotaure*. Sanity, rational order, is determined by *distinction* from the environment; the morphological mimicry of environment by insects might serve as a model for a madness driven by a *'temptation by space'* (70). The T-cell occupies 'impossible', overdetermined spaces, spaces which do not 'work', or which confuse the real and the boundaries of the art-work. Even the unstable name of the T-cell disappears from the closing sections in a way which anticipates the erasure of Tyrone Slothrop from the manically proliferating surveillance devices in *Gravity's Rainbow*. But this disappearance enacts the schizophrenic as understood by Caillois: 'space seems to be a devouring force. Space pursues them, encircles them, digests them in a gigantic phagocystosis. It ends by replacing them. Then the body separates itself from thought, the individual breaks the boundary of his skin and occupies the other side of his senses . . . He feels himself becoming space, *dark space where things cannot be put*' (72). *Atrocity* is thus firmly in the tradition of Surrealism's problematic celebration of 'madness'—a surrender which, very soon, might turn around to become startlingly aggressive and sadistic.

Bürger argues that the appearance of the avant-garde, the very possibility of its strategies, was opened by the 'end' of the historical development of 'artistic means'; all previous methods, bounded then by their historical evolution, were now open to citation and combination. Setting in motion Bürger's 'end of art history', refusing this termination, it is plain that *Atrocity* begins to re-cite 'Cubism' or 'Surrealism' as themselves open to re-contextualization and re-combination. This is neither posited identity with the 'historical avant-garde' (Ballard as 'modernist') nor a hollow and savagely ironic repetition of it (Ballard as 'postmodernist'); the relation is more complex than that.

Paranoia-criticism's extreme subjectivism is disturbing in its communicability and rational mimicry. For Perry and Wilkie, *Atrocity* is to be read through the T-cell's obsessional interpretive frame, and is to be 'vindicated' as the only 'sane' response: 'Owing to the absence of fixed, determinate values, the only relevant measure of meaning is subjective conviction' (183) This is opposed to David Punter who suggests that *Atrocity* concerns the erasure of Self, subjectivity 'transcended by mechanism and the massive systems of information and data' (9–10). This again evokes the difficulty of establishing the status of Ballard's fictional worlds: are his landscapes to be seen as inner spaces, or as threatening the self with annihilation? Where the Surrealist emphasis privileges the former, it is important to signal how Surrealist desire is absolutely transformed by the media landscape of the 1960s. This is where Ballard's simultaneous deployment of neo-avant-garde Pop Art strategies becomes just as important to trace.

The Atrocity Exhibition, Mass Culture
and the Neo-Avant-Garde

If mass culture has already become one great exhibition, then everyone who stumbles into it feels as lonely as a stranger on an exhibition site . . . Mass culture [is] a system of signals that signals itself (Adorno, *The Culture Industry,* 71).

What does *The Atrocity Exhibition* exhibit? Does this 'stylish anatomy of outrage' (Theroux, 56) anatomize or embody? Is this body of texts negating or affirming what it exhibits? With its mass cultural concerns, how can *Atrocity* be positioned in relation to that mass culture from which in part it derives?

I have suspended what is evident at the outset: *Atrocity* concerns the explosion of the 'media landscape'. Televisions, film festivals and billboards project images from Vietnam. The Zapruder film of Kennedy's assassination endlessly replays. The content of these images suddenly matches the violence that had been for so long accorded to the form of the media channels of mass culture. Reality is defined as that constituted by the media: for the T-cell, the fragmented projections of Elizabeth Taylor renders her 'a presiding deity', for 'the film actress provided a set of operating formulae for their passage through consciousness' (16). The T-cell's hope for unitary identity seems to be premised on whether Monroe's suicide can be 'solved', whether it is possible 'to kill Kennedy again, but in a way that makes sense'. The media have released irresolvable traumatic material which can only induce repetition of the trauma, in a futile attempt at mastery. This is the media as the embodiment of the death drive, the compulsion to repeat.

Punter's statement that in *Atrocity* subjectivity is 'transcended by mechanism and the massive systems of information and data' corresponds with a narrative of the effect on the subject of technologization in advanced industrial capitalism that has been endlessly told and re-told. If, for Jameson, postmodernism marks the invasion of the unconscious, the evisceration of 'the bourgeois ego or monad' and so 'the end of psychopathologies of that ego' ('Postmodernism', 64), then Jacques Ellul used virtually the same terms for the triumph of 'technique', its 'mechanical penetration of the unconscious' (404) in the 1950s. Ellul's account of a society dominated by the logic of the machine is not a simple determinism, for 'technique' can inhabit any sphere. However, 'when technique enters into every area of life, including the human, it ceases to be external to man, and becomes his very substance'(6).

Human society becomes a test ground to discover the greatest 'efficiency'. Central to this is mass culture which aims for 'the simultaneous fusion of . . . consciousness with an omnipresent technical diversion' (380). Ellul sees in mass culture the 'disappearance of reality in a world of hallucinations' (372).

This is a long way from the Surrealists' avant-garde assault on what Breton called 'the paucity of reality' through the injection of irrational dream, desire and hallucination. Surreality was premised on a sublation of dream and reality, the communicable and the incommunicable; many commentators claim it is advanced capitalism that is seen to have achieved this, and not the revolutionary avant-garde. The historical avant-garde in effect posited that the return of the repressed (desire) could explode the instrumental rationality of a mechanized social, but postmodernism, defined as the cultural logic of late capitalism, manipulates and routinizes the very desire now recuperated to the system. The impasse of the historical avant-garde in this respect can be precisely measured: when Ellul posits that 'Man' has become a 'device for recording effects and results obtained by various techniques' (79), it immediately recalls Breton's definition of automatism in the first Manifesto, that the experimenters aimed to be 'the silent receptacles of so many echoes, modest recording instruments' (*What is Surrealism?*, 123). Again, when Breton later admits 'we remain as little informed as ever regarding the origin of the voice which it is open to each of us to hear and which speaks to us, in the most singular fashion, of something different from what we believe we are thinking' (*What is Surrealism?*, 133), then a new and disturbing origin for this voice begins to be suggested by these mass media accounts. If 'technique' has penetrated even the unconscious, then the 'voice' automatism tried to capture can no longer be fantasized as self-presence, but is an 'external' implantation. Dali's paranoia-criticism was also founded the subject's desire. Ellul refuses the essentialization of desire: desire is the programmed expression of *L'homme machine*.

Could not the T-cell be seen as *l'homme machine*, his desires encoded by media circuits, his compulsions instigated by televisual trauma? The text is tediously repetitive: Karen Novotny is repeatedly killed in conceptual deaths that replay the irresolvable violence unleashed by television: Kennedy's assassination, Monroe's suicide, the invasive cameras that wait outside the Hilton Hotel for Elizabeth Taylor's death to be announced, the cycle of reports on atrocities from Vietnam. The Zapruder film of Kennedy's death is replayed, both to signify collective trauma and the attempt at mastery, but also to affirm the power of the media, to celebrate its capacity to capture the full horror, and with triumph to 'hook' the nation to its networks in a 'prodigious new display of synchronicity' (Jameson, *Postmodernism*, 355). *Atrocity* mantrically repeats proper names—Kennedy, Taylor, Nader, Oswald, Reagan, Monroe—and key phrases: 'geometry', 'formulae', 'modulus'. The cipher, a final signified that would stop this circulation, can only itself be repeated, remaining forever unreadable: 'an immense cipher' (21), 'elongated ciphers' (23), 'muffled ciphers' (39), 'a random cipher' (41), 'unravelling ciphers' (48).

Does *Atrocity* 'negate' this mediatized disaster or embody it? Marshall McLuhan argues that 'experimental' art gives 'the exact specifications of coming violence', information on 'how to re-arrange one's psyche in order to anticipate the next blow from our own extended faculties' (64) For Ellul, however, the 'psychic shock absorber' is developed out of technique, for 'only another technique is able to give sufficient protection against the aggression of techniques' (332). David Porush argues that Burroughs and others 'seek a way to innoculate themselves against technique by injecting its hardness into the soft body of their texts' (x). If *Atrocity* belongs to this strategy, there is an intolerable uncertainty as to intent. Andrew Ross' description of McLuhan's deep ambivalence might be transcribed for Ballard here : 'chillingly grave, apocalyptically nonchalant and swollen with emancipatory promise' (*No Respect*, 118). The remorseless, machinic, clinical rhetoric of *Atrocity* renders its distance or proximity to the violence of media networks profoundly ambivalent.

Nathan's didactic explanatory role shifts from a view of the technological penetration and disruption of subjective integrity ('. . . the failure of his [the T-cell's] psyche to accept the fact of its own consciousness, and his revolt against the present continuum of time and space'[12]) to one which appears to *advocate* the T-cell's project of complete inter-penetration of body and technology. The 'authorless' scientific reports centre solely on how 'the latent identity of the machine is ambiguous even to the skilled investigator' (98), and where the car crash is 'a liberation of sexual and *machine* libido' (my emphasis, 98), this is a startling moment which would seem to posit not the cathecting of technology, but gives technology a desire of its own.

Cautionary or affirmative, *Atrocity* oscillates. Technology in this text, like Ellul's 'technique', extends beyond the machinic: as the introduction to *Crash* states, reality is fiction determined by 'mass merchandizing, advertising, politics conducted as a branch of advertising, the instant translation of science and technology into popular imagery, the increasing blurring and intermingling of identities within the realm of consumer goods . . .' ('Introduction', 97–98). This is the iconography of mass culture, but it is also the context for the transformed strategies of neo-avant-garde Pop Art.

The sequence of rooms in the Warhol Retrospective exhibition at the Hayward Gallery in London in 1990 was an uncanny embodiment of *Atrocity*, both in terms of 'visual', thematic parallels (darkened, chapel-like rooms housing the Jackie Kennedy and Elizabeth Taylor sequences; brash, overlit spaces for the 'Death and Disaster' series), and as an enactment of the 'maze of billboards' the T-cell negotiates. There are two elements to be discussed here: Pop Art as neo-avant-garde, and Ballard's relation to the English artists of the Independent Group. Each one evokes specific concerns of the problematic of the avant-garde.

Where Bürger and Jameson agree on the avant-garde is the question of space and distance. Against the depth and spacing of Van Gogh's shoes are Warhol's 'Diamond Dust Shoes', too close, in this epoch of instantaneity, to effect a critique. However, the perception of a disrupted and transforming avant-garde practice would refuse this fixity of what constitutes an 'avant-garde'. Ambivalence, oscillation, is central to Pop Art, as Lucy Lippard suggests of one key artist: 'it is the narrow distance between the original and the Lichtenstein that provokes the tension and the great drama of his best work' (90) Bürger's third route of attack on the institution—reception—is also in Lippard's account: 'Parody in Pop Art largely seems to depend on the viewer's response' (86). This is what Thierry de Duve means by the irrecoverable intention of the works: Warhol does not promise, he simply *testifies*.

Just as the T-cell's modulus becomes a plug with which he is 'jacked' into networks that annihilate any traces of identity, so Warhol famously desired to be a machine, to erase and de-subjectivize the 'artist'. Breton's 'modest recording device' speaks not of the authentic self, but the market. Repetition and seriality in the Factory production of silk screens structurally repeats the mass-produced commodity. It is difficult to know if Warhol's work is serious or parodic (the 'oxidized' metal works are literal 'piss-takes', of course).

Whilst Warhol represents for Bürger the end of the avant-garde, Benjamin Buchloh has carefully reconstructed the initial reception of Warhol's early shows. If these early exhibitions did shock, breach the institution, Buchloh is not simply claiming an avant-garde status which, in repeating the historical avant-garde, was then recuperated. From the very beginning, Warhol's work played on the undecidable edge between negation and affirmation, denying easy 'access to a dimension of critical resistance' (Buchloh, 'Andy Warhol's One Dimensional Art', 57). The later work (which *becomes* advertising) if anything intensifies this ambivalence, as David James suggests.

Both *Atrocity* and Warhol are repetitive, use similar 'visual' contents and appear to express a 'machinic' desire. Just as Warhol's 'non-art' commercial graphics deployed the gestures of 'high' art and his 'high' art commercial sources, so Ballard's 'experimental' phase cannot be delimited to after his 'commercial' science fiction beginnings, as in McHale. In the late 1950s, Ballard put together a series of collages (figs. 1 and 2), which were plans for a putative novel based purely on typography, on the styles of type and spacing of text, with little concern for meaning. Ballard entertained the notion of using billboards as the site for this new novel to unfold. Later, he paid for a series of 'adverts'— having failed to get an Arts Council grant—to 'sell' the ideas of his text, the product's name being his own signature (fig. 3). It is the use of billboard space which transforms the historical avant-garde's concern with textual spacings (Mallarmé), typographic play (Apollinaire and Dada poetry), and found scientific texts (Ballard collaged material from scientific journals, just as Ernst did) into a neo-avant-garde focus on the very institutional *framing* of the text. To disperse texts across the public spaces of the city evokes the strategies begun in the 1960s by artists like Daniel Buren, and which continue with Jenny Holzer's 'Truisms' flashing up on Times Square and Piccadilly Circus electronic boards in the 1980s. To *détourne* (in Situationist language) those spaces, not by gestures of refusal but by occupation and trans-formation, is a model that could assist a reading of *Atrocity*'s position in relation to mass culture.[3]

There is another connection to Warhol to be considered. In one of Warhol's last projects, the 'Myths' sequence, his most famous icons were silk-screened onto a single canvas. There too was one of his own self-portraits. This might recall the presence of a character called 'Ballard' in Crash; loss of distance and control, the 'author' within the space of his own text, no longer writing it, but being written by it. This is not the main point, however. It becomes difficult in Warhol to mark a line where parody lurches towards self-parody: so too with Ballard. *Atrocity* is frequently hilarious in its clash of registers. The highly technical listings often end with Captain Kirby/Webster's banal questions ('You say these constitute an assassination weapon?' (34), 'So you think the Novotny girl is in some kind of danger?'(56), 'And all these make up one picture?' [83]) puncturing the portentousness. The

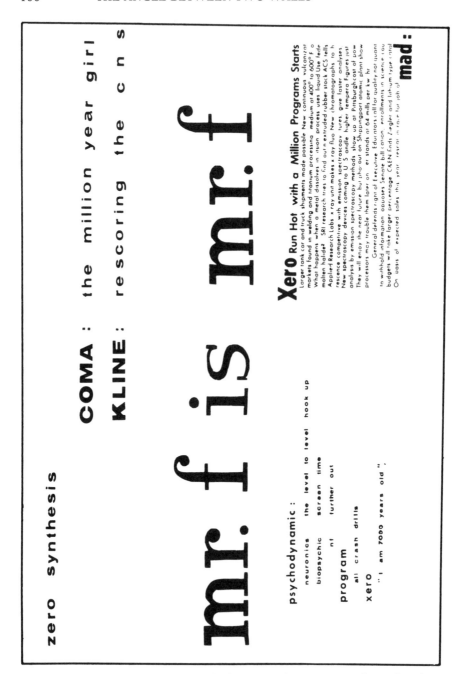

Figs 1 (above) and 2 (opposite) Ballard's 'Project for a New Novel', produced in the late 1950s

time probe

Volcano Jungle: vision of a dying star-man

Editor's Note: Feature of the March 1957 Scientific American was an article by David S. Jenkins, director of the Office of Saline Water, U.S. Department of the Interior. This article, which described generally the various salt water conversion methods being investigated under Interior's sponsorship, said partially of the Rudger Hickman still. In the past three years interest in conversion distillation has been heightened by an exciting new system. In essence what Hickman has added is a simple device for increasing phenomenally the rate of heat transfer to the water, namely spreading it out in a thin film. The salient feature of this device is a rotating drum, shaped something like a child's musical top. IAEC's article on the succeeding pages describes in detail the development of this still. At this article went to press, the editors were advised that the semicono than those obtainable from government sources, which provide a much larger price increase from 1939 to 1947 and for the over-all period considered. A correlation shows that the very moderate price increase in industrial chemicals from 1939 to 1953 (compared with the sharp price increase experienced by the rest of the economy) is related to the rapid expansion of the chemical industry during this period. The result has been more goods at relatively low prices ultimately for the consumer, on these bases it can be concluded that the industry is fulfilling its function satisfac-

• • 'Coma,' Kline murmured, 'let's get out of time.'

T·12

▲ ▲ ▲ ▲ ▲

███████ servo maze ███████████████

███████████ time sea █████

██ ▌▐ ▌▐ ▐▌ ██████████

▐██████████ total bureau ███████

██████ the nth root of wonderful ██████

███ yes ███ yes ███ yes ███ yes ████

█████████████ blood house ██████

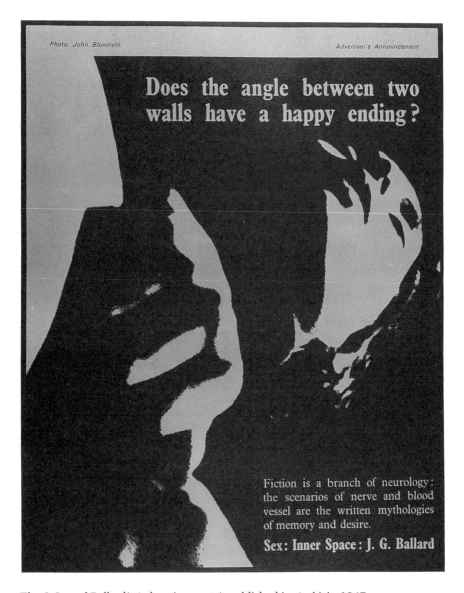

Fig. 3 One of Ballard's 'advertisements', published in *Ambit* in 1967

descriptive sentences can also teeter on a self-parodic edge. Consider: 'This strange young woman, moving in a complex of undefined roles, the gun moll of intellectual hoodlums with her art critical jargon and bizarre magazine subscriptions' (70). This is as meaningless as the description of Buddy Holly: 'the capped teeth of the dead pop singer, like the melancholy dolmens of the Brittany coastline, were globes of milk, condensations of the sleeping mind' (74). It is precisely the *jargon* that is important, its repetitive combinations and re-combinations, that have the effect of 'closing' the space of the text into its own logic, meaning giving way to pure effect. An impossible demand is requested of the reader: too close misses the parodic element, but too far makes the text collapse into self-parody.

Questions of 'high' and 'low' are brought into focus by moving to British Pop Art. The convergence of method and image amongst artists in America was initially without a stable name. 'Pop Art' was taken up from the English critic Lawrence Alloway. Alloway was the first to narrate a 'secret history' of the 1950s experimental group that met at the Institute of Contemporary Art: the Independent Group. Ballard subsequently associated with some of its key members (especially Eduardo Paolozzi and Richard Hamilton) in the 1960s and participated in 'performances' and readings at the ICA.

The links of the IG to science fiction are often noted: in two documented seminars at the ICA, Paolozzi displayed the vibrancy of American popular art by referring to gaudy science fiction magazine covers (he later declared: 'It is conceivable that in 1958 a higher order of imagination exists in a SF pulp produced on the outskirts of LA than [in] the little magazines of today' [cited Lawson]), and Alloway himself developed a non-Aristotelian aesthetic (in opposition to the predomi-nant ICA aesthetic of Herbert Read) through a reading of A. E. Van Vogt (!). Reyner Banham was also enthusiastic about science fiction: the influence of Banham's work on the commercial architecture of Los Angeles is everywhere evident in the stylized spaces of *Atrocity*. Eugenie Tsai suggests that the IG were fascinated by science fiction 'as a genre that was particularly in touch with the radical technological changes that were underway' (71). This fitted with a kind of post-Futurist celebration of the machine. Tsai details Ballard's visit to the famous 'This is Tomorrow' exhibition in 1956 and the narrative produced from this visit is fascinating. Not yet a science fiction writer, Tsai links the publication of Ballard's first story, four months later, exactly to this visit: 'while it remained tied to traditional science fiction, "This is Tomorrow" contributed to the more critical and cynical "new wave" through its influence on Ballard' (73); in turn, in a kind of feedback loop, Ballard influenced the work of Robert Smithson (see Finkelstein).

The mistranslation that occurred in exporting Alloway's 'pop art' into American 'Pop Art' is crucial. As has been noted by Massey and Sparke, Alloway's pop art referred only to sources that were to be worked on within 'high art'; pop was not conceived as an erasure of the boundary between high and low. A 1962 Alloway article makes this plain: 'The term refers to the use of popular art by fine artists: movie stills, science fiction, advertisements, games boards, heroes of the mass media'. Alloway, however, goes on to criticize Derek Boshier for 'seem[ing] to use pop art literally, believing in it as teenagers believe in the "top twenty" ' (1087).

However, the perception of lack of critical distance accords with the definitional centre for pop moving from England to America—and Warhol's work is difficult in its indiscernible distance from its commercial sources. This shift is important to any analysis of *Atrocity*; *Atrocity* seems too mobile, too oscillatory to 'fit' an equation of the 'high' with critical distance and negation and of the 'low' with mindless complicity. Tsai's story of Ballard's entry into science fiction via Pop Art depends on a legitimation of 'low art' by its recontextualization in a 'high' art setting. Many, however, including the artists of the IG, would refuse this distance of ironic quotation. Brian Wallis sees the IG as having the 'whole-hearted enthusiasm of consumers' (9), and Alloway himself quotes Hamilton's insistence that his work is not 'a sardonic comment on our society' (1085), but purely celebratory (at least in its early phases; his later work, from 'Swingeing London' on, displays clear critical content).

Tsai glosses over the fact that 'This is Tomorrow', using conventionalized science fiction imagery, managed to inspire Ballard to non-conventional science fiction work. In fact, as Massey notes, 'This is Tomorrow' had only two display environments (of twelve) that could be coded as pop; the rest were constructivist pieces. Rather than visual connections, then, methodology is again a more appropriate link. In 1953, the ICA allowed Paolozzi and others to put on an exhibition called 'The Parallel of Art and Life'. This contained 'sampled photographs, all blown-up to the same size and ranging from "art" contents to images of radio-valves, televisions, radiograph readouts, burnt-out forests, tribal ceremonies and car designs' (Massey, 240). Reviews of the time were shocked at the implicit equivalence being proposed by this semiotic range and its violent staging. As Lawson suggests: 'the aggressive all-over organization of the images made the exhibition itself a microcosm of the intrusive reality of pop culture' (Lawson, 24). The IG seminars covered popular imagery, car-styling, helicopter design, modern architecture and A. J. Ayer's philosophy. Such semiotic promiscuity and implicit equivalence is more clearly related to the strategy of *Atrocity*.

Like Surrealism, then, it is not shared iconography that puts *Atrocity* and Pop into the same frame, but a methodology, one which contracted the space of a simple critique, and set in motion oscillation. The seriality and machinism of Warhol, the knife-edge of complicity and critique of Pop Art in general, produces the same difficulties of reading as Ballard's text. By the 1960s a simple opposition of subjectivity to instrumentalized technologization is no longer sustainable. In Ballard's disturbing imbrication of the subject and media networks, it is possible, perhaps, to see a trace of Marcuse. In the 'humanist' account of Ellul and Porush the history of the liberatory potential of technology is erased, but for Marcuse post-scarcity results from the increase in 'technological forces'; utopia is 'inherent in the technical and technological forces of advanced capitalism' (*One Dimensional Society*, 4). These are the forces which can potentially burst the stasis of capitalist relations of production and induce revolution. Marcuse insists on taking technology to the end of its logic. Technological post-scarcity is precisely that which necessitates the re-invention of the 'biology' of Man. How far within or beyond is *Atrocity* in this scheme? If Marcuse invokes Eros in this liberative potential, he tends to erase its counter-force, Thanatos, the death drive, which Ballard does not. This is Ballard's 'thesis': 'Just as sex is key to the Freudian world, so violence is the key to the external world of fantasy that we inhabit. There's this clash between what we all believe to be true, such as that violence is bad, in all its forms, and the actual truth, which is that violence may well serve beneficial roles' (Henessy, 63). This link of liberation with violence allows a final consideration of *Atrocity* as avant-garde in its perhaps most problematic set of concerns.

The Avant-Garde, Violence and the 'Feminine'

In the smooth neutralizations of Ballard's oeuvre into narratives of transcendence, what is nearly always evaded, *skirted*? Warren Wagar's efficient schematization sweeps *Atrocity* into the model without much difficulty: 'The point, again, is simply to transcend reality, including the technological landscape of the late 20th century, by passing *through* it rather than *around* it' (64). Whilst a dubious reading at best, Wagar does not consider the violence of this strategy, or consider that this 'passing *through*' is staged, repetitively, on a shattering of the female body in the conceptual deaths that recur through the text. The extremity of violence toward the feminine in *Atrocity* is nearly always evaded by critics.[4] If held as an avant-garde text, however, this thematic becomes dramatically foregrounded: *Atrocity* finds itself in the notorious company of de Sade and Bataille, and returns to expose the sadistic aggressivity that insistently haunts the 'liberatory' potential of desire in Surrealism. The T-cell's compulsive actions could well be figured as answers to Bataille's provocative questions: 'What does physical eroticism signify if not a violation of the very being of its practitioners?—a violation bordering on death, bordering on murder?' (*Eroticism*, 17). As avant-garde text verging on the pornographic, *Atrocity* discomfitingly demonstrates the imbrication of sexuality and the death drive.

The 'meat' of *Atrocity* is Karen Novotny, the switching centre, the 'modulus' (for it is nearly always her), the traversed site on which discursive regimes simultaneously condense and disseminate meaning. She is consistently manipulated and brutally re-functioned by the obsessive T-cell. The choice of the name must be a reference to the call-girl Marielle Novotny, allegedly a mistress of John F. Kennedy and involved in the Profumo scandal in 1963. The 'geometry' of Novotny's body is collapsed into architectural space (the smoothness of walls, the angles of balconies), and 'translates' for Hollywood icons. To seize the 'secrets' of her geometry, the T-cell places her in a series of postures and draws 'chalk outlines on the floor around her chair, around the cups and utensils on the breakfast table, and lastly around herself' (25). He is already chalking out the posture of a dead body, as indeed she is repeatedly killed, sometimes as herself, sometimes playing roles. At one point Novotny is simply the list of objects in a 'sex kit':

> It contains the following items: (1) Pad of pubic hair, (2) a latex face mask, (3) six detachable mouths, (4) a set of smiles, (5) a pair of breasts, left nipple marked by a small ulcer, (6) a set of non-chafe orifices, (7) photo cut-outs of a number of narrative situations—the girl doing this and that, (8) a list of dialogue samples, of inane chatter, (9) a set of noise levels, (10) descriptive techniques for a variety of sex acts, (11) a torn anal detrusor muscle, (12) a glossary of idioms and catch phrases, (13) an analysis of odour traces (from various vents), mostly purines &c., (14) a chart of body temperatures (axillary, buccal, rectal),

(15) slides of vaginal smears, chiefly Ortho-Gynol jelly, (16) a set
of blood pressures, systolic 120, diastolic 70, rising to 200/150 at
the onset of orgasm . . . (54)

Affectless scientific language mixes an obsessive medical penetration
and disassemblage of the body with the reduction of Novotny to a
mannequin. In perhaps the most startling synaesthetic translation of
the female body into car styling, a paragraph entitled 'Elements of an
Orgasm' simply lists the fourteen precise muscular movements it takes
for the T-cell to exchange seats with Novotny so that she can drive (63).
This is Ballard's wicked parody of the sexological discourses of the
1960s which had finally claimed to determine the exact physiology of
the 'mysterious' female orgasm (a parody made sense of by Lynne
Segal's attack on 1960s sexology in *Straight Sex*). Obscenity is abstracted
to the conceptual level and the 'authorless' scientific reports are a wider
analysis of bodies, judging the effects of car-crashes and atrocity films
on mentally and physically disabled test groups. It is this very choice of
language which for Baudrillard (as it also operates in *Crash*) and for
Warren Wagar denies erotic titillation in its sheer functionalism and
repetitiveness. Moral outrage, they suggest, misreads the intent.

But the 'terminal irony' of Ballard's text has a corrosive effect on
intention. The marginal comments of the Re/Search edition only
heighten the difficulty. The 'found texts' on cosmetic surgery are
framed by two contradictory marginal notes. The first states: 'the
present pieces . . . show, I hope, the reductive drive of the scientific text
as it moves on a collision course with the most obsessive pornography'
(111); the second is a eulogy to Mae West and the Hollywood screen
stars. It continues: 'Beyond our physical touch, the breasts of these
screen actresses incite our imaginations to explore and reshape them.
The bodies of these extraordinary women form a kit of spare parts, a set
of mental mannequins . . . As they tease us, so we begin to dismantle
them, removing sections of a smile, a leg stance, an enticing cleavage'
(114). What 'voice' is Ballard using here? Against the assertion of
distance in the first statement, this seems to be a continuation of the
T-cell, an affirmation that 'our' spectatorship is nothing other than
'obsessive pornography'. This is all the more alarming given the
brilliant stroke of placing the proper name 'Mae West' in this description of reduction mammoplasty. It suddenly injects an elegiac tone to
the medical discourse, as if this operation figured for the loss of the
Hollywood stars of the studio system, and as this desperate attempt to
maintain eroticism is failing, so indeed the mammoplasty risks 'losing

all', since the last, devastating sentence concludes: 'The ultimate results of this operation with regard to the sexual function are not known' (116). What Wagar terms the non-moral 'value-neutral' (64) language of science cannot simply be used as a protective, distancing strategy ascribed to Ballard. It is not only the continuation of this language 'outside' the fictive frame in the marginal note here; Ballard's oscillation can also be seen within Bataille's insight that sexology, the reduction of sex to a determinable object of the scientific gaze, cannot evade the enticement, the radical complicity, that the disruptions of the sex act induces even in its allegedly neutral observers (*Eroticism*).

This entanglement with problematic conceptions of the feminine is, in fact, an inevitable result of *Atrocity*'s constitution as avant-garde text. A peculiar assertion, no doubt, but it is one which can be tracked along converging lines in art history and psychoanalysis. Rosalind Krauss has consistently sought to recover an avant-garde suppressed by the dominant histories of Modernist art. Clement Greenberg's conception of the avant-garde as the pursuit of a transcendent, pure opticality, reaching its zenith in Abstraction, works by displacing a Surrealism he denounced as 'a reactionary tendency which is attempting to restore "outside" matter' to art (*The Optical Unconscious*, 7). Krauss reconstitutes Surrealism as invoking an 'optical unconscious' which contests the transcendent eye that never blinks in its reification of the indivisible moment of seeing. The optical unconscious is 'a projection of the way that human vision can be thought to be less than a master of all it surveys, in conflict as it is with what is internal to the organism that houses it' (*The Optical Unconscious*, 179–80). In other words, the historical avant-garde sought to link vision to carnality, to *re-corporealize* opticality through 'the optical system's porousness to the operation of its internal organs' (*The Optical Unconscious*, 124)—that is, the beat of carnal desire. To *re-embody* vision, to re-sexualize it by re-integrating it to the networks of the unconscious, is to link rebellion with the lifting of repression.

That de-sublimation, in Lacanian terms, is a refusal of the Father's law: the avant-garde artist becomes, in effect, a rebellious son who disobeys the founding Oedipal moment of acceding to repressive Law. And the first object to open to this 'pervert' is that which was the aim of the Father's interdiction: the mother's body. 'The emblematic subject of male avant-garde practice', claims Susan Rubin Suleiman, 'is . . . a transgressive son' (87) who enacts his violent refusal over the body of the woman, now seen as the (silenced) stage of a battle between father and son. It is Barthes' *The Pleasure of the Text* which emphasizes that what is de-sublimated is not simply desire but also aggressivity, a violence toward the feminine: 'The writer is someone who plays with the body of the mother: in order to glorify it, to embellish it, or to dismember it, to take it to the limit of what can be known about the body. I would go as far as to take *jouissance* in a *disfiguration*' (cited, Suleiman, 9).

Ballard's debt to Surrealism in *Atrocity* can now be considered in different—and much darker—terms. There is no doubt that Breton's oft repeated declaration that 'The problem of woman is the most marvellous and most disturbing in the world' is continued here: Karen Novotny embodies the modulus that will provide a solution to the compulsions induced by the media landscape. But if Woman veils the truth she must be *mutilated*, ripped open, in order to reveal it. Again and again this mutilation must be enacted, for she is put in the place of the bearer of Truth precisely by the Law. The son's transgression remains bound to the taboo installed by the father, and the desire that is directed to Woman is bound by aggressivity, sadism and the deathly compulsion to repeat.

In *Atrocity*, 'The Great American Nude' contains a paragraph entitled 'Baby Dolls', which opens: 'Catherine Austin stared at the object on Talbert's desk. These flaccid globes, like the obscene sculptures of Bellmer, reminded her of elements of her own body transformed into a series of imaginary sexual organs' (53). The marginal commentary note expands: 'Hans Bellmer's work is now totally out of fashion, hovering as it does on the edge of child pornography . . . his vision is far too close for comfort to the truth' (53). Bellmer's *poupées* (dolls) takes the locus of the female body as the site of avant-garde rebellion to its extreme.

The test-crash mannequins that pepper *Atrocity*, *Crash* and 'The Terminal Beach' have a link to the set of female mannequins for the 1936 International Surrealist exhibition, which were in fact inspired by Bellmer's first Doll, constructed in 1933 after Bellmer had seen 'Tales of Hoffmann'. The inevitable recourse here is to Freud's essay 'The Uncanny' where Hoffmann's 'The Sand Man' is the central document, concerning as it does a mechanical doll mistaken for a woman. Bellmer is uncomfortably more exact to Hoffmann's tale, which involves *dismemberment* of the doll. A sequence of staged photographs, Bellmer's dolls are obsessional dismemberments, perverse combinations of limbs and bulbous protuberances: his view (echoed in Ballard's comments on the Hollywood stars cited earlier) is that 'The body is like a sentence that invites us to rearrange it' (cited Foster, *Compulsive Beauty*, 103).

For Krauss, these represent 'the obsessional re-invention of an always-same creature—continually re-contrived, compulsively re-positioned within the hideously banal space of kitchen, stairwell, parlour' ('Corpus Delicti', 86). That the T-cell's similar dismemberments of Novotny in stylized scenarios find an equivalent male sadism toward the feminine is made clear by Bellmer's own commentary: 'Wasn't exactly that which the imagination seeks in desire and intensification to be found in the doll (in the image of precisely her dollishness), *who only had life insofar as one projected it onto her*, who despite her limitless submissiveness understood that she was reserved for despair?' (cited, Peter Webb, my emphasis, 33). And yet the context shifts slightly when it is observed that Bellmer was the son of an enthusiastic advocate of fascism who built the doll as a staging of his own simultaneous rebellion and abjection to his Father's law. Bellmer's commentaries insist that the work figured his father's threat in terms of castration and the refusal of his father in terms of a fetishized displacement onto the doll. In some ways, the dolls 'perversely' traverse sadism *and* masochism, objectification *and* identification, and 'masculine' *and* 'feminine'. Hal Foster whilst accepting this narrative, worries that Bellmer uses precisely a 'fascist' strategy—dismemberment—to counter Nazism ('Armor Fou'). The avant-garde son's perversity yet comes to mimic the Father's law.

In *Atrocity* the question of oscillation between complicity and critique, refusal or absorption, the textual 'world' as subjective projection or objective penetration of the T-cell, cystallizes around the obsessive re-functioning of the doll-women. As sadistic act it recapitulates the delusion of woman as Truth; as masochistic identification, it can only pre-figure his own disappearance into the tabulations of scientific taxonomies. As avant-garde text, *Atrocity* reiterates the blindnesses of the project with regard to the violence toward the feminine. And could not its scopophilic epistemology go much further than that, and become pornography?

Linda Williams has attempted to trace pornography's premise of 'maximum visibility' in a frame derived from Foucault's first volume of *The History of Sexuality*: the implantation of the compulsion that sex speak the entire truth of being. Muybridge's stop-action scenarios of female movement and Charcot's photographic record of hysterical seizures constitute voyeuristic atrocity exhibitions, recalling *Atrocity*'s newsreels of Vietnam, car crashes and assassinations. Hard-core 'obsessively seeks knowledge, through a voyeuristic record of the confessional, involuntary paroxysm, of the "thing" itself' (49). This 'frenzy of the visible' is, for Williams, impossibly contradictory, however. Hard-core films are directed towards unrepresentable on the woman's body (the 'absence' of a visible record of female orgasm), but this is displaced onto the ejaculating penis as signifier of the other's pleasure.

Is there an analogy to *Atrocity* here?

> **Questions, always questions** . . . 'What are you trying to build?' she asked. He assembled the mirrors into a box-like structure . . . 'A trap'. She stood beside him as he knelt on the floor. 'For what? Time?.' He placed a hand between her knees and gripped her right thigh, handhold of reality. 'For your womb, Karen' (32–33)

The T-cell tries to capture the 'secret' truth of Novotny's body precisely in the 'vanishing point' of her genitalia. The compulsion to repeat the mutilations of her body record the inevitable failure but reiterated attempts to grasp that 'truth'. And that is because this epistemology works, according to Elisabeth Bronfen, in a logic in which 'to attribute a fixed meaning to a woman, to solve the mystery of her duplicity is coterminous with killing her'. The inevitable death, Bronfen continues, 'can be read in part as a trope for the fatality with which any hermeneutic enterprise is inscribed' (294). This accords with Peter Brooks' analysis of the body of Emma Bovary. For a novel that centres on the body of Emma so obsessively, Brooks notes that that body is rarely represented as a whole; as she undresses, there is always a turning away, onto the clothes, onto fragments. It is 'repeatedly "metonymized", fragmented into a set of accessory details rather than achieving coherence as either object or subject' (48) This does, in fact, echo, with the billboards throughout *Atrocity*, those which display 'a segment of the lower lip, a right nostril, a portion of the female perineum . . . At least five hundred signs would be needed to contain the whole of this gargantuan woman' (15). With Freud, the visual field, as the privileged field of knowledge, is shot through with desire and disavowal: the female body is never fully knowable because the (male) scopophilic gaze is seeking an imaginary object, a body without lack. Emma's body is finally only seen 'whole' in death, and Brooks states: 'At one extreme, the body must be killed before it can be represented, and indeed Freud acknowledges the link of the instinct for knowledge to sadism' (63) For the Sadist to kill, as de Beauvoir notes in 'Must we Burn de Sade?', means not the victory of power but its complete loss; the other's suffering no longer affirms power.[5] The death must be repeated again and again therefore. Does this explain *Atrocity's* repetition?

And yet . . . and yet it could be argued that despite the pervasive logic of violence toward the feminine that uncomfortably reiterates Bellmer and the pornographic, the operation fails because something radical has happened at another level of the text. The composition of the text in its overdetermined, 'impossible' spaces collapses levels and sets in train a promiscuous and unending semiosis even to the extent of displacing both the phallic economy and the ultimate truth of being in sexuality. Nathan ponders that

> it's an interesting question—in what way is intercourse per vagina more stimulating than with this ashtray, say, or with the angle between two walls? Sex is now a conceptual act, it's probably only in terms of the perversions that we can make contact with each other at all. The perversions are completely neutral, cut off from any suggestion of psychopathology—in fact, most of the ones I've tried are out of date. We need to invent a series of imaginary sexual perversions just to keep the activity alive (61–63).

The unending translation between levels prevents a single containment of desire within a phallic economy. On this point there is a certain agreement with Barthes' distinction between Sade and Bataille. Sade is merely expansive; taxonomical and encyclopaedic, it is, as Susan Sontag says, 'the body as machine and of the orgy as an inventory of the hopefully indefinite possibilities of several machines in collaboration with one another' ('The Pornographic Imagination', 99). *Crash* opens with an encyclopedic array of extremities, and forever moves towards epiphanies that are little more than taxonomical listings of perversity; Vaughan's photojournal of crash victims and their subsequent sexual 'swerves' is the zenith of the text, which works through a remorseless accumulation of the 'unacceptable'. Barthes, in contrast, sees Bataille's *The Story of the Eye* working through metonymical chains of association that begin to cathect objects 'beyond' the sexual, and entrains these objects to the movement of desire. Such associative chains and bizarre cathecting of 'non-sexual' objects has been seen to operate in *Atrocity*. Further, Barthes sees Sade as remorselessly phallic, whilst Bataille's chains move across the eye and the eye-like: triumphantly non-phallic, even 'feminine' (this is not the eye of the 'male gaze', but one 'pregnant' with associations), Bataille transgresses the phallic economy. *Crash*, I would argue, is obsessively phallic; the centre of the text is the spreading stain of repeatedly discharged semen on the crotch of Vaughan's jeans. If 'Ballard' comes to desire Vaughan, and finally consummates this desire, it is not so much a 'gay' act as the desire to *be* Vaughan's phallus, the 'modulus' which unlocks the logic of the eroticized car-crash. *Crash* tries, clinically and affectlessly, to list perverse acts; the sexual performances with Gabrielle, crippled and supported in a set of leg and back braces (an echo of Frida Kahlo's injuries?), moves away from the vagina to a dream of 'other orifices' 'opened' by the scars and indentations of the car-crash, the grooves and weals produced by the braces. These still remain, however, to be penetrated. If wounds are fetishized, this is exactly because the fetish disavows and displaces—but also affirms—the lacking phallus.

Atrocity's locus is difficult to determine. There is no privileged 'level' or term; chains of association are always reversible. The action of desire can be read either as the T-cell's or the implantation of the 'machine libido' of mass culture. What shifts this beyond the simple celebration of subversive desire by the Surrealists, or the 'liberation' narrative of Marcuse is the emphasis that Eros and Thanatos are equally unleashed by de-sublimation, that violence and death are concentrated obsessively on the figure of the Woman. This remains intractable and troubling.

And yet . . . and yet I want to risk reading *Atrocity* one final time in a way which re-writes this violence toward the feminine in figural terms, and which returns to the impossible place of Ballard's work between high and low art.

Does the Angle Between Two Walls have a Happy Ending?

What has happened to science fiction in this treatment of *Atrocity*? In part, I have been concerned to track the emergence of a possible place for Ballard's most experimental work in the moment between the historical avant-garde and the neo-avant-garde, the 1960s as the ambivalent site of transfer and transformation erased by the monolithic opposition of modernism and postmodernism. But it has also been necessary to depart from the science fiction milieu in order to treat *Atrocity* seriously in the bewilderingly dense connections it makes to a century of artistic practices which the critics of *Atrocity* have hitherto failed to consider. Now it is time to return to the thesis that Ballard's work constitutes the very edge, the limit, both the inside and the outside of science fiction, and how the oeuvre returns to allegorize that limit in displaced forms.

A marginal note in *Atrocity* praises Sontag's essay, 'The Pornographic Imagination', which wants to save a *literary* pornography, where 'inherent standards of artistic excellence pertain' against the 'avalanche of pornographic potboilers' (Sontag, 84). The former is clearly coded as avant-garde; they are limit texts, beyond good and evil. Sontag has constant recourse to science fiction in relation to pornography, surprisingly perhaps after the dismissal of science fiction film in 'The Imagination of Disaster'. 'As literary forms', Sontag suggests, 'pornography and science fiction resemble each other in several interesting ways' (84). The de-legitimation of pornography as literature—because it has an uncomplex address, single intent, a ruthless functionalism with regard to language, and no interest in character—meshes, to some extent, with the ghettoization of science fiction. For Sontag, however, 'Pornography is one of the branches of literature—science fiction is another—aiming at disorientation, at psychic dislocation' (94).

Anxious to avoid the fall into sociologizing pornography, Sontag proposes—for a specific French 'high' tradition—an ahistorical expression of the sexual drive in extremity. For de Sade and Bataille, Sontag suggests 'the "obscene" is a primal notion of human consciousness' (103); it has been the ambivalent 'gift' of these writers to reveal the 'authentic' extremity of sexual ecstasy, that Man has, in his 'sexual capacity', an impetus which 'can drive a wedge between one's existence as a full human being and one's existence as a sexual being' (104–05). Sontag's emphasis on the responsibility of these works recalls Simone de Beauvoir's Sade-as-existentialist. Avant-gardism becomes inseparable from this discharge of desire which is both beyond the self and simultaneously more 'authentic' than that merely human self.

This strategy takes the 'high' pornographic text into a space beyond moralism (which is left for 'low', generic pornography). That science fiction should cross her argument is significant, for this division of high and low echoes the legitimations of Ballard's work. Ballard's texts have 'value' in their unacceptability in science fiction, their outraging and out-reaching of the ghetto.

If the strategy of legitimation by appealing to 'high' art status has been questioned throughout (and ought, perhaps, to be particularly questioned in this context),[6] does not treating *Atrocity* as an avant-garde text insist on its 'high' literary status? This is where the figure of Woman becomes important again. I want to consider the violence to the feminine in highly figural terms, as it operates in 'You: Coma: Marilyn Monroe'. The 'chapter' concerns the use of Novotny as the 'modulus' through which the T-cell 'had come to this apartment in order to solve (Monroe's) suicide'(42). After this statement, Novotny is obliquely murdered:

> **Murder** . . . At intervals Karen Novotny moved across it [the room], carrying out a sequence of apparently random acts. Already she was confusing the perspectives of the room, trans-forming it into a dislocated clock. She noticed Tallis behind the door and walked towards him. Tallis waited for her to leave. Her figure interrupted the junction between the walls in the corner on his right. After a few seconds her presence became an unbearable intrusion into the time geometry of the room. (42)

Later, when Coma arrives at the apartment, Novotny's death is explained thus: 'She was standing in the angle between two walls' (42).

Now, just as this phrase is the leitmotif of *Atrocity*, so I have adopted it to site Ballard in the non-site between high and low, the 'hinge' of both. It is possible to argue that it serves precisely that function here. Andreas Huyssen's 'Modernism's Other: Mass Culture as Woman' is a well-known essay that displays how the mass was coded feminine by modernism. Huyssen's sources are largely from late nineteenth century German writers, but it possible also to consider English sources at the same moment which reverse this coding: high culture as Woman. I have already shown how Haggard's revitalization of the romance attacks Naturalism as 'carnal and filthy', but Haggard also notes that the American novel has developed worrying characteristics: 'their men . . . are emasculated specimens . . . with culture on their lips . . . About their work is an atmosphere like that of the boudoir of a luxurious woman, faint and delicate' (175). Between the high and the low, each marks the other as Woman, each projects at its edge a feminine form.

That Woman is in the liminal position, the 'angle between two walls', connects to Lynda Nead's treatment of the female nude as a troubling category for art history. 'More than any other subject, the female nude connotes "Art" . . . it is an icon of western culture, a symbol of civilization and accomplishment' (1); on the other hand, the nude woman must be contained and idealized within the frame, otherwise it threatens collapse into obscenity: 'The obscene body is the body without borders or containment and obscenity is representation that moves and arouses the viewer rather than bringing about stillness and wholeness' (2). At once idealized and denigrated, art history polices this figure so insistently because it at once the site on which the border between 'high' art and 'low' obscenity is affirmed, but is also the *internally* divided moment where that distinction may collapse.

Could the conceptual death of Novotny perhaps signal the attempted destruction of this mutual projection, to clear the space of the 'angle between two walls' for an impossible occupation, precisely by Ballard's texts? It is important that the angle is maintained, for this is no erasure of the border between high and low, but rather a 'double' death, of the low's high and the high's low. Whilst Bellmer's strategy is problematic, there is a reason for Ballard's echo of it: as the doll is placed in banal spaces *between*—in stairwells and in the angle between two walls—so Ballard deploys his figure of Woman to stage an occupation of the limit between high and low, modernism and postmodernism, science fiction and mainstream. Neither a simple definitional postmodernism (erasure of the border), nor simple avant-gardism (sublation of the border); the angle remains intolerably present. Does the angle between two walls have a happy ending? Yes and no: oscillation.

This is the most tentatively 'positive' reading of the conceptual deaths of *Atrocity*. However, it unacceptably waives the physicality of violence towards Woman. It repeats, too, Breton's denial of *les femmes* for *La Femme*—the object, the image of the feminine. If, in the disaster novels, Beatrice and Suzanne Clair stand for veiled apocalyptic knowledge, *Atrocity* may mark a new stage in the dismemberment of the feminine cipher, a violence to force a giving up of the truth.

Hal Foster's work on Bellmer's dolls and Ernst's collages is concerned that these may participate in the very devices they seek to criticize. For Foster, Ernst's body-as-tank, body-as-diagrammatized-engineering-plan, has a worrying analogy with Theweleit's analysis of the fascist Freikorps soldier: the state-manufactured body, metallized armour replacing the ego. Such armour is constantly under threat, tested only by pain. Anything which threatens is violently attacked, most particularly the 'oozing', non-bounded state of the feminine. If Ernst's collages of the body-as- machine serve to 'shore up a disrupted body image or to support a ruined ego construction' (Foster, 'Armor Fou', 68), the machines are dysfunctional, as wild and fantastically inoperative as any in Roussel's fiction (to which *Atrocity* also refers in two cited titles of Roussel's fiction, *Locus Solus* and *Impressions of Africa*). Bellmer's sadism and mastery the doll, however, may mean his 'misogynistic effects . . . may well overwhelm his liberatory intentions' (Foster, 'Armor Fou', 87).

To take the violence towards Woman in *Atrocity* in such terms may be the most positive statement, that Ballard, like Bellmer, is 'ambiguously reflexive about masculinist fantasies rather than merely expressive of them' (Foster, 'Armor Fou', 87)—the same undecidability that has been emphasized throughout this chapter. If Woman holds the truth, a sadistic attack must be launched, a compulsive re-killing of Novotny. And yet Nathan's narrative of the T-cell's activity may begin with this attempt to shore up the ego, but the T-cell himself is eventually dispersed into traces, footnotes of a main document that has now been lost. No object or subject can hold the truth or the gaze that would pierce the truth.

The oscillation I have ascribed to *The Atrocity Exhibition* is an over-determined one, moving between high and low, affirmation and negation, 'historical' and 'neo' avant-garde. I hope to have displayed that if the text has exemplary 'postmodernist' concerns, it also adopts strategies more properly ascribed to 'modernism'. The art-historical and literary frames that would distribute the places of texts discretely between these categories seem too monolithic, troubled by a text that coils them within one another in a complex simultaneity. One leitmotif of the text, the phrase 'the angle between two walls', determines the impossible site of *The Atrocity Exhibition* itself.

CHAPTER FOUR

Mediation, Simulation, Recalcitrance:
Crash to *Hello America*, with Detours

The Atrocity Exhibition intensifies the thematic of the 'mediated subject' in Ballard's work. At a pivotal moment, it hinges on whether the mediascape is a screen for the projection of perversities or is a device for the *implantation* of machinic desires. Surrealist derealization, directed by the subversive unconscious, or interpellation of the subject, the text actively fuses these apparently incompatible narratives in the compacted space of its condensed paragraphs.

The hinge question of the media, of mediation, is a major thematic in Ballard's fiction. It is not, however, initiated by *Atrocity*, nor is the 'take' on mediation finalized in its pages. It is important to traverse the full range of Ballard's fictions of the media in order to track the multiple and contradictory theoretical models that are proffered there, especially once attention shifts to *Crash*, a text now freely adopted as a proto-typical postmodernist narrative, in which mediation becomes solely identified with simulation. Media *means* 'middle', and theories of mediation precisely contest how intervening spaces—between screen and audience, say—act as conductors of information. That mysterious, interstitial, even ethereal space allows for theories ranging from indoctrination and submission to active and resistant challenge. Ballard's texts simultaneously adopt and suspend such assumptions: tracking his media fictions thus insists on a traversal of these intervening spaces that entertains modes of mediation, simulation and recalcitrance. This is the project of this chapter.

Media Stories

Two stories: 'The Subliminal Man' (1963) and 'The Intensive Care Unit' (1977). The first is a classic narrative of alienation in consumer society, the instrumentalization of desire via the indoctrination of command-screens, an economy sustained by accelerating cycles of obsolescence and enforced by shopping channels, advertising barrages and an insistent social pressure to conform. Hathaway's jamming of the flickering billboards, revealing the subliminal dictatorial commands (BUY NOW BUY NOW BUY NOW), is an act of demystification, the last revelation, before complete control, of the extent of the *inauthenticity* of social relations. The second story almost completely reverses this narrative: social relations are conducted entirely via media channels. Couples meet through video linkups, court and marry 'within the generous rectangle of the television screen' (*Myths of the Near Future*, 197), produce children via artificial insemination. The 'authenticity' of meeting 'in the flesh' can only re-introduce 'all the psychological dangers of a physically intimate family life' (197): the retrospective narration takes place in a hiatus as the family grouping re-gathers strength to complete its first, murderous embraces.

Between these two texts, what has occurred? Has Ballard shadowed the transformations in theories of the media, replaced a crude model of psychological coercion with a Baudrillardian conception of simulation? The dating of the stories seems to confirm this, for the crudity of 'The Subliminal Man' should neither belie the historical specificity of the constellation of ideas that generates it nor its generic roots. Vance Packard's *The Hidden Persuaders* (1957) popularized the notion of conspiratorial advertising techniques. Packard analysed the increasing dependence of advertisers on Motivational Research, the application of crude psychological techniques on consumers with the aim of increasing excitation/anxiety and tying its neutralization to the purchase of specific products. Depth persuasion offered a panic scenario of the *incitement* of psychic imbalance rather than its pacification: an insidious psychoanalytic treatment in reverse.[1] Ballard's portrait of Franklin's wife in 'The Subliminal Man' as representative consumer dupe accords with Packard's fascination and revulsion at the ease with which supermarket spaces could hypnotize housewives into involuntary over-consumption. William Whyte's emphasis on a newly emergent anonymous collectivity in *The Organization Man* (1956)—a possible source for Ballard's own title?—also isolated the new sciences of 'personality testing' as subtly sedimenting an oppressive social conformity. Adding these elements to Jacques Ellul's thesis of the triumph of technique instrumentalizing the human as 'test ground' for its own cybernetic efficiency (and his assertion, as per Hathaway's paranoid conviction about the subliminal billboards, that 'only madness is inaccessible to the machine' [404]), and the matrix for Ballard's story becomes clear.

A more immediate route, however, is likely to have been the politicized satire of H. L. Gold's *Galaxy* magazine, for these media theories are clearly the same context for stories like Frederick Pohl's 'The Tunnel Under the World' (1955), which details a series of progressive revelations about the control advertisers have gained. The tunnels beneath the town lead directly to the factory, a front for an advertising laboratory, with Tylerton's (read: Taylorized town)[2] populace an experimental set for testing the effectivity of advertising techniques. Metaphorical mechanization becomes literal: the populace are test robots; one better—they are miniaturized on a table top. The story ends with a kind of psychotic vent opened onto the Real, as Buckhardt stares down at the chasm to the floor, before being re-programmed and once more locked into the cycle of mindless consumption.

There is an alienated reality to be unveiled here, but one based on a performative contradiction in the sense that both 'The Subliminal Man' and 'The Tunnel Under the World' must insist on the impossibility of escape from a totalitarian system precisely by engineering a privileged, momentary vision of the system from its 'outside'. Their negation is reliant on giving over to the media a fictive power in excess of their actual operations, a simplistic model of domination; they have to *produce* this domination in order to arrive at its negation. In contrast, 'The Intensive Care Unit' abandons a didactic narration, deploying an indeterminately ironic mode, perhaps the only available one where notions of the real or alienation from reality are seemingly meaningless. The narrator and his wife conduct themselves entirely through prior representational codes: 'I relished the elegantly stylized way in which we now presented ourselves to each other—fortunately we had moved from the earnestness of Bergman and the more facile mannerisms of Fellini and Hitchcock to the classical serenity and wit of René Clair and Max Ophuls' (201–02). There is no coercive or conspiratorial control exercised in this atomizing system. In Guy Debord's terms, this may be the society of the Spectacle, in which 'isolated individuals [are] recaptured and *isolated together*', even in the 'family cell', through the 'widespread use of receivers of the spectacular message' (172), but the 'outside' of this mediatized realm seems only more perverse than its interior. Surely, in this inversion of model and copy, couples contouring their intimacies to *auteur* styles, can only be explained via Baudrillard's version of the simulacra, where signs exit the 'gravitational pull' of the real, have 'no relation to any reality whatsoever' (*Simulacra*, 6), and merely circulate within endlessly self-citational mediatized codes.

Does Ballard's trajectory, from didactic demystification through the densely theorized mediations of *The Atrocity Exhibition* to the glazed irony of 'The Intensive Care Unit' follow a path of increasing 'sophistication'? Two more stories complicate this pattern. 'The Watch-Towers' (1962) is set in an undetermined city under the panoptic gaze of evenly distributed surveillance towers, inhabited by unseen powers. An interpretation of the story as an allegory of 1950s social conformity seems likely, the disapproval of the council elders directed at Renthall's adultery and his Angry Young Man attempts to expose the mysticism surrounding the attributed authority of the towers. But the security of this reading is unsettled by the closing pages, in which Renthall's planned confrontations are disabled by the populace's sudden indifference and eventual scotomizing of the very presence of the towers. Possible readings suddenly proliferate: Renthall may be the surviving witness of the transition from repressive apparatuses of the maintenance of power to the internalization of ideological self-regulation; on the other hand, his insistent attempts to force people to see the towers may satirize oppositionality as precisely inventing the very totalitarian system it claims to denounce. That Renthall may have hallucinated the negative hallucination of his fellow citizens renders the final sentences profoundly ambivalent: does his sighting 'the watchers' constitute a final confirmation of his thesis of panoptic control, or actually undermine the 'mystical authority' of the towers which gives his rebellion meaning? The genuine hesitation at the close of the story could not be further away from the didactic narrative of 'The Subliminal Man', written the year after.

On the other hand, 'The Secret History of World War Three' (1988) is a *jeu d'esprit* which returns, knowingly, to the most mechanical conception of television consumer dupedom. The narrator documents the virtual disappearance of reports of a limited nuclear exchange between Russia and America on newscasts which obsess solely about the ailing health of Ronald Reagan, brought back in sublime senility for a third Presidency. Spectacular decoy for the *absence* of power, the enforcement of pseudo-community is wonderfully suggested by the permanent broadcast of Reagan's heart-rate monitoring, a kind of signature ('Transmitted live from the Heart of the Presidency') beneath vacuous B-movie output which responds to the swings of melodrama and sentimentality , and on which the mass audience models its own response. Based, perhaps, on the obsession with Reagan's cancer of the nose, Ballard's story alarmingly predicts the media circus around George Bush's irregular heart-beat in 1990. Pushed to the margins, then, the nuclear exchange takes place unnoticed, and the story returns back to notions of 'hidden persuasion', the figure of the duped wife, as in 'The Subliminal Man', standing in for a wholly distracted culture.

The point of displaying this double movement, the path of one set of stories from the coercive to the simulacral being reversed by the other set, is at once to resist a teleological advance in Ballard's work, and to restore the diverse and historically embedded media theories that can be employed to read his texts. If *The Atrocity Exhibition* seems to invite a reading of the determination and destruction of the subject via mediation, other texts in the oeuvre explore an absolute limit to media penetration, from the numinous 'The Greatest Television Show on Earth' to 'The Reptile Enclosure', which, as previously analysed, connects the completion of a satellite carapace to instinctual mass suicide. This is an important matrix to re-establish, for Ballard criticism of late has lifted *Crash* from the series and established it as a text to govern over the whole oeuvre.

Crash

The move from the polylogue of *The Atrocity Exhibition* to the remorseless monologism of *Crash* is a startling transition. The complex compositional techniques of collage, juxtaposition and condensation are abandoned for a single, sustained, intolerably intense narrative voice. There is only one transaction here, mantrically asserted: between semen and engine coolant, body and car, the bruises of medallions, steering wheels and instrument binnacles flowering subcutanously, as if the technology had been wholly incorporated. Or, to reverse the formulation, as if the body had been imbibed by the circulation of inhuman traffic. The compaction and intertextual overlayings of *Atrocity*'s urban landscapes are replaced by a verbal equivalent of photographic hyperrealism: Vaughan and the character Ballard ceaselessly traverse the same 'enchanted domain' (39) of multi-storey carparks, Heathrow terminal buildings and the Westway motorway interchange. In such an alienated terrain 'the human inhabitants of this technological landscape no longer provided its sharpest pointers, its keys to the borderzones of identity' (40). Guy Debord indicates that 'The dictatorship of the automobile, pilot-product of the first phase of commodity abundance, has been stamped into the environment with the domination of the freeway, which dislocates old urban centres and requires an ever-larger dispersion' (174), and yet Ballard seems more concerned with the sexualization of this car economy. 'Its future does not belong in the area of transportation', McLuhan noted, and with 'the violence of millions of cars in our streets', he worried that people could not be 'expected to internalize—live with—all this power and explosive violence, without processing and siphoning it off into some form of fantasy' (*Understanding Media*, 219). McLuhan was probably not calculating the kind of fantasy of these technological 'extensions of man' that Ballard clinically explores: the transcoding of the *petit mort* of orgasm into the fatal car-crash, Vaughan's fantasied front-end collision with Elizabeth Taylor the apotheosis of sexual ecstasy. This is the closed economy of the motorway: 'These unions of torn genitalia and sections of car body and instrument panels formed a series of disturbing modules, units in a new currency of pain and desire' (113–14).

The literalization of the death drive, the fatal cathexis of the car crash as ambivalent symbol of the extent of alienation in the technological landscape—these possible theories are erased by the reading of *Crash* that Baudrillard presents as a centre piece in his *Simulacra and Simulation*. It is the only text Baudrillard considers worthy of lengthy citation, with paragraphs incorporated into his own theory, as if there were an absolute identity of strategy, rhetoric and concern. For Baudrillard, *Crash* exemplifies the order of simulation, the abandonment of both reference to the real and to the signified as present absence standing in for the real. In the staged history of the sign, from reflection to masking absence to acceleration beyond the 'gravitational pull' of the real, *Crash* dramatizes a new economy of ceaseless simulacral circulation, the clinical unfolding of motorway logic, the imbrication of sex and technology, entirely divorced from any possible psychoanalytic interpretation of perversity or deviation. 'The non-meaning, the savagery, of this mixture of the body and technology is immanent, it is the immediate reversion of one to the other' (*Simulacra*, 112). This fusion, this equivalence or indifference of signs, can only take place, however, through the mediation of a third element, Vaughan's camera: 'Only the doubling, the unfolding of the visual medium in the second degree can produce the fusion of technology, sex and death' (117). Indeed, the simple inversion of roles in 'The Intensive Care Unit' pales into insignificance against the complexities of mediation in *Crash*. Most commentators quote the same dizzying moment from the simulated car crashes at the Road Research Laboratory. A test crash is repeated in slow motion on monitors:

> The audience of thirty or so visitors stared at the screen, waiting for something to happen. As we watched, our own ghostly images stood silently in the background, hands and faces unmoving while this slow-motion collision was re-enacted. The dream-like reversal of roles made us seem less real than the mannequins in the car (110).

Any grounding outside this feedback is swept into the circulation of images: if, for 'Ballard', his own crash 'was the only real experience I had been through for years', then that 'real' is immediately rendered simulacral: 'Like everyone else bludgeoned by these billboard harangues and television films of imaginary accidents, I had felt a vague sense of unease that the gruesome climax of my life was being rehearsed years in advance' (32). The accident, death itself, Baudrillard avers, has become a calculable element of the 'era of simulation', not its limit of finitude.

Baudrillard's reading, whilst provoking some violent reaction from science fiction critics themselves ensnared in Ballard's 'terminal irony' (making a reading of *Crash* as admonitory unlikely),[3] has nevertheless been highly influential in developing a new interpretation of Ballard's oeuvre. That Baudrillard lavished attention on a text previously considered beyond the 'lunatic fringe' (Martin Amis, cited Pringle, *Bibliography*, 99) of science fiction grants an exponential increase in the legitimation of Ballard's work as central to a certain narrative of postmodernism to the extent that, for Scott Bukatman, 'postmodernism itself' is unthinkable without Ballard's work (sic: *Terminal Identity*, 46). And yet, in the subsequent essay to the piece on *Crash*, 'Simulacra and Science Fiction', Baudrillard entirely conforms to legitimating modes analysed in chapter one. Ballard is crucial because his texts leave 'good old' science fiction, with its model of extrapolation from the real, to enter a new simulacral order where the real itself becomes an inaccessible utopia. Inside simulation '*Crash* . . . is without a doubt (more than . . . *Concrete Island*) the current model of this science fiction that is no longer one. *Crash* is *our* world, nothing in it is "invented" ' (*Simulacra*, 125).

This is not a mere elevation of *Crash* above generic boundaries, however, for this science-fiction-which-is-not constitutes the mediated real itself, as well as the only possible mode of theoretical writing: 'the good old imaginary of science fiction is dead and . . . something else is in the process of emerging (not only in fiction but in theory as well)' (121). No wonder, then, that Baudrillard can incorporate Ballard whole inside his system without attention to the differences of fictional or thetic framing, for the order of simulation renders such boundaries irrelevant. Theory is (science) fictional. When not attacking analysis or critique for its quaint tie to delusions of demystification, Baudrillard either portrays the loss of history or the social in science fictional terms (the 'black hole' of the masses, the 'zero gravity' of aleatory events replacing history, the 'satellization' of the real, as in 'The Year 2000') or, on occasion, looks to science theory-fiction as a lever against the new order: 'the only strategy of opposition to a hyperrealist system is pataphysical, a "science of imaginary solutions" . . . a science fiction about the system returning to destroy itself' ('Symbolic Exchange', 123).

As seen in Chapter One, this conjunction (a theory/fiction Ba(udri)l-lard construct) transforms a marginal generic practice into the modulus of contemporary cultural experience: science fiction enters the 'quoti-dian consciousness of people living in the post-industrial world' as a 'mode of apprehension' (Csicsery-Ronay, 388). A retrospective re-writing of Ballard's output narrows it to *The Atrocity Exhibition* and *Crash*, now retrofitted as proto-cyberpunk texts which 'prefigure' Fredric Jameson or 'anticipate' Baudrillard and Virilio (Bukatman, 6). Indeed, this narrative is seductive, for does not visual mediation become the only guarantor of experience, paradoxically an erasure of any grounded experience, in Ballard's work? The T-cell attempts to displace trauma by transcoding it into iconic moments of mediated violence (Kennedy, Vietnam, Biafra), just as Vaughan attempts to crash onto the far side of the screen. Moments of dizzying doubling become set-pieces: the corny cowboy shoot-out between Wayne and Ricci in *Hello America*, itself staged within a Wild West theme park, is peculiarly ennobled by the vast film projections of John Wayne and Henry Fonda above them (102); 'Ballard', too, enters a vertiginous sequence of re-duplications in *The Kindness of Women* as the film of *Empire of the Sun* guarantees an experience more 'genuine' than his own. The *immanence* of all signs, their endless re-duplication, becomes the defining signature of Ballard, displacing the narratives of *transcendence* that had previously governed his work. All of Ballard, it might be said, can be found in Baudrillard.[4]

What worries me about this elision is the abandonment of Ballard to Baudrillard's very specific take on the Simulacra. To enter an 'era of simulation' is to accelerate beyond 'the real' and beyond 'history': 'In a sphere foreign to history, history itself can no longer reflect or prove itself' (*Fatal Strategies*, 16). That move (a nonsensical 'era' which would evaporate the notion of era itself) both triumphantly erases all competing theories of the media, which, as I have shown, continue to operate in Ballard's work, and renders *identical* not only Ballard to Baudrillard, but every Ballard text: each tells the same story. *Crash* provides the metaphor for the oeuvre: an indifferent circulation of equivalent signs trapped in a single logic. The thrust of the readings of *The Atrocity Exhibition* was to display a recalcitrance to this narrative, but does *Crash* mark a transition into a new, self-enclosed order? Is there no 'outside' or internal resistance to simulation?

Scott Durham's 'rescue' of *Crash* works within Baudrillard's model but develops an internal separation of the ideal of simulation from the comic failure to attain it. That Vaughan draws 'Ballard' into a logic of the accident, of the orgasmic transgression of death, might constitute a strategy of breaching the endless circulation of traffic. As has been seen though, Baudrillard transcodes death into a fully operational counter of this system. Death, pre-programmed, reinscribes transgression as perfect confirmation of a system that can have no outside. Durham's reading finds a comic gap, an internal ironizing distance, between this operational system and Vaughan's failed attempt to join it, for the 'joke' is that his ultimate crash misses Elizabeth Taylor and merely plunges into his fellow audience of fascinated rubberneckers. He falls 'outside' simulation, never reaching 'inside' the screen at all. Where Baudrillard argues for the completed success of the order of simulation, Durham proposes that the repeated *failures* of Vaughan's, Seagrave's and Ballard's crashes attest to 'the nonidentity of the simulation model across its repetitions and appropriations, even for the subject who imagines its domain to be totalitarian and absolute' (168).

This notion of nonidentical modulation points to Baudrillard's traduction of the concept of the simulacrum. Deleuze states: 'The simulacrum is not a degraded copy, rather it contains a positive power which negates both original and copy, both model and reproduction' ('Plato and the Simulacrum', 53). At times Baudrillard accords with this 'positive power'; more often his most potent effects derive from inversion (Disneyland is 'real', the America outside it 'simulacral') or a *blurring* of the distinction between model and copy. Where, however, Baudrillard arrives at the 'era of simulation' from a teleological trajectory of the sign's progressive separation from the real, Deleuze emphasizes how the Platonic simulacra is of an entirely different order. Why the Platonic operation seeks 'to hunt down' and 'define the being (or rather non-being) of the simulacrum' (47) is related to its dissimulation *from the very beginning*. It does not *depart* from an originary resemblance or correspondence, but is 'constructed around a disparity, a difference' (49). The simulacra is demonic because it wrecks the return of the Same, the correspondence of copy to model, inserting an operator of difference. Baudrillard reverses this. *His* version of the simulacra is the clone, a perfect reproduction, so perfect that any indication of original and reproduction is erased. Cloning 'enshrines the reiteration of the same: 1 + 1 + 1 + 1' (*Simulacra*, 97). Deleuze's simulacrum is precisely the uncanny double which Baudrillard abolishes, for the double insidiously introduces differences which result in anarchic, non-identical proliferation. Nothing could be further from the similitude of Baudrillard's 'era of simulation', in which everything is reduced to indifferent equivalence, the same story (the story of the Same) told over and over again for every cultural event.[5]

This at least resists turning Ballard's work into a cloned product, one of a series of terms in *Simulacra and Simulation* which carries the same 'genetic code' indifferently. A Deleuzian conception of the simulacrum might direct a reading of Ballard's obsessively reiterative oeuvre to attention on the *-iter*, the alterity or difference, that demonically occupies and sabotages an endless repetition of the same (and thus, too, of any single-thesis reading of Ballard's work, whether immanental or transcendental). The concern with difference and repetition is the subject of the next chapter; here I wish to focus on Ballard's media stories that evidence a recalcitrance to the post-historical world of simulation, by returning the difference of historical density to the work.

There are no doubt new systems of information and accelerated cycles of capital that affect forms of knowledge, modes of representation, the archivization and narrativization of history—transformations which Ballard texts repeatedly work over. Undoubtedly, too, *Crash* intersects with these shifts at the level of affect in a tonality that plays undecidably between performance and ironization. Baudrillard links this heightened affect (mantric repetition, the technical language of a pornographic writing evacuated of sexuality) to *Crash*'s ecstatically ungrounded economy of traffic in signs, just as Jameson connects the 'hysterical sublime' or the experience of euphoric intensity to the vertiginous loss of history ('Postmodernism'). But this use of what Ballard calls 'terminal irony' is not the only strategy, and placed back in a differential sequence of texts, the peculiar narrative of *Crash* is revealed as one device which may intersect with simulation but is more properly seen as one mode of approaching media penetration and reinscription of the experiential. It is a remorselessly monologic extension of a trajectory first sketched in *The Atrocity Exhibition*. There are, however, multiple lines of traversal of the mediascape, and those recalcitrant to the ecstatic mode of immersal in the extremities of mediation are the ones I want to follow here.

Supermodernity and the Uncanny

'My last meeting with Vaughan—the climax of a long punitive expedition into my own nervous system—took place a week later in the mezzanine lounge of the Oceanic terminal' (166). No better (peculiarly specific) space could sum up the anonymous zones in which *Crash* unfolds: buildings devoid of cultural accretions, temporary housings for transient travellers, transitional areas for those between meaningful destinations—'the strange tactile and geometric landscape of the airport buildings, the ribbons of dulled aluminium and areas of imitation wood laminates' (34). Like the suspended state of duty-free malls, a zone at once inside and yet outside the legal parameters of the country it exists in, Vaughan and Ballard experience the motorways as weirdly detached from an embedded culture or history or morality. The implicit analogy between nervous system and the anonymity of an airport mezzanine perfectly equates with the detachment and suspensive nature of Ballard's (non)relation to the world beyond the network of motorway traffic.

In Marc Augé's terms, the airport terminal and the motorway constitute non-places, 'which cannot be defined as relational, or historical, or concerned with identity' (77). Augé sketches a crisis in ethnology, which concerns itself with 'anthropological place' as determining a referential grid for meaningful cultural inhabitation and act. In an over-abundant supermodernity (for Augé the obverse of 'postmodernity'—not a collapse of meaning or the loss of history, but the *excess* of meaning and history [30]), meaningful place is increasingly exchanged for existence in non-places:

> A world where people are born in the clinic and die in hospital, where transit points and temporary abodes are proliferating under luxurious or inhuman conditions (hotel chains and squats, holiday clubs and refugee camps . . .); where a dense network of means of transport which are also inhabited spaces is developing; where the habitué of supermarkets, slot machines

and credit cards communicates wordlessly, through gestures, with an abstract, unmediated commerce; a world thus surrendered to solitary individuality, to the fleeting, the temporary and ephemeral, offers the anthropologist (and others) a new object (78).

Supermodernity marks the proliferation of these 'immense parentheses' (111): transnational, indifferent to context, resistant (as Clifford Geertz would say) to 'thick description'. Margaret Morse, too, in somewhat more apocalyptic terms, has attempted to define a new 'ontology of everyday distraction' in which the television, the shopping mall and the freeway sustain a continuum of ungrounded space, each producing an 'attenuated *fiction effect*' (193). Such 'derealized spaces' dehistoricize and delocalize their inhabitants, who are pacified and 'liquified', set adrift on planned itineraries of commodity consumption. The mall, freeway and television hook up the distracted to a homogeneous space: 'The viewer as mobile subject has remote control over trajectories and channels plus power to take the off ramp and leave the zone of televisual space. However, the television viewer who enters a car to go shopping, or even to work, hasn't left nonspace behind' (207).

'A person entering the space of non-place is relieved of his usual determinants' (103), Augé states, and in many ways *Crash* could be seen to investigate this psychological effect, especially as Augé isolates the motorway as the exemplary non-place. But Augé's lengthy description cited above might also illuminate other Ballard texts—the way, for instance, that 'The Largest Theme Park in the World' (the kernel for his novel, *Cocaine Nights*) investigates 'the linear city of the Mediterranean coast, some 3000 miles long and 300 metres wide' (*War Fever*, 78) as a zone of transnational leisure complexes increasingly detached from culture, history and work in the North. Another treatment of the theme, 'Having a Wonderful Time', elides Augé's 'luxurious' hotels with 'inhuman' refugee camps by envisaging Mediterranean holiday complexes as holding camps for redundant middle managers. All the way back to 'Zone of Terror' (1960), in fact, Ballard has been concerned with the psychological effects of non-places, these transitional spaces between, here a 'complex . . . operated the electronics company . . . as a sort of "recreational" centre for senior executives and tired "think-men". The desert site had been chosen for its hypotensive virtues, its supposed equivalence to psychic zero' (*The Disaster Area*, 123). That the non-place moves from the desert to the heart of the anonymous suburb, as in 'The Enormous Room', might mark an increasing trajectory of invasive non-places that both displace and evacuate the accretions of 'anthropological place'.

The non-place, for Augé and Morse, is ahistorical, non-relational, indifferent to locale, and renders equivalent everything within it. And yet, if Ballard is being portrayed as a fictionalist of non-place, how is this different from Baudrillard's simulacral world of the indifferent circulation of self-citational signs? The answer lies by slightly shifting the focus of the non-place, and the erasures it allegedly performs. Anthony Vidler's reflections on the contemporary anonymity of the city contains this usefully summational statement:

> In this city, where suburb, strip, and urban centre have merged indistinguishably into a series of states of mind and which is marked by no systematic map that might be carried in the memory, we wander, like Freud in Genoa, surprised but not shocked by the continuous repetition of the same, the continuous movement across already vanished thresholds that leave only traces of their former status as places (184–85).

The reference to Freud is to the famous moment in 'The Uncanny', where Freud finds himself unaccountably caught in a compulsion to return to the same dubious street even as he tries to escape it (359). Altering the definition of the rootlessness of non-place to emphasize its 'unhomeliness' or 'uncanniness' (*unheimlich*, literally means unhomely) transforms the perspective on these Ballardian non-places, for the uncanny is 'that class of the frightening which leads back to what is known of old and long familiar' (340). And yet an uncanny of the supermodern non-place initially appears as a flat contradiction: how could that which erases relation, history and identity be 'haunted' by anything at all, since haunting implies the interruptive absent presence of an unacknowledged *past*? The non-place, however, may aim to displace or erase historical accretions, but it is that very attempt at active forgetting which turns the recalcitrant traces (in Vidler's terms) into inexplicably frightening objects.

It seems more acute to conceive of a certain strand of Ballard's work as exploring the *uncanniness* of contemporary posturban spaces than to portray him in accord with the emptied simulacral world of Baudrillard: Ballard is of that 'contemporary sensibility that sees the uncanny erupt in empty parking lots around abandoned or run-down shopping malls, in the screened *trompe l'oeil* of simulated space, in, that is, the wasted margins and surface appearances of postindustrial culture' (Vidler, 3). It is significant, I think, that Baudrillard marginalizes

Concrete Island to a parenthetical dismissal in his commentary on *Crash*, for this is the place in the topography of simulation where circulation halts, coming off the rails, and repeatedly trips over the recalcitrant and uncanny wasted margins or ruins of a forgotten twentieth century history. Before analysing that novel, however, it is worth pausing on the aspects of a supermodern uncanny that Ballard explores in other texts.

'Motel Architecture' concerns a television critic, Pangborn, who is entirely isolated within his sanitized and digitized room, able to walk yet wheelchair-bound as a symbol of his passivity before the TV screen (it is, after all, the model of the human in Paul Virilio's 'teletopia', where the subject becomes 'a terminal citizen who will soon be equipped with interactive prostheses whose pathological model is that of the "motorized handicapped" ' [10]). Pangborn's existence might well be simulacral: in a reversal typical of both Ballard's and Baudrillard's media stories 'He preferred the secure realities of the television screens to the endlessly bizarre fictions of ordinary life' (*Myths*, 181). In this sealed realm, Pangborn aims for perfect transparency (doubling the space on his surveillance cameras) and for a transcendence over his repulsive body. The arrival of Vera Tilley, however, inserts a flicker of non-identical difference: once she unseals the space of the apartment Pangborn tracks the tantalizing traces of an intruder on the surveillance cameras and is repeatedly assailed by the bodily sweat and heavy breathing of his double. Like *Crash* this is mediated through the third space of the television screen; Vera is murdered in exactly the same manner as the shower sequence in *Psycho* that Pangborn ceaselessly analyses. And yet this intruder is not the Baudrillardian clone but the double as 'the uncanny harbinger of death' ('The Uncanny', 357). The over-explanatory final page of the story does not surprise in Pangborn's realization that 'over the years in the solarium he had become so detached from external reality that even he himself had become a stranger' (194) to the extent he can murder both Vera and, by the close, himself, for this perfectly accords to Freud's own anecdote of an intruder in his railway carriage who Freud realized too late 'was nothing but my own reflection in the looking-glass on the open door' (371). This is not the cloned return of the Same within a sealed order, but the demonic double which separates self from self.[6]

In a long review of the first Edward Hopper exhibition in France, Ballard contrasted the haunting spaces of Hopper's uncanny city scenes to the new complex being built near the exhibition site at Antibes-les-Pins where 'Fibre-optic cables and telemetric networks will transmit data banks and information services to each apartment, along with the most advanced fire, safety and security measures. To cap it all, in case the physical and mental strain of actually living in this electronic paradise proves too much, there will be individual medical tele-surveillance in direct contact with the nearest hospital' ('In the Voyeur's Gaze', 23). The designers of Antibes-les-Pins seem to retain a belief in the Modernist utopia of a 'Radiant City' divorced from the nightmare of history—a perfectly enclosed and self-sustaining fortress fending off contingency. As Le Corbusier stated: 'If we eliminate from our hearts and minds all dead concepts in regard to the house . . . we shall arrive at the "house-machine" ' (quoted Vidler, 63). Like Hopper's inexplicably frightening canvases, however, Ballard's psychological horror stories of supermodern non-places (unhomely homes) like 'Motel Architecture' and 'The Intensive Care Unit' track the violent eruption of uncanny traces—the 'dead' concepts that cannot be eliminated. Pangborn's desire to transcend the body equals the Modernist architectural desire to transcend its context. The result is the same: 'A "machine for living in" has been transformed into a potentially dangerous psychopathological space populated by half-natural, half-prosthetic individuals, where walls reflect the sight of their viewers, where the house surveys its occupants with silent menace' (Vidler, 161).

The scenario of 'The Thousand Dreams of Stellavista', the last story in the compulsively repetitious *Vermilion Sands* collection, explicitly the-matizes this sense of silent menace. Psychotropic houses, which record and respond to the emotional range of their inhabitants, decay along a once-fashionable street for movie stars and media folk in the Vermilion Sands resort. Talbot moves into the house of Gloria Tremayne, a dead film star disgraced by her outrageous acquittal of the murder of her husband, Miles Vanden Starr. Traces of this traumatic history are inscribed in the pulsating structure of the house: 'The responses were undefined, but somehow eerie and unsettling, like being continually watched over one's shoulder, each room adjusting itself to my soft, random footsteps as if they contained the possibility of some explosive burst of passion or temperament' (192). 'Something that ought to have remained secret and hidden but has come to light' is Schelling's definition of the uncanny that Freud elaborates, and in the interstices of this story Ballard is satirizing the Modernist belief that haunting history could be banished from returning. Talbot remembers Vanden Starr in photographs 'glowering out of 1950-ish groups with Le Corbu-sier and Lloyd Wright, stalking about some housing project in Chicago or Tokyo like a petty dictator' (199). Talbot's own tenancy of the house will recapitulate a secret history—unwittingly he compulsively repeats Vanden Starr's cruelty to his wife to the point of inducing the psychic traces of the house to repeat Tremayne's self-defensive murder of Vanden Starr/Talbot. The functionalist Modern is countered by the Surrealist Modern: Matta proposed houses that 'must have walls like damp sheets which deform themselves and join with our psychological fears' (quoted Vidler, 153). Ballard's story, like Matta's proposal, *installs* the recalcitrant historical trace in its design rather than erasing it: it induces uncanny effects, making the fragmentary, glimpsed secret past the lever for splitting open the glazed surfaces of what might appear to be the simulacral supermodern.

It is *Concrete Island* that takes this to another level—taking the uncanny out of the house and into the strange spaces of the metropolis. *Concrete Island* is the shadowy double of *Crash*, in the very first page ostentatiously smashing through the protective barriers that had restricted *Crash*'s economy. Just as *Concrete Island* repeats *Crash* by displacing its symbolic investment in circulation and collision, so Maitland is immediately dislodged from self-identity, becoming his own double: 'In the driving mirror he examined his head . . . The eyes staring back at him from the mirror were blank and unresponsive, as if he were looking at a psychotic twin brother' (8).

'The Uncanny' offers several competing attempts to grasp the effect, a definition stalled by the very nature of its indefinable unease. Initially, Freud offers Jentsch's proposal that it is generated by 'intellectual uncertainty', particularly with regard to *spaces*: 'the uncanny would always, as it were, be something one does not know one's way about in. The better oriented in his environment a person is, the less readily will he get the impression of something in regard to the objects and events in it' (340). If this is rejected for a treatment of the repressed which returns (in the famous treatment of castration anxiety in Hoffmann's 'The Sand Man') what is less noted is the bipartite source for uncanny effects that the essay concludes with. Certainly one route is the return of repressed infantile fantasies, but Freud considers this less common than the momentary return of 'primitive' beliefs that one had believed one had *surmounted*. The uncanny 'associated with the omnipotence of thoughts, with the prompt fulfilment of wishes, with secret injurious powers' derives from that the fact that 'our primitive forefathers once believed that these possibilities were realities, and were convinced that they actually happened. Nowadays we no longer believe in them, we have *surmounted* these modes of thought; but we do not feel quite sure of our new beliefs, and the old ones still exist within us' (370–71).

In his treatment of *Concrete Island*, David Punter casually refers to the island as a 'desolate pubic triangle' (15). Maitland's confused attraction/repulsion to staying on the island, this 'wound that had never healed' (12), may certainly indicate a primal uncanny effect: 'This *unheimlich* place [of the female genitals], however, is the entrance to the former *Heim* of all human beings . . . the *unheimlich* is what was once heimisch, familiar; the prefix 'un' is the token of repression' (368). My concern, however, is to read *Concrete Island* as producing a kind of technological uncanny, in which surmounted and abandoned technologies and artifacts live on in the interstices of new economies. The rubble and ruins of the concrete island constitute the surmounted urban spaces that *Crash*, in its glazed, ecstatic rhetoric, seeks to repress but cannot. As Michel de Certeau states:

> Epistemological configurations are never replaced by the appearance of new orders; they compose strata that form the bedrock of a present. Relics and pockets of the instrumental system continue to exist everywhere . . . Tools take on a folk-loric appearance. They nevertheless make up a discharged corps left behind by the defunct empire of mechanics. These populations of instruments oscillate between the status of memorable ruins and an intense everyday activity. They form an intermediary class of objects, some already put into retirement . . . and others still at work. (146)

This slight alteration of Freud's terms seems to me to grasp extremely well the uncanny effect of Ballard's landscapes, littered with redundant technologies and inexplicably haunting icons (the drained swimming-pool, for instance, is one repeated—weirdly uncanny—image). It also issues an imperative to read 'simulacral' landscapes not as completed systems of an 'era of simulation', an era which casually erases all prior historical moments, for Ballard, if anything, constructs narratives out of the brute intrusion of the recalcitrant fragment from 'the defunct empire of mechanics' into new or emerging orders. And the sur-mounted fragment becomes the lever of critique of such systems.

'Comparing it with the motorway system, he saw that it was far older than the surrounding terrain, as if this triangular patch of waste ground had survived by the exercise of unique guile and persistence, and would continue to survive, unknown and disregarded, long after the motorways had collapsed into dust' (50). Maitland's gaze is reversed from that of Ballard's in *Crash*; from the island he can see the anonymous balconies of the high-rises—the type of place where Ballard convalesced (and whose functionalist order atavistically degenerates in *High Rise*). His abandonment is secured by the affectless economies of work and desire in which he operates: his company will assume work-related absence; his wife and mistress will each assume his staying with the other. Like the initially confining spaces of 'The Enormous Room' or *The Unlimited Dream Company*, the concrete island begins to exponentially expand, this time in a kind of archaeological depth. In fragments, Maitland reconstructs the traces of an erased history: ruins of a 'stucco Victorian house' (30) exist on an Edwardian pattern of streets (50); the shelter of a World War Two bunker (29) opens a first buried space, followed by 'the ground-plan of a post-war cinema' (50), complete with basement. Here, 'A faded cinema poster hung from the wall at the foot of the bed, advertising a Ginger Rogers and Fred Astaire musical' (57), but if that is assigned to a surmounted epoch of mechanical reproduction, so is the ideology of the Sixties in the psychedelic designs and Che Guevara posters that fade alongside it. In such a zone of suspended history, where even the obliterated churchyard has had its dead unearthed and relocated, it is no wonder that Maitland contrasts this fragmentary depth to a memory of 'the futuristic resort complex' at La Grande Motte where 'the ziggurat hotels and apartment houses, and the vast, empty parking lots laid down by the planners years before any tourist would arrive to park their cars [were] like a city abandoned in advance of itself' (48). Maitland has fallen into the interstices of the new economy, and rather like the analogy Freud repeatedly draws on, analysis as archeological excavation in 'Dreams and Delusions in Jensen's *Gradiva*', his suspension in this technologically uncanny zone begins to unearth clumsy Oedipal memories from his childhood (51).

Maitland has no representational means either to escape the island or to turn these fragments into meaningful narrative: it is significant that he recalls La Grande Motte as he recuperates in the ruins of a printing-shop, with 'copper-backed letterpress blocks [lying] at his feet' (48). The scriptural economy, surmounted, cannot compete with the ceaseless circulation of traffic that mark the confines of the island. All his attempts at writing messages are either erased by the rain or by the hidden presence of Proctor; later attempts at teaching Proctor to write merely result in 'garbling the letters into an indecipherable mess' (109). As Punter notes, even the motion of the grass on the island itself 'provides a continuous production and erasure of meaning, a maze which really requires no interpreting effort since its patterns do not endure' (17).

Punter suggests that the narrative of *Concrete Island* 'symbolizes a renunciation of the impulse towards the ideal society, and replaces it with a wish for abdication, yet in that act of abdication the self reasserts a useless sovereignty, apparently free from technological compulsion but free also from any location in discourse' (17). This is an acute comment: whilst 'abdication' might misread the leverage ruins supply *against* simulacral trafficking, Punter correctly reads the tendency in the latter half of the novel for Maitland to exploit the space for a colonial assertion of subjecthood. *Crusoe* parallels are evident; so too the echoing, in Jane, Proctor and Maitland, of the principal figures of *The Tempest* (even down to Proctor's first steps in writing being a 'learning to curse', like Caliban). Resonant with these classic colonial fictions, Maitland's need to 'dominate' the island is obsessively reiterated (45, 46, 99, 126); increasingly, Maitland identifies the zone of the island with his own body or fevered/fantasmatic projection: 'These places of pain and ordeal were now confused with pieces of his body . . . He would leave his right leg at the point of the crash, his bruised hands impaled on the steel fence. He would place his chest where he had sat against the concrete wall. At each point a small ritual would signify the transfer of obligation from himself to the island' (51). It remains uncertain whether Maitland's fevered identifications are being affirmed or ironized. The inability to exploit the colonial machinery of the transformation of 'virgin' territory into discursively mapped province ('mazed' script remaining unreadable) would suggest the latter. To the final discovery of Proctor's altar relicry of Maitland in the Church crypt, Maitland fails to master the hidden pockets of the island. Ruins, recalcitrant to the networks of the motorway, also problematize the triumphal assertion of subjecthood.

Perhaps this reads against the grain of the island as another zone of 'inner space' (the island, after all, becomes 'an exact model of his head' [51]), but the logic of the uncanny ruin and surmounted technologies can be read in a way which opens the matrix of Ballard's texts in unforeseen ways. *Concrete Island* dislodges a sector of the present moment, plays detritus against the depthless chrome and speed of the motorway. What happens when the contemporary itself is projected as a ruin *of the future*?

The Temporality of Future Ruins

In 'Myths of the Near Future' Sheppard's Cessna 'soared to and fro above the abandoned space grounds, unsettling though they were, with their immense runways leading to no conceivable sky, and the rusting gantries like so many deaths propped up in their tattered coffins. Here at Cape Kennedy a small part of space had died' (*Myths*, 9). Like the accompanying stories set in the ruins of Cape Kennedy, 'The Dead Astronaut' and 'Memories of the Space Age', 'Myths' generates peculiar unease by rendering spectacularly redundant the most advanced technological site. Mystical events take place in these future ruins: somewhat like *The Crystal World*, this site is a place which produces fugues in their itinerant population, states which go beyond life and death, and outside chronological time. In the terms of the Surrealist Manifesto, this is the exact state of the *sur*-real: a point beyond the oppositions of subject and object, reality and imagination, life and death. No wonder, then, that both 'Myths' and 'Memories' reference Surrealism: for Sheppard, his obsessional behaviour includes 'gazing for hours at reproductions of Chirico's Turin . . . Magritte's dislocations of time and space . . . and Dali's biomorphic anatomies' ('Myths', 15); for Mallory, 'The forest oaks were waiting for him to feed their roots, these motionless trees were as insane as anything in the visions of Max Ernst' ('Memories', *War Fever*, 137).

For Walter Benjamin, it was the Surrealist movement that first comprehended the radical power of cultural detritus and ruins:

> [Breton] was the first to perceive the revolutionary energies that appear in the 'outmoded', in the first iron constructions, the first factory buildings, the earliest photos, the dresses of five years ago, fashionable restaurants when the vogue has begun to ebb from them . . . No one before these visionaries and augurs perceived how destitution—not only social but architectonic, the poverty of interiors, enslaved and enslaving objects—can suddenly be transformed into revolutionary nihilism ('Surrealism', 229)

Now, it would be preposterous to ascribe to Ballard an equivalent 'revolutionary nihilism', but this does not mean that his own rigorously Surrealist intertexts, as the last chapter demonstrated, cannot be read within the same matrix (indeed a Benjaminian would no doubt criticize Ballard for the same reasons as Surrealism: a *maintenance* of the intoxicating dream-state, a dependence on the mysticism and the desire for, though not achievement of, transcendence). Where Benjamin focused on unmodishness of objects of the recent past to prise open the eyes from a collective commodity dream-state, Ballard de-modes the contemporary by projecting it as the detritus of the near future. Susan Buck-Morss explains Benjamin's strategy thus: 'In the era of industrial culture, consciousness exists in a mythic dream state, against which historical knowledge is the only antidote. But the particular kind of historical knowledge that is needed to free the present from myth is not so easily uncovered. Discarded and forgotten, it lies buried within surviving culture, remaining invisible precisely because it was of so little use' (x). Later, she adds: 'Benjamin sought out the small, discarded objects, the outdated buildings and fashions which, precisely as the "trash" of history, were evidence of its unprecedented material destruction' (93). In Ballard it is the present in ruins (in *Concrete Island*) and the present as the ruins of the near future which performs the same task. Uncannily surmounted, our technologies are hauntingly doubled, divorced from their self-identity, given, suddenly, as useless, futile junk.

Benjamin's work was inspired by Breton's hymn to the detritus of flea markets in *Nadja* and *L'Amour Fou* but particularly by Aragon's *Paris Peasant*. Aragon's evocation of the Passage de l'Opera, a covered shopping arcade, gained its edge from its destruction in the urban clearings ongoing in Paris. Benjamin took up the arcades, the enclosed iron constructions of World Expositions and dioramas, all of which emerged in the mid-nineteenth century, as the exemplary symbols of a new economic order of the commodity phantasmagorization of the world. No 'experience' as such is available in this regime, no 'real' outside this spectacle, no history that is not caught in the accelerated cycles of commodity fashion, each wave obliterating the last. If this sounds like Baudrillard's 'era of simulation', that's because it produces the same effects, only Benjamin seeks a counteracting critique from *within* the phantasmagorical world by exploiting the outmoded and the waste of the system to recover an erased history. Hence his interest in Baudelaire's 'poet as ragpicker' ('Everything that the big city threw away, everything it lost, everything it despised, everything it crushed underfoot, he catalogues and collects' (*Baudelaire*, 79)—hence the adaptation of Proust's 'involuntary memory', which calls up lost experience from tiny, marginal objects—hence his appropriation of Surrealism, for with them 'we begin to recognize the monuments of the bourgeoisie as ruins even before they have crumbled' (*Baudelaire*, 176).

That Ballard sends the gantries of Cape Kennedy into the near future as ruins is an equally inspired exploitation of an exemplary symbol. Dale Carter's extraordinary history of the space race, *The Final Frontier*, sees the Apollo programmes as the primary mechanism of the Rocket State, the 'apotheosis of the Spectacle' of a post-war America using the military rocket technology of coercive Fascism (the V-2) to generate a transmutation into a mediatized realm of 'voluntary totalitarianism': a nation televisually united in their conquest of the 'final frontier'. The sick joke of Ballard's 'The Dead Astronaut', in which a melancholic woman is reunited with a dead beloved astronaut after his twenty years of orbiting the earth only to find his remains are radioactive from the secret atomic bomb on board, captures perfectly the imbrication of frontier wonder with the hard facts of its purely military and Cold War motivation. Space technology expands in perfect accord to the growth of television in the 1960s: the Apollo XI landing on the moon, Carter states, reveals an audience 'passively finding their collective identity via wilful subordination within an elaborate drama of state' (181). 'The launching towers rose into the evening air like the rusting ciphers of some forgotten algebra of the sky' (*Low-Flying Aircraft*, 108), and the narrator of 'The Dead Astronaut' has a momentary 'feeling that the entire landscape of the earth was covered with rubbish and that here, at Cape Kennedy, we had found its source' (114). The task of trash, for Benjamin, is to provide a lever to awaken us from the collective dream-state in a phantasmagorical world; 'The Dead Astronaut', in its temporal defamiliarization of the advanced technologies of the space race, exploits the uncanny ruin for a similar effect. The NASA beacon that guides space trash back to base exposes this apotheosis of the spectacle, its monuments become ruins 'even before they have crumbled' (*Baudelaire*, 176). It remains important, however, to avoid simply collapsing Ballard into Benjamin's project: both 'Myths of the Near Future' and 'Memories of the Space Age' retain a purer Surrealist edge in their elaboration of an alternative 'dream-state', the fugues that announce a truer space age journey to the surreal amalgamation of past, present and future selves in mythic atemporality. Nevertheless, the effect of the ruin works, as in *Concrete Island*, to reveal the erasures of the phantasmagoric, simulacral world.

Post-war America is the Rocket State, America is simulation achieved. The final Ballard text to be considered here, *Hello America*, traverses the critical/cultural terrain which announces America as the apotheosis of the mediatized, ahistorical New World Order, but which complicates this move by the same device of near future disadjustment.

My Re-Found Land: *Hello America*

Two stupendous set-pieces stand out in *Hello America*: the Tombstone shoot-out and the automata at the Sahara Hotel. In the first, the expeditionary team to an America abandoned one hundred years previously finally disintegrates at the heart of the Great American Desert in Kansas. Even dying of thirst Wayne is somewhat embarrassed by his clichéd environs: 'were they all part of a theme park tableau, the last reel of a western?' (97). It gets worse: shots ring out in the desert streets, and 'as the swing doors rocked behind him he stepped out into the sun-filled street' (98). The final confrontation with Ricci begins:

> He realized that the whole secret logic of their journey across America had been leading them to this absurd and childish confrontation in a theme park frontier street, in a make-believe world already overtaken by a second arid West far wilder than anything those vacationing surburbanites of the late twentieth century could ever have imagined (99).

Dizzying reversals accompany this scene: in a mummified 'fake' past re-authenticated by the renewed desert, actions are nevertheless performed entirely through film clichés; this self-conscious imitation, however, is once more asserted as fake as Wayne's stagey dying moments in the Boot Hill cemetery is presided over by vast holographic projections of authentic 'fake' icons of Western mythology. John Wayne and Gary Cooper appear, 'heroes resurrected from the tombs of Boot Hill and the theme park saloons of Dodge city' (102). No direct 'experience' for the expedition: as Baudrillard states: 'you should not, then, begin with the city and move inwards to the screen; you should begin with the screen and move outwards to the city. It is there that the cinema does not assume an exceptional form, but simply invests the streets . . . with a mythical atmosphere' (*America*, 56). Indeed, Wayne is saved in 'the last minute of the final reel' (110).

The second scene takes place in a tropicalized, apparently empty Las Vegas. Music strikes up; Wayne, McNair and Anne enter the Sahara Hotel to find Sinatra, joined by Dean Martin and Judy Garland ending their rendition of 'My Way': 'This was the Sinatra of the latter period, the Sinatra of the endless farewell appearances and testimonial concerts, when America had clung to its last great icons' (124–5). Wayne topples the Sinatra automaton, causing chaos: 'The players in the orchestra had lost their scores, the violinists were calmly breaking their bows . . . the conductor stabbed himself in the eye with his baton. Sinatra lay on his back, legs kicking, gesturing at the ceiling' (127).

Holographs and 'animatronic' robots constitute a specifically American way of historiographic practice, according to Umberto Eco. For the past to be represented at all, it must reside in a 'full scale authentic copy', an Absolute Fake, in which 'the sign aims to be the thing, to abolish the distinction of the reference' (*Travels in Hyperreality*, 6). America, without the density of a European past, anxiously and compulsively attempts to capture its perfect reproduction, in doing so volatizing any distinction between model and copy and thus, in the bizarre juxtapositions of the dioramas of its waxwork museums, abolishing any coherent historiographic narrative. Everything is rendered equivalently 'real', which is to say indifferently simulacral. 'Holography could only prosper in America, a country obsessed with realism, where, if a reconstruction is to be credible, it must be absolutely iconic, a perfect likeness, a "real" copy of the reality being represented' (4). As in the moments of astonishment before Wayne exposes the Sahara Hotel concert as a robotic fake, so Eco leaves the animatronic robots of Disneyland knowing that 'afterwards reality will always be inferior to it' (46). Ballard's take on the wholly mediated culture of America is itself, seemingly, wholly mediated by a pervasive European cultural critique of American historical and representational practices.

Is *Hello America*, then, a satire of contemporary America which works by extrapolating its simulacral tendencies in the desert *it already is*? It is in the desert, too, that Baudrillard sees American culture's 'ecstatic form of disappearance' (*America*, 5)—an insight available only to the European traveller: 'It may be that the truth of America can only be seen by a European, since he alone will discover here the perfect simulacrum—that of the immanence and material transcription of all values. The Americans, for their part, have no sense of simulation. They are themselves simulation in its most developed state, but they have no language in which to describe it' (*America*, 28–29). Concurrence with Julia Kristeva, therefore: the European intellectual will be valued in this '*nonverbal*' culture, because s/he can 'speak in a place where it [i.e. America] doesn't speak' ('Why the United States?', 275). America is iconic, not verbal: this distinction even governs Todorov's liberal account of the Spanish victory over Mexico, a victory won by the more 'evolved' language of Spain's 'higher civilization' over the pictograms of the Aztecs (*The Conquest of America*, 81).

If satire is an adequate term, however, *Hello America*'s satirical aim is directed more *against* European projective fantasies of America. This is a text densely freighted with a knowingness about the successive waves of the fantasmatic investment in 'America'. Ballard's standard tropes of 'inner space' are present here ('they were about to begin that far longer safari across the diameters of their own skulls' (76), 'The first settlers to cross America were driven by their fantasies too' (93), and so on) but like *The Drought* competing fantasies clash and are unable to resolve the landscape into the desired image. The additional device of *Hello America* is to deploy a terrain that is not 'new found land', a virgin territory awaiting discursive inscription, but a 're-found' land that is the very epicentre of late twentieth century 'dream production'. Ruination, once more, uncannily doubles and *disadjusts* (rather than clones) the American spectacular as theorized by a succession of European intellectuals.

This is not so much, then, an empty repetition of a classic East to West coast journey through the icons of simulation; rather, it switches back on itself at every stage to excavate a history of the projections that announce America's lack of history.

A reading of the opening chapters fully indicates this overlaid density. The first noun of the book—gold—condenses temporally disjunct utopian projections. From Columbus' use of lure of gold to finance his explorations, to the mythic El Dorado that propelled Cortez and Pissarro (and which becomes, in this text, Las Vegas), to Frobisher's shipping home of over one thousand tons of what proved to be fool's gold from Meta Incognita in the 1570s, gold drives the movement towards America *even before it is 'discovered'*. As many note, America is never 'unknown', but a space prepared for by a creative mix of divine, materialist and classical authorities. Stephen Greenblatt speaks of the real-world effects of these fantasmatically anticipatory representations as 'a set of images and image-making devices that are accumulated, "banked," as it were' (6), and Ballard's bravura opening self-con-sciously raids these image-banks.

As the SS *Apollo* arrives in New York (thus reversing the exploration from outer to inner space) from Plymouth (like the Founding Fathers), McNair can only resort to established cliché: 'The streets of America *are* paved with gold!' (7) Wayne's surveyal of the New York skyline is also anticipated by 'the ancient slides in the Geographical Society library in Dublin', yet he has the banally familiar tourist response: 'he was unprepared for the spectacular size and mysterious form' of New York (8). Docking at the Cunard terminal, evoking the golden age of transatlantic glamour cruising in the 1920s, this is overlaid by Wayne's evidently post-World War Two inspired 'need to get away from a tired and candle-lit Europe with its interminable rationing and subsistence living' (9–10). The desired iconography of America that Wayne devours in ancient *Time* and *Look* magazines serves the same function of escape as it does for Jamie in the Lunghua camp in *Empire of the Sun*, trading the magazines for dangerous tasks set by the glamorous survivalist GIs. The text can evoke 1950s austerity, imagine the crew in Renaissance doublets and armour (23) and speak of the expedition as Ellis Island immigrant arrivals (24) in quick succession, overlaying significant moments of primary encounters with the New World.

The description of New York as a deserted and desertified ruin also, curiously, evokes a particular post-War response. Wayne's description of 'the soundless city with its great towers and abandoned streets, a million empty windows lit by the afternoon sun', with 'dunes that filled the floors of these deserted canyons' (23), recalls Jean-Paul Sartre's essays on America written in 1945–46. 'The skyscrapers . . . seem like . . . rocks and hills, dead parts of the urban landscape one finds in cities built on turbulent soil' ('American Cities', 107); later the 'vertical disorder' of the skyline is described as a 'rocky chaos' (115). And the uncanny ruination of these advanced technological structures is already there for Sartre in 1946:

> The man who walked about in New York before 1930 saw in the big buildings that dominated the city the first signs of an architecture destined to radiate over the whole country . . . Today . . . they are already mere historical monuments, relics of a bygone age . . . Far away I see the Empire State or the Chrysler Building reaching vainly towards the sky, and suddenly I think that New York is about to acquire a History and that it already possesses its ruins ('New York, The Colonial City', 123).

This is the uncanny effect that Anthony Vidler ascribes to the 'discovery' of Pompeii for the nineteenth century imagination, archaeology 'revealing what should have remained invisible' (48). In the twentieth century, New York is insistently projected as a future ruin, a space in which catastrophe always already inheres, and which thus inspires a geological or archeological gaze rather than an anthropological one:

> A day will come when amateurs of archeological digs will look for the location of New York City. A whole forest of these great oiled steel trees, which are the backbone of elevators, will be found. Scientists will try to guess whether these remnants date

from the twentieth century or the Aztec period (Paul Morand, quoted in Mathy, 183)

The image of the desert that already occupies the gleaming citadels of American modernity is one which Ballard firmly adopts from a well established image-bank. A haunting double of the known city emerges here, an uncanny effect produced by the apparent *untimeliness* of its death. For Wayne, 'The ancient desert cities of Egypt and Babylonia were safely distanced from them by the span of millennia. But for all its rusting neon signs, the New York around him seemed preserved in limbo, its vast buildings abandoned only the previous day' (35–36).

That the gold that McNair and the crew see is, of course, rust is also a neatly presented standard narrative about the ironic gap between image and reality, American Dream and Nightmare—the illusion of riches shattered for the conquistadors, the arrival of Eden on Earth destroyed by the return to the fallen history of corrupt European time for the Puritans.

The density of reference to prior contacts—Ballard even takes time to include a passing satire of anthropological misprision, Ricci mistaking the drowned Statue of Liberty for 'a local marine deity . . . The Americans of the eastern seabord worshipped a pantheon of under-water creatures' (20)—is one which is consistently flagged and ironi-cally deflated. Orlowski's early role is to transcode their 'first' contact with the exotic Other into absurd modern forms: 'I feel like Columbus. By rights the natives should appear now, bearing traditional gifts of hamburgers and comic books' (34); 'What's this, Captain? A whole bunch of Man Fridays . . . Have you saved us from the cannibals?' (69) Even more unsettling is the rather alarming similarity between the expedition force—an indestructible captain, a Russian, an enthusiastic Scottish engineer, amongst others—and the crew of *Star Trek*. Perhaps this is why critical reception of the novel was lukewarm: Ballard adapts the very narrative to melodramatic cliché of 'American' popular fiction: the disaster novel, the Western, the nuclear countdown, the crazed psychopathic leader. What better form, however, for the journeying back to the 'origin' of ghettoized science fiction, America?

What Jean-Philippe Mathy calls the 'paradigm of discontinuity' (2) between Europe and America produces a reiterated narrative: 'The crossing of the Atlantic, like the passage of a modern Lethe, means forgetting the Old World, which cannot be remembered, let alone conjured up or resurrected, but only simulated' (168). And yet *Hello America*, whilst being driven by the utopian investment of an America beyond a newly austere Europe, reflexively announces a history of those fantasms not in order to repeat them but to interrogate and ironize them.

There is a serious element to be extracted from Baudrillard's provocations in *America*. The extremity of European reaction to the United States in part derives from melancholia, he suggests. America, as part of the West, nevertheless divorced itself from Europe before the revolution of 1789 established a particular paradigm of modernity. There is no mirroring of this modernity in America, which succeeded in becoming absolutely modern in a way that Europe has never achieved. The attraction/repulsion towards America is to be explained in a melancholic entrapment of Europe within a superseded model of the modern: 'We in Europe are stuck in the old rut of worshipping difference; this leaves us with a great handicap when it comes to radical modernity, which is founded on the absence of difference. Only very reluctantly do we become modern and in-different' (97). One does not have to accept Baudrillard's distribution of difference/indifference to discern a crucial point about the investments in the United States. *Hello America* itself might be conceived as a process of analysing melancholic entrapment in a certain demand for America to conform to a desired image.

'Like his unknown ancestors centuries before him, he had come to America to forget the past, to turn his back forever on an exhausted Europe' (14). This repetition of the Puritan impulse, however, is stalled by the precision of the anticipatory fantasies of the crew, which they desire to reenact. Orlowski is correct to believe that 'the real contraband was their collective dream of America' (27). Within ten days of arrival 'everyone was retreating into their own dreams' (55): Anne Summers 'brought back her own little booty, a full-length black evening gown from Macy's Fifth Avenue' to fulfil her narcissistic Hollywood fantasies; Wayne sees Ricci 'sitting in the back of an antique limousine . . . [wearing] a pin-striped suit of extravagant cut with lapels like wings, and cradled a rusty Thompson gun between his knees' (55–56); Steiner grabs horse and hat and becomes an inscrutable cowboy. Wayne's initial mourning of the lack of iconic American cars—'His childhood in Dublin had been fed by dreams of an America filled with automobiles, immense chromium mastodons with grilles like temple facades' (43)—does not prevent his ceaseless attempts to revive the dead icons of power. He cleans the Oval Office, returns the Lincoln Memorial from its burial in the sand, and nurses dreams of reversing the climactic changes that have desertified America.

The melancholic refuses to work through loss by denial and an internalization of the lost object. Secretly installed in the ego, the incorporated object retains the traces of 'countless separate struggles . . . in which love and hate contend with one another' (Freud, 'Mourning and Melancholy', 266), and begins to dominate a now vilified ego, driving it to compulsively repetitive behaviour in order to keep the lost object 'alive'. The incorporated object may even infect the superego: 'The destructive component has entrenched itself in the superego, and turned against the ego. What is now holding sway in the superego is, as it were, a pure culture of the death instinct' (Freud, 'The Ego and the Id', 394). The propulsion of the crew and their behaviours constitute a melancholic repetition, even to the extent of driving them (like previous expeditions) towards death in the desert. The dream-state of ruling phantasmagorias of America continues, even in the face of its ruination. A series of gestural reenactments of American iconography is mediated entirely through the remaining archives of its culture in Europe. Whilst they are all secretly relieved that Washington is empty, 'that they were alone here at the heart of their dream' (72), it is Manson's more powerful 'lunatic fantasy' (230) that begins to dismantle their melancholic entrapment.

Charles Manson, bearing an 'uncanny' resemblance to Nixon and living his existence by reiterating the later years of Howard Hughes, has revived Las Vegas, its casino economy translated with minimal difficulty into a form of nuclear roulette. It is his holographic displays that reconvene the panoply of American lost culture. The first critique of this is significantly given by one of Manson's *Mexican* recruits: 'In his eyes it was an excess of fantasy that killed the old United States, the whole Mickey Mouse and Marilyn thing, the most brilliant technologies devoted to trivia' (149). If Wayne continues his melancholic attempts to revive the corpse of a lost America (re-opening the drugstores and fast food bars), his eventual rejection of Manson's revival of the Rocket State is couched in terms that initiate a process of mourning. 'I'm not an American!' (218), he proclaims, and the final paragraph of the text announces: 'The old dreams were dead, Manson and Mickey Mouse and Marilyn Monroe belonged to a past America, to that city of gamblers about to be vaporized fifty miles away' (236). The final assertion that 'it was time for new dreams' (236) does not exactly instance a *healthy* mourning since this is premised on the wipe-out of Las Vegas, a nuclear effacement of old cultural accretions and, perhaps, a restatement of a 'blank slate' on which to inscribe new fantasmatic constructions. Nevertheless, it is a shattering of entrapment within European productions of 'America'.

The evident, if ambivalent, love for American iconography in *Hello America* is not apparent in the 1977 short story, 'Theatre of War', which (according to an appended note) transcribes a Vietnam commentary onto an imagined invasion of England by American troops propping up a puppet English regime and seeking to repress an indigenous rebel army. Ballard here deploys an obverse yet equally standard set of narratives about invasive Americanization. *Hello America*'s facility with American stereotypes seems much more in accord with the openly complicitous use of iconography by the Independent Group of Pop artists, Richard Hamilton's appropriation of car stylings, Eduardo Paolozzi's celebration of junk culture, and Reyner Banham's enthusiastic accounts of the 'Autopia' of Los Angeles. This group is in fact cited by Duncan Webster in his account of English paranoid fantasies about Americanization as finding solution to the problem of 'how to reconcile unavoidable admiration for the immense competence, resourcefulness and creative power of American commercial design with the equally unavoidable disgust at the system that was producing it' (247). Ballard's fascination with American culture is consistent throughout the oeuvre, and if *Hello America* is principally concerned with investigating and undermining the projection of America as the apotheosis of simulation, this need not necessarily curtail a reading of the text as *also* concerned with interrogating America as neo-imperialist state, thus connecting with the scenario of 'Theatre of War' and the implied criticism in the stories that 'ruin' Cape Kennedy.

The representational capital of the image-bank of colonialism works on 'the colonial space [as] the *terra incognita* or the *terra nulla*, the empty or wasted land whose history has to be begun' (Bhabha, 246). The monumental temporality of modernity, post-colonial critics suggest, insists on the colonial other coming before its tribunal in ways which can only judge on its belatedness or regression. Homi Bhabha's project, as previously discussed, is to shatter the monumentality of modernity by re-examining the anxious reiterated assertion of the inferiority of the other, and to exploit the gap between the event and its narration in the singular frame of modernity. This gap Bhabha calls the *time-lag*, the catastrophic space *between*, in which a marginalized agency can seize and transform the locus of thought, speech and historiographical authority: 'the project of modernity is itself rendered so contradictory and unresolved through the insertion of the "time-lag" in which colonial and post-colonial moments emerge as sign and history' (238).

This formulation owes much to Walter Benjamin's famous critique of the 'empty homogeneous time' of modernity, and the function of the Now (the event) as bearing elements which might cause it to 'blast open the continuum of history' (Theses on the Philosophy of History', 254). This explosive power is available from the fragment. It is possible, then, to consider the temporality of the future ruins in Ballard's novels, and particularly in *Hello America*, as inserting a time-lag *inside* the contemporary moment, uncannily doubling it as its own ruination. The space opened by this act not only exposes the mechanics behind simulacral or phantasmagoric projections, giving it back a repressed history, but also operates to unveil the *colonial* imperative in which it is engaged (a kind of double movement that was suggested as one way of reading the catastrophe novels). Such are the multiple effects of this interruption that *Hello America* can simultaneously reveal the machinery of European and American colonial projections. The text is not about the ruin of representation, as in Baudrillard, but deploys the representation of ruins as a challenge to the triumphal assertion of possession. This was suggested in the section on *Concrete Island*, but *Hello America* intensifies the effect.

The projection of America into the near future produces overdeterminations at once neo- and post-colonial. The private fantasms of the expedition occupy and are directed by the archives of media representations; if repeating an entrenched European history of projection, their quaintness is emphasized by the stark neo-imperialist tendency in Manson's revival of American militarism. A Las Vegas built once again by Mexican labour, the gun-battles above the forest canopy transpose the Vietnam ecocide and genocide inside American borders. Whilst the melodramatic narrative and architecture of ruination displace and expose the pathology of this melancholic repetition, the very estrangement of Las Vegas nevertheless depends on another set of colonial encounters with American landscape. The overwhelming plenitude of tropicalized Western America reiterates von Humboldt's influential rendering of South American landscape as a superabundant tropical space of 'impenetrable forests' (Mary Louise Pratt, 131). Wayne initially thinks longingly back to the desert, its 'bonelike towns and grain silos, abstract elements of a private dream waiting for him to act out anything he wished' (117). In the tropical West, however, 'his voice was lost in the chittering of thousands of tropical birds, tenants of a demented aviary': 'Here, in this raucous madhouse, one could never be alone' (117). The time-lag induced by the uncanny ruins of America, therefore, produces contradictory effects: the landscape of the novel is at once a knowing and disadjusted reiteration of colonial projections, satirizing neo-colonial repetition via disjunctive post-colonial temporal effects, but the extent of that satire remains undeterminable—the space between identical and differential repetition of colonial images uncertain. Whatever the effects, they all move between mediation, simulation and recalcitrance.

This chapter's traversal of Ballard's manifold approaches to the question of mediation, from early media stories of brainwashing advertisements to the complex and knowing strategies of *Hello America*, has sought to emphasize that the scenario of simulation supplied by *Crash* cannot be taken out of context of the series in which it is written and work to supply a single thesis for the oeuvre, miraculously in accord with current accounts of postmodernism and cyberpunk. Whilst the 'hysterical sublime' of *Crash*'s ecstatic narration can clearly be read inside this framework, to privilege it is to forget the recalcitrant ruin, the demonic double, the margins and abandoned wastelands, in which much of Ballard's fiction is set. These are, in effect, the remaining traces of 'anthropological place' which provide levers to return history to the evacuated non-places of the contemporary: it is the spaces *between*, as ever, on which Ballard focuses.

CHAPTER FIVE
The Signature of J. G. Ballard

This book has been concerned with frames and borders throughout, and the strange lapsus in their operations that Ballard's texts produce. Being between science fiction and the 'mainstream', modernism and postmodernism, avant-garde ('high' texts in advance) and après-garde ('low' texts dragging behind), have been positions carefully examined, as have Ballard's explicit thematization of permeability, invagination, the peculiar space between catastrophe and catastrophe, and the uncanny protrusions into the empty spaces of supermodernity, those zones of transit that lie between elsewheres.

Every critic would desire (for wouldn't every reader demand this?) to capture the essence of their chosen texts, squaring possible hermeneutic violence with an advance in understanding. But in some ways, this has been a book about Ballard's means of escaping capture, the 'lines of flight' that leave contextual, generic and theoretical frames somehow inadequate. This is not in itself a disaster; rather, it is the nature of my interest in Ballard—a writer of texts that lure theoretical framings only to throw them into question in enlightening ways.

But perhaps this is not enough; one more effort (that is always the lure) might reach the essence, the singular affectivity of Ballard's work, the core of its oscillating fascination/repulsion. If the focus was tightened, could that enigmatic core finally offer itself up? What would it take to render Ballard's texts transparent, finally readable?

Un/Readability

In his monograph on Ballard David Pringle lists a series of objects that he considers 'unforgettably "Ballardian" ': abandoned airfields, sand dunes, half-submerged buildings, advertising hoardings, drained swimming pools. The list continues on and on, carried away by the pleasure of nominalizing the 'Ballardian'. Pringle then asks:

> What do all these heterogeneous properties have in common? They are Ballardian—any reader with more than a passing

acquaintance with his work will vouch for that—but what do they mean, and are they interconnected in more than a purely private and autobiographical manner? (*Earth is the Alien Planet*, 15–16)

Harlan Ellison also states: 'Ballard . . . seems to me to write peculiarly Ballardian stories—tales difficult to pin down as to one style or one theme or one approach but all very personally trademarked Ballard' (458). Tautology is the only way to determine this object: Ballard writes Ballardian texts. Both of these statements hint, in those phrases 'purely private and autobiographical' and 'very personally trademarked', at a fear of the fundamental *unreadability* of the texts, the reader trapped forever in tautology, never getting beyond the surface. Private iconography is one way of opening a reading, determining a singularity; everything returns to the name, even as what is said in that name remains enigmatic, for the 'purely private' leads beyond the text into the body of the writer. The other route is into the texts themselves, grouping them, following the structures of repetition of theme, image and character. However, a similar disappearance is affected, for to analyse the style is, in Ellison's words, like looking at '[t]he most exquisite Wyeth landscape' which, 'when examined more and more minutely, begins to resemble pointillism, and finally nothing but a series of disconnected coloured dots' (459).

Pringle and Ellison attempt to establish the absolute singularity of Ballard's texts, to isolate the core of their fascination, but both also signal the difficulty of this project, for to project meaning 'outside' the text into the signature of Ballard is to close it off from reading; on the other hand, to locate meaning in the innermost recess of the text, is either to witness its disappearance into 'disconnected coloured dots' or else to transform the text into private language, one which is equally unavailable for reading. That Pringle's questions are *rhetorical*, that he begins to elaborate a reading of Ballard's texts, indicates that reading is, of course, possible; even when 'ultimate' meaning is projected 'outside' or encrypted 'inside', the texts partake of general language, of a relative recognizability according to generic codes, of the institution of literature. And yet those forms of access—language, generic code, institution —all situate Ballard's specificity within the general; the 'uniqueness' of his work undergoes dispersal once more. For Pringle and Ellison, it might be said, reading is possible, but this impetus to read is driven by the seductiveness of that tautologous core—Ballard's Ballardianism—

which either refuses to give itself up, remaining private, or which gives itself up only to disappear in general codifications.

No text, however, is totally 'private' or totally 'public', in the sense of being dispersed through general language. As Derrida states: 'A text lives only if it lives *on*, and it lives *on* only if it is *at once* translatable *and* untranslatable . . . Totally translatable, it disappears as a text, as writing, as a body of language. Totally untranslatable, even within what is believed to be one language, it dies immediately' ('Living On', 102). In another way, no text is completely ascribable to the *signature* (for that would situate all meaning in the body of the signer, 'outside' the text), and no text is purely *idiomatic* (for that would be a private, unique language wholly internal to the text and inaccessible to laws of reading). The enigma, the fascination that compels a desire to *pin down* the specificity of an oeuvre, is in fact generated in the space between readability and unreadability, in the tensions created by this space.

Ballard's work lends itself well to an analysis in terms of signature and idiom, for these two directions, one leading outwards the other inwards, have possessed a certain governance over the critical compulsions to render his fiction readable. Once Ballard published his two 'autobiographies', *Empire of the Sun* and *The Kindness of Women*, they were seized on, in effect, as signed confessions, detached from fictional space but working as decoding machines to render autobiographically readable the body of his work. If that produced difficulties, for the operation of the signature is not so straightforward, this is nothing to the tensions of readability and unreadability that complicate the attempt to isolate Ballard's 'unique' idiom, his *textual* signature; a text like *Vermilion Sands* begins to promise a pure instance, only to find itself bewilderingly disseminated. These are the texts that will be the focus of my one last effort, moving between what is allegedly transparently autobiographical to the frustrations of the opacity of Ballard's peculiar idiom.

The Paraph: *Empire of the Sun* and *The Kindness of Women*

J. G. Ballard has been mystifying and embarrassing readers for much of his career. Praise is mixed with comments on the awkwardness of his prose, perplexity at his intent and the impossibility of *siting* his work within comfortable frames. I have attempted to display the effect in which Ballard is situated within the SF/mainstream binary only as he is projected elsewhere: when science fiction critics praise him, it is for

transcending the genre; mainstream critics celebrate his transformation of science fiction tropes as long as they remain inside genre
boundaries. This process effectuates a constant double displacement,
and the difficulty of siting his work results from this uncertain nonsite
between science fiction and the mainstream. Both groupings reacted
violently to pieces like *The Atrocity Exhibition* and *Crash*, which were left
in lengthy suspension outside any frames of readability until very
recently.

One way of dealing with such extremity is simply to refuse it, to
render it external either to science fiction or the mainstream. An
attendant effect of this, however, is Ballard's occupation of the strange
space of the 'cult writer'. The cult can cut a swath through institutional
framings of the high/low, serious/popular binary to appeal to an
unforseeably admixed sodality of readers. As Umberto Eco notes, 'cult'
texts are read transgressively: the 'low' can be elevated to the 'high' or
vice versa ('*Casablanca*: Cult Movies and Intertextual Collage', *Travels in
Hyperreality*). However, cults coagulate around secrets, arcana, are
performed through private languages, gestures and rituals, and depend
for their survival on an uncomprehending exteriority, whose disappro-
bation merely intensifies the lure of the cult. One way of 'saving'
Ballard becomes only another form of marginality.

This secrecy has nevertheless been breached on two occasions. In a
way that apparently ejected him from the double marginalization of
'science fiction' or the 'cult author', Ballard has been *received and
understood*, with massive critical and commercial success, in his two
'autobiographical' novels, *Empire of the Sun* (1984) and *The Kindness of
Women* (1991).

The sudden visibility of Ballard and Ballard's work in 1984 (Booker
prize nominee, Guardian Fiction Prize) is no less astonishing for the
equally sudden disappearance and then repeated 'discovery' in 1991
(the week of publication saw major interviews on Radio 3, Radio 4, a
documentary on BBC2, serialization in *The Independent* newspaper, and
later, that most English of accolades, Ballard on Desert Island Discs).

The reason for this sudden acceptability—a conjunction of mass
audience with critical elevation to 'serious' novelist—can be incontra-
vertibly traced to a perceived generic shift: SF to 'autobiography'. More
than this, *Empire* could be rendered generically safe in another sense: it
was a Second World War novel. These terms of acceptance are problematic, however. The logic of the argument proceeds thus: *Empire* and
Kindness can be detached from the oeuvre in their generic shift; both can
be read as new additions to an honourable 'confessional' mode, thus

escaping the derogatory appellation of 'science fiction'. At the same time these texts can then be re-attached to the oeuvre as the 'straight' texts which finally decode the bizarre and perverse aberrations that had gone before, rendering the fiction autobiographically comprehensible.[1] In other words, the autobiographies supposed another contract—one, if not of transparency, then of authentification by a *signed* confession. To the name that adorns the cover of a fiction is added the *paraph*, the flourish of the signature, that seemingly guarantees authorial sincerity as a bulwark against the dangers and seductions of the fictive.

The dominant media reception of these works clearly deployed them as autobiographical decoding machines. Of *Empire* it was said that it was 'the key to the rest of an extraordinary oeuvre and central to his project' (Webb), 'the first stage in a comprehensive decoding' (Murray); of *Kindness*, that it 'provides a framework for comprehending much that is disturbing in his writing' (Blow), that it 'loops together all the strands of a story that, in the course of fictionally processing his life, reveals how and where Ballard acquired his distinct gallery of images for his literature' (Kemp). It now becomes 'tempting to see all his earlier fiction as a kind of displacement activity' (Barber, 'Alien at Home').

The logic of this repeated argument is a retrospective rereading of the prior science fiction as encrypted autobiographical performance. Inverting the order of the series, *Empire* and *Kindness* become the paradigms that decrypt and displace the science fiction from simple self-identity; a nongeneric 'secret' can now be implanted to explain Ballard's perverse attachment to such a juvenile genre.[2] Peter Brigg detects the model Vonnegut provided for the writing of *Slaughterhouse-5* in these proposals, that 'the authors worked through a series of science fiction novels to develop the style to express the almost inexpressible aspects of their own experiences' (*J. G. Ballard*, 106)—something, apparently, that could not be performed within science fiction. This downgrades the science fiction texts to 'drafts' of a 'final' literary text. However, this move cannot be limited to an attempt to legitimate writers associated with science fiction; it often informs the theory of autobiography in general. The autobiography is 'the symptomatic key to all else he did' (Olney, 4); the 'autobiographical key' (Gusdorf, 46) unlocks the work, it is 'the magnifying lens, focusing and intensifying that same peculiar creative vitality that informs all the volumes of his collected works' (Olney, 3–4). Lejeune suggests that this produces an 'autobiographical space' (12), which retrospectively occupies and 're-reads' the fictional work.

Autobiographical readings have a clear explanatory power whose lure cannot be simply rejected, and yet they are dangerous if they reductively claim to establish the correct reading. For Gusdorf, the peculiar force of autobiography is inextricably connected to Western concepts of individualism. It offers the unity of identity across time, interpreting life in its totality, 'a second reading of experience . . . truer than the first because it adds to experience itself consciousness of it' (35). Gusdorf, though, abandons any claim to factual truth in the text, preferring the somewhat religiose 'theodicy of individual being' (39).

Olney too dispenses with simple considerations of 'truth-telling', as well as genre or historical development, and argues that autobiography comes from the 'vital impulse to order that has always caused man to create' (3). Any systematizing knowledge arises from this 'innate' patterning. Olney proposes that this 'vital principle' is outside any notion of life as linear narrations, outside 'experience' or even 'memory'. Lejeune is more pragmatically concerned with defining the genre: autobiography is a retrospective prose narrative, written in such a way as to clearly identify author, narrator and character as the same person (as distinct from biography and the novel). At this stage, the slightest non-coincidence of terms bars entry to the autobiographical. This is the terms of the pact, signed by the author and countersigned by the reader. The proper name ensures fixity; Lejeune is almost patholo- gically concerned to counter the problem of the textual 'I' as shifter (an empty, non-referential place within the enounced which is filled, every time, by specific contextual factors) by tying it back to the proper name of the author which appears on the cover. Once again, this is a formulation which is not concerned with fact or truth (which can never be textually established, as Mansell states), but with the sincerity of the enunciation, the condition of the signed/countersigned pact.

Autobiography is therefore given a transcendent position, in relation to the oeuvre as a whole and in itself: it accesses 'deeper being'. A cursory reading of *Empire* and *Kindness* can witness a certain conformity to these debates. There is no problem, for example, with their 'distortions'. The decision to separate Jim from his parents in the Lunghua camp, unlike Ballard's real experience, and the displacement of the manner of his wife's death causes no difficulties. As Ballard states: 'It's literally true half the time, and psychologically true the whole of the time' (Barber, 'Alien at Home'). *Kindness* is also, far more explicitly than *Empire*, apparently structured in terms of the retrospec- tive discovery of a patterning which informs the writer's life and work, with 'Each of my novels . . . reflected in a section of the book' (Pickering). So far so good, but there seem to me to be three related problems with this autobiographical theory and the structure of detachment/reattachment to the oeuvre when applied to Ballard.

The first revolves around the terms in which autobiography is delineated: sincerity of the pact. This does not refer to the text itself, but to the *edges* of the text, the contextual determination which establishes autobiography *as* autobiography. Since the fictive has a disconcerting ability to mimic the textual appearance of autobiography, 'our expectations depend heavily upon all sorts of obvious clues to authorial intention such as a preface, autographs, even cover blurbs or literary classifications' (Stone, 6). Philippe Lejeune's theorization of the pragmatics of the 'autobiographical pact' may try to determine genre through retrospection, the identity of the author, narrator and central character, but ultimately Lejeune concludes that 'the fringe of the printed text . . . *controls* the entire reading (author's name, title, subtitle, name of the collection, name of the publisher, even including the ambiguous game of prefaces)' (29).

John Sutherland has argued for the importance of covers in determining responses and takes as his opening example the hardback edition of *Empire of the Sun*. He states:

> What will condition the reader's experience of the novel are 3 points, all stressed as being important in the jacket material: (1) *Empire of the Sun* draws on autobiographical experience and therefore carries a more complex, ethical cargo than most fiction; (2) it is a 'departure' from Ballard's normal (science fiction) work; (3) it is the crowning achievement of his work in fiction—the point to which all his previous novels tend. It seems clear to me that someone entering *Empire of the Sun* via the jacket apparatus must have a different set from the reader (particularly the reader new to Ballard) with a bald library copy (4).

Framing devices direct and constitute readings. That both this jacket material and the reviews cited earlier are crucial enframing devices is helpfully theorized by Gérard Genette in the concept of the paratext. For Genette, the paratext is that set of framing apparati which includes the framing on and around the text (*peritext*) and those at more distance (*epitext*: reviews, interviews, conversations). Since a text cannot appear in a naked state, unadorned, this edge determines a reading, however 'auxiliary' (261) it may appear.

One might expect that this welcome attentiveness to the textual edge would assist in an analysis of the insertion of a generic frame which strategically aims to distance Ballard's 'autobiographies' from his science fiction. Genette, however, and in spite of arguing that the paratext is 'fundamentally heteronomous' (261), suggests that this frame is 'always the bearer of an authorial commentary either more or less legitimated by the author' (262). In proposing that the multiple discourses of the paratext are fully traceable to a singular author-ity, Genette's foregrounding of the paratext is yet a frame that is marked only to be immediately effaced. In this, it performs according to Jacques Derrida's analysis of the *parergon* (the frame of the art-work): 'the parergon is a form which has as its traditional determination not that it stands out but that it disappears . . . [and] melts away at the moment it deploys its greatest energy' (*The Truth in Painting*, 61). It is as if the work generates its own frame, completely and exhaustively determines its own contextual enframing. It is significant in this respect that Genette cites Lejeune on autobiography to assert that the responsibility of the paratext always reverts to the author. For Lejeune it has to if the pact is to be at all functional, if the boundary between fictional oeuvre and autobiographical text is to remain in place. This is exactly the same for Gusdorf, Olney, and others, like Barrett Mandell, who asserts that autobiographies 'ultimately emanate from the deeper reality of being' (50). Jonathan Loesberg's comments on such statements are useful here: 'the problems theorists attribute to writers of autobiography, the problems involved in accurately inscribing consciousness within a text, are actually problems faced by a reader of autobiography unwilling to accept textual indeterminateness as inherent in an autobiographical text' (169).

In Ballard's case, it is evident that the enframing is not purely self-generated. It is the product in part of a mechanism to detach the 'autobiographies' in order to give them the textual sanction to operate as decoding machines for the oeuvre. And yet *Empire* and *Kindness* slip the fixity of the division that would render transparent the fictional code because they are, of course, autobiographical *novels*. Ballard's own epitextual work in interviews and other framing activities is to issue a double injunction that these texts both are and are not autobiographical. They are, in the sense that the Preface to *Empire* states that it is based 'for the most part' on his own experiences, and they are not, because the fictionalizing goes much further than the alteration of a few facts: *Kindness* often contradicts, rewrites and even erases sections of *Empire*. No simple identity, either, can be established between J. G. Ballard and the Jamie/Jim figure in the texts. This creates a 'zone of indetermination' (Lejeune, 19), in which, as a novel, it belongs too closely to the coincidence of author-protagonist, but the distance between them cannot allow it full autobiographical status. What the initial reviewers believed they had found in these texts—the key to unlock the opacity of his fictions—already founders over the indeterminate zone between fiction and autobiography which *Empire* and *Kindness* occupy.

The second problem extends this difficulty since it hinges on the relation between autobiography and oeuvre. The injunction to decode is performed by reading Ballard's oeuvre backwards: the landscape of *The Drowned World* finds its generation in the Shanghai skyline reflected on the paddy fields beyond the Lunghua camp; the obsession with dreams of flight in much of Ballard's work reverts back to childhood obsession and the 'liberation' of Shanghai by the American Air Force, staged in *Empire* as an almost theatrical performance just beyond the limits of the camp. *Kindness* accelerates this process of identification: Ballard's brief career as an Air Force pilot ties in to Traven's obsession with nuclear war in 'The Terminal Beach'; the experience with LSD equates with the visions of *The Crystal World* no less than the transmogrification of Shepperton in *The Unlimited Dream Company*.

The separation on which this decoding depends is problematic for reasons which centre on repetition. No simple 'departure' comes with *Empire*; 'The Dead Time' is woven out of the ambivalent space between the official 'end' of the war and the beginning of 'peace' in the zone around Shanghai. Given the peritextual blurbs on each of his books, which always contain reference to his internment in China, this can already be read as generated out of 'autobiographical' elements. Secondly, there is the curious paragraph in *Atrocity*, the longest of the book, which is the T-cell's entry on his early life in Shanghai. It begins: 'Two weeks after the end of World War II my parents and I left Lunghua internment camp and returned to our house in Shanghai' (72). This entry is startling not least because it is closer to the facts than the subsequent 'autobiographies'. The paragraph details the T-cell's attempt to travel to Japan on the invitation of a Captain Tulloch, and the oblique sense that the Japanese prisoners in the hold of the ship are victims of an impending American atrocity. This scene is repeated in *Kindness* (60–61), but witnessed from the ship on which Jim leaves for England. Tulloch appears in *Empire*, but as one of the roving bandits who is shot attempting to raid the Olympic stadium (see Chapter 39). A Tulloch is also a river-steamer Captain in *The Drought*. There is a sense here of a constant permutation of details, weaving between fiction and supposed autobiography.

This oscillation is further emphasized by the relation of *Empire* to the first part of *Kindness*, which returns to the Shanghai childhood.

Although there is repetition (the same bizarre anecdote of the English driving out to survey battlefields, where, in *Empire*, 'the rotting coffins projected from the loose earth like a chest of drawers' with 'dead soldiers . . . as if they had fallen asleep together in a dream of war' [29, 32], and in *Kindness* 'open coffins protruded like drawers in a ransacked wardrobe' with 'dead infantrymen . . . as if asleep in a derelict dormitory' [25]), *Kindness* is far from a reprise. Of the three opening chapters, the first predates *Empire*, the second would need to be inserted between parts I and II of *Empire* (which jumps to the end of internment rather than detailing any time between arrival and the weeks before release), and the third at points openly re-writes *Empire*. There is, for example, a casual reference to the bombs at Nagasaki and Hiroshima: 'Some of the prisoners even claimed to have seen the bomb-flash' (42); those prisoners, in *Empire*, include Jim himself, and this gesture seems to defuse the vital image-chains of apocalyptic light in *Empire*. Also, the Jim of *Kindness* only learns from television reports of war crimes that 'the Japanese had planned to close Lunghua and march us up-country' (58); this effectively negates fifty or sixty pages of the forced march in *Empire*, some of its most powerful sequences. This includes the eventual escape from the march by lying amongst the dead, imitating them (272); a scene also in 'The Dead Time'.

One should also consider the completely different emphasis of *Kindness*, the centrality of Jamie's relation to Peggy Gardner in the camp, entirely absent from *Empire*, and the key event which resonates through *Kindness*; the casual murder of the Chinese prisoner, tortured and asphyxiated on the derelict station platform. This seems to replace the intensity of the identification with and guilt over the youthful Kamikaze pilot in *Empire* (which itself had resonated with the fictive dialogue between Traven and the Japanese figure at the end of 'The Terminal Beach').

These interleavings and rewritings between fiction and perceived autobiography, between *Empire* and *Kindness* themselves, undermine the enframings that would separate putative decoder from code. The border of demarcation necessary to allow this model to operate is repeatedly transgressed. And in a complex effect of invagination, Ballard's work draws these 'external', parergonal questions into the very 'inside' of his texts. Again it has to be noted that the problematic siting of Ballard's work is repeated in the strange spatiality of border effects as a thematic throughout his work; this is no less the case in *Empire* and *Kindness*.

Empire continues that obsessive concern of Ballard's work and my reading of it: the permeability and impermeability of boundaries. Strictly speaking, it is a mistake to view *Empire* as a novel about World War II; the time of the war takes place in the blank space between parts I and II. Rather, it is about the impossibility of determining a clear boundary between beginnings and ends, ends and re-beginnings. Early in the book, Jim's father's joke 'You might even start the war' (24) haunts Jim after his torch signals appear to produce the first barrage from the Japanese warships (43). The latter half is full of obsessional conversations attempting to find an end, a closure. As the Japanese guards leave the camp, Jim proclaims 'the war has ended!', to which the weary response comes: 'Ended again, Jim? I don't think we can stand it' (231), and a few pages later: 'Sure enough, the war's end proved to be short-lived' (234). On the forced march, the ending seems more pressing: ' "The war must end". "It will". "It must end soon". "It has almost ended. Think about your mother and father, Jim. The war has ended" ' (edited, 225–26). If this seems definitive, Jim's immediate question opens a further border: 'But . . . when will the next one begin?'(256). Official endings are meaningless: 'The whole of Shanghai and the surrounding countryside was locked into a zone where there was neither war nor peace, a vacuum . . .' (305). Leaving Shanghai certain that 'World War II had ended', but wondering 'had World War III begun?' (332), it is unsurprising that only the final part of *Kindness*, after the 1960s, can be entitled 'After the War'.

Between these blurred beginnings and endings, *Empire* moves from one bounded zone to another. 'Walls of strangeness separated everything' (50), strange not least because of the inversions that attend these zones. The charmed life of the ex-patriates continues until 1941 because the International Settlement is a peculiar pocket within the colonial landscape. Once overrun, the zone retracts to the 'sealed worlds' (86) of the abandoned houses on Amherst Avenue. Jim is constantly on the wrong side of the border: initially misplaced to a Navy hospital (and within that, to a misplaced ward), he misses the round-up of European and American civilians and finds it impossible to surrender ('Jim had pondered deeply on the question of surrender, which took courage and even a certain amount of guile. How did entire armies manage it?' [110]). 'Safe' as a prisoner, there is the farcical attempt to find a prison camp that will accept him. In Lunghua much of the time is spent strengthening the camp defences in order to keep the Chinese *out* (the fence, for Jim, is, as ever, permeable—he is sent out by Basie to determine the terrain beyond the edge). With peace as the threat of starvation, liberation as death, the dead providing life (Jim's mimicry), perhaps the most persistent inversion is praise for the Japanese over the dour and apathetic English, that 'the Japanese, officially his enemies, offered his only protection'(60).[3]

Borders stretch and contract, values are inverted, there are zones within zones (Jim's battle for space with the Vincents over the moveable walls of their shared room [172]): this repeats and recalls the infinitely expanding interiors of 'The Enormous Room', 'Report on an Unidentified Space Station', *Concrete Island*, and the strange border effects Blake encounters at the limits of Shepperton in *The Unlimited Dream Company*.

If *Empire* directs attention to the frame, *Kindness* introduces difficulties into that which the frame is said to engender: the 'autobiography' as decoding machine. It is directed (not least by Ballard's epitextual work) that *The Kindness of Women* is to be read as a re-tracing of the writer's life. It is strange, given that each chapter 'reflects' one of the novels, that no explicit link is ever made to the fiction. These linkages are there, but they are *encrypted*. Reviewers have insisted on a rigorous division of the 'autobiographies' from prior texts; the 'bullshit apocalyptics' (Strawson) have been left behind. In terms of image, style and pattern of verbal repetitions between the 'fiction' and the 'autobiographies', this seems an astonishing claim to make. Although the fiction itself is never mentioned, there is a kind of game of reference-spotting of titles and phrases grafted from prior texts. A drunken publishing agent, touring Soho for prostitutes has his action described thus: 'The atrocity exhibition was more stirring than the atrocity'(146). The next page contains an embedded reference to a 'drowned world'(147). Phrasal echoes continually appear: in Spain, 'the peculiar geometry of these overlit apartments' where 'stylized' sex acts are performed (121) immediately keys into *Atrocity*, whose thesis on 'the death of affect' is repeated here (158). Lykiard's likely view of Armageddon as 'merely the ultimate happening, the audience-storming last act in the theatre of cruelty'(151) echoes Nathan's view that 'For us, perhaps, World War III is now little more than a sinister pop art display' (*Atrocity*, 12). In the car-crash sequences, the obsessional phrase 'the jut and rake of the steering wheel' is repeated (182). Relationships are repeated too: Richard Sutherland tussles for Miriam's affections by taking her flying (just as, in an internal repetition, David Hunter later takes Sally up in the air [221]), recalling any number of erotic triangles in the fiction where the narrator competes with a rogue pilot.

The chapter on LSD takes repetitive phrases from *The Crystal World* ('carapace', 'coronation armour' [161]). In the epitextual interviews on the publication of *Kindness*, Ballard both asserts that 'The LSD experiences are *The Crystal World*' (Pickering) and that 'I took LSD long after the publication of that book. *Crystal* was the product of a completely unaided visionary imagination' (Thomson). The latter has long been Ballard's position in interview; *Kindness* demonstrates a process of re-jigging elements into 'mythology' and possibly (yet who could determine intention from these flatly contradictory statements in supposedly extrafictive utterances?) Ballard's quiet derailment of the attempt to bind text to life.

Also strange is the absence of any but casual and dismissive references to the writer's milieu, so central to the 'science fiction' enclave. In fact, the one chapter title that repeats another title is not to his own work. 'The Final Programme' details Richard Sutherland's attempt to film his own death, or rather perpetuate life through electronic media. That this *final programme* is *a cure for cancer* is an embedded reference to the first two works of Moorcock's Jerry Cornelius quartet. This is so encrypted that it promotes paranoia in the reader; what other cryptic references are missed?

There is no interdiction on reading these repetitions 'backwards', that these repetitions, cited in 'autobiography', decode the fictional texts. Equally there is no interdiction on reading them 'forwards', as further fictions produced out of the obsessive elements that are repeatedly combined and re-combined in the oeuvre. And yet it is clear that the decrypting reading cannot do without the encrypting reading. The detachment of the 'autobiography' cannot be too radical; there must be repetitive elements to re-attach, even as that re-attachment threatens their separation. This problem is discussed by Ann Jefferson in her article on the disruptive 'autobiographies' of Robbe-Grillet and Barthes. *Roland Barthes* by Roland Barthes toys with the role of autobiography as 'metatextual commentary' on prior works, but then sets about destroying the authority of the meta-: 'my texts are disjointed, no one of them caps any other; the latter is just a further text, the last of the series, not the ultimate in meaning: text upon text, which never illuminates anything' (*Roland Barthes*, 120).

Does *Kindness* occupy the same deliberately enigmatic space as Barthes' teasing (non)autobiography? Is there no authority to the gestures of decryption offered by the text? I emphasize decryption because *Kindness* repeatedly deploys the image of the crypt. Internment becomes interment; in the constant inversions encountered here, the prison camp becomes a safe and secret tomb from the anarchy on the other side of fence: 'Far from wanting to escape from the camp, I had been trying to burrow more deeply into its heart' (41). This begins a chain of tombs and wombs: dissecting his medical school cadaver's womb, it is revelatory, 'displayed like a miniature stage set' (81); Jim's decision to leave Canada, to pursue a different mythology, is dictated by the unborn child in a prostitute's womb, which had 'given me my new compass' (99). This is followed by a chapter devoted to the inaccessible mysteries of childbirth, Miriam's withdrawal and return, encryption and decryption (111–14). In 'a secret logic' (146) Miriam's burial is overcoded with the mourning of Jacqueline Kennedy, the atrocities of the 1960s and the Chinese dead. The book's final movement contains the unearthing of a World War II fighter pilot in the Cambridge fens and a pacifying re-burial; a scene echoed by the rescue of a child from drowning, entombed in a sinking Range Rover.

This set of images could offer a tempting narrative of *Kindness* as a coming to terms with the melancholic compulsions that have driven the fiction, the 'autobiography' as accepting loss and enacting the work of mourning. Indeed, it could be seen as a working through of Nicolas Abraham and Maria Torok's theorization of the 'cryptophoric subject'. In what Nicholas Rand terms a 'general theory of psychic concealment' or a 'poetics of hiding' (57), the melancholic erects a crypt in the ego in which the dead are incorporated, kept alive, in secret: 'Grief that cannot be expressed builds a secret vault within the subject. In this crypt reposes . . . the objective counterpart of the loss ('Introjection', 8). What the crypt seals is an absolutely unutterable secret, and yet the living dead within the crypt may find ways of breaking the seal: 'the phantom of the crypt may come to haunt the keeper of the graveyard, making strange and incomprehensible signs' (8); this phantom 'works like a ventriloquist, like a stranger within the subject's own mental topography' (Abraham, 'Notes', 290). That the title of the final section of *Kindness*, 'After the War', ambivalently references the 1960s, its televisual violence, Miriam's death, as well as the haunting remainders of World War II, might invoke a form of melancholic ventriloquizing whose 'secret logic' is pacified in the closing moments of decrypting the Air Force pilot and the child in the Range Rover.

It may seem that in invoking this psychoanalytic theorization of the crypt, I am suggesting that *Kindness* offers a revelation of the 'secret', the encrypted 'primal scene' that motors the Ballardian oeuvre. This would be the interpretive dream of ascribing to the text the role of decrypting autobiography. But given the complex, obsessional repetitions within the 'autobiographies', his work displays rather a *textual* anatomy of melancholic compulsion. This is to say nothing of any putative psychopathology of Ballard; what is meant is that while a reading of this *thematic* of decryption may gesture toward an autobiographical decoding, the patterns of textual repetitions maintain the encryption, spinning out the code rather than working to decipher it.

Both 'autobiographies' *mythologize*, which is to say that they take elements of the same compulsively repetitive landscapes, scenarios, and images and recombine them in fictions which yet teasingly and forever undecidably play within the frame of the autobiographical. There is no authenticity here, no revelatory discourse of (in Gusdorf's insistent phrase) 'deeper being'.

This brings me to the third problem with the autobiographical theory delineated above; I have analysed textual framing and the difficulty of extricating the autobiography from the fiction. The third problem returns to the claims of 'depth' ascribed to autobiography, Olney's belief that 'wholeness and completion' comes through epiphanic moments where opposites are sublated and a unified pattern is the result (25). In a sense, this has already been considered in terms of the repetition which returns Ballard's 'autobiographies' to the level of the code. There is, however, another chain of images that demand attention; a chain that I have already followed in the oeuvre in relation to simulation.

Throughout both *Empire* and *Kindness* is a sense of doubling, of an uncanny re-staging that accompanies every significant event. Theatrical and cinematic analogies pervade both texts. The opening page of *Empire* establishes this immediately:

> Jim had begun to dream of wars. At night the same silent films seemed to flicker against the wall of his bedroom in Amherst Avenue, and transformed his sleeping mind into a deserted newsreel theatre. During the winter of 1941 everyone in Shanghai was showing war films. Fragments of his dreams followed Jim around the city . . . (11)

This has a confusing circularity. No priority can be established between the dream of war (as both passive residua and active fantasy projection: later Jim is 'dreaming of the war and yet dreamed of by the war' [260]), its filmic representation and the reality of the streets. To Jim, 'the landscape now exposed in many ways resembled a panorama displayed on a cinema screen' (186), and the prisoners were 'like a party of film extras under the studio spotlights' (254) (as the British visiting the battlefields are 'like a group of investors visiting the stage-set of an uncompleted war film' in *Kindness* [25]). Shanghai had always dissolved the boundaries of the cinema: the two hundred hunchbacks hired for the opening of *The Hunchback of Notre Dame* ensured that 'the spectacle outside the theatre far exceeded anything shown on its screen' (37). In war this effect is intensified:

> He rested in the padlocked entrance to the Nanking Theatre, where *Gone with the Wind* had been playing for the past year in a pirated Chinese version. The partly dismantled faces of Clark Gable and Vivien Leigh rose on their scaffolding above an almost life-size replica of burning Atlanta. Chinese carpenters were cutting down the panels of painted smoke that rose high into the Shanghai sky, barely distinguishable from the fires still lifting above the tenements of the Old City (59)

Again the interpenetration of the real and representation is profoundly disruptive. It becomes impossible to limit this figure, since it structures both texts: then, vertiginously, *Kindness* literalizes this blurring of the cinematic and the real by ending with the filming of *Empire* by Steven Spielberg. This has the strange effect of lending a sense of pre-programming to this figural chain. Everything is doubled and re-doubled: filmed in Shepperton, his home town, the sense of a re-staged suburbia, surrounded as it is by the sound stages of the film studios, becomes re-re-staged; his neighbours are recruited as the extras they had always been. Discovering a virtual simulacra of his childhood home just outside Shepperton and reflecting that the film team was 'working to construct a more convincing reality than the original I had known as a child' (275), Jim's response is that this is 'uncanny'. This is itself being filmed, within the film, by a documentary crew. Later, Ballard arrives in a Los Angeles with his own name emblazoned on billboards, television and cinema hoardings (the apotheosis of *Atrocity*). The text ends with the launch of Heyerdahl's papyrus ship on the Pacific. This is not a replica ship, but a fibreglass replica of the original replica, which had sunk in the Atlantic. The doubles, the repetitions, multiply in a vertiginous spiral. In closing *Kindness* by enfolding a version of *Empire* within it, Ballard may create a sense of completion, but this closure comes from a *textual* incorporation of *Empire* into *Kindness* and the literalization of the figural chain of the always already restaged, rather than any sense of 'deeper being'.

Summarily, then, the double injunction, this is and is not auto-biography, problematizes the reading that would lead the signature beyond the text to ground it in the referential body of the signatory. The privileging of autobiography must appeal to the textual frame, of the preface, generic mark and so on—appeal, that is, to a *cartouche*. This is a term that Derrida introduces in his discussion on Titus-Carmel. Titus-Carmel made 127 drawings of a model coffin and in a written statement, an appended cartouche, Titus-Carmel asserts that the drawings follow the model. The model 'paradigm' inspires the series, but is also outside it. But what, in the series, prevents a reversal of this reading, seeing the model as a result of the sketches, or inserted somewhere in the series? What is the status of the appended cartouche?

> If I place the cartouche outside the work, as the meta-linguistic or meta-operational truth of the work, its untouchable truth falls to ruins: it becomes external and I can, considering the inside of the work, displace or reverse the order of the series, calmly reinsert the paradigm at any point . . . If, conversely, I make room for the cartouche on the inside, or on the inside edge of the frame, it is no longer any more than a general performance, it no longer has a value of truth overbearing. This result is the same, the narrative is reinscribed, along with the paradigm, in the series (*The Truth in Painting*, 220)

I am suggesting, then, that *Empire* and *Kindness* occupy that uncertain place between paradigm and series in Derrida's de-stabilization of the cartouche. Detachment of the 'autobiographies' insists that a new contract has been established; the necessity of re-attachment undermines that contract. But even if it was possible to divide the signature in this way, nothing, according to Derrida, could be guaranteed, for the signature itself is already divided, it already functions like a cartouche, given its uncertain position as an *appended* mark. Where does the signature take place?

> First case: the signature belongs to the inside of that (picture, relievo, discourse and so on) which it is presumed to sign. It is in the text, no longer signs, operates as an effect within the object, has its part to play within that which it claims to appropriate to itself or lead back to its origin. Filiation is lost. The signature deducts itself. Second case: the signature holds itself, as is generally believed, outside the text. It emancipates as well the product, that can get along without the signature, from the name of the father . . . The filiation again gives itself up, is still betrayed by what remarks it (*Glas*, 4)

Like the relation of 'autobiographies' to the fiction, the signature either falls inside the frame of the text, thus losing authority, or falls too far outside, leaving the text to get on very well without the signatory, and thus without finally determinable sanction.

This is not simply to abolish author-ity, for, as Derrida states elsewhere, literature could not be thought of at all as institution 'without the development of a positive law implying authors' rights, the identification of the signatory, of the corpus, names, titles' and so on ('No Apocalypse', 26). Of course it is possible to identify an oeuvre and read it under the name of 'Ballard'—it is the condition of possibility for a book such as this. Nevertheless, as I have insisted so often, the discomfort and uncertain siting of Ballard's work is related to his exposure of the operations of these silent framing devices, a work which, almost, *voices* these mechanisms.

Where does Ballard's signature take place? Consider Colin Greenland's words: 'J. G. Ballard is unmistakable. His habit of introducing a story with a tableau, meticulous and stylized, proclaims his hand no less distinctly than a name signed in the bottom right-hand corner of a canvas or flashed in capitals across a screen' (92). Greenland here elides appended signature with Ballard's 'unmistakable' style. But that elision is understandable, for the recognition of a distinctive idiom operates like a *textual* signature. Perhaps, then, a closer attention to the idiomatic could crack open the tautology of Ballard's Ballardianism.

> Vapour trails left by the American reconnaissance planes dissolved over my head, the debris perhaps of gigantic letters spelling out an apocalyptic message. 'What do they say, Jamie?' (*Kindness*, 42)

All by itself?: Idiom in *Vermilion Sands*

Idiom, that metaphor of the signature conventionally understood, is recognized through its repetitive recurrence in and across texts whose signature piece is performed within the frame. It is the textual trait 'coming along to sign all by itself, before even the undersigning of the proper name' (Derrida, *The Truth in Painting*, 193). Anyone who reads Ballard over a number of texts comes to recognize patterns of repetitions—from reiterated plots, character relations, imagery and syntactical structures. The textual signature of Ballard's texts is indeed immediately recognizable without the need of a confirmatory signature. It is perhaps this demonic repetition-in-difference that ensnares the reader of Ballard's work, seduces him or her. It has become a standard practice of Ballard criticism to arrange and re-arrange these repetitive elements into interpretive structures (Pringle's 'four-fold symbolism', for instance, or the narrative of transcendence employed by Wagar and Stephenson to unite the oeuvre), but is the idiomatic trait any less problematic than the waywardness of the signature? For idiom is defined through a nexus of terms that are contradictory. The idiom must be unique, absolutely singular. But in order to be recognized as such, it must be repeatable. This can be summed up in the dictum that a style is inimitable exactly to the extent that it is imitable. And then to rely on the recognition of patterns of repetition need not in itself come to any understanding, either in one element of the series, or across it. Repetition, even with modulation, can be merely additive. Repetitions, that is, whilst being read, are also, in some senses, unreadable in that they give no access to interpretation but merely reinforce the enigma. And curiously, the remarking of obsessional repetition itself becomes obsessive, the reader caught in structures of repetition. Obsessive texts uncomfortably interpellate the reader as obsessional, in the grip of a compulsion that is incomprehensible.

In what follows, I want to concentrate on *Vermilion Sands* as a text that, dazzlingly and maddeningly, intensifies the problematic of the idiomatic trait. For on the macro level this text exponentially increases the repetitions that are a mark of the oeuvre as a whole: the nine stories virtually repeat the same plot, a plot that is itself about repetition compulsion. On the micro level, *Vermilion Sands* has perhaps the most extreme concentration of Ballard's idiomatic tic: his use and abuse of the simile.

In idiom, the trait is there like 'a name signed in the bottom right-hand corner of the canvas' (Greenland, 92), it 'com[es] along to sign all by itself' (*The Truth in Painting*, 193). In *Vermilion Sands* 'Studio 5, The Stars' details a literature generated purely from computer randomizations of a set of permutations: 'Fifty years ago a few people wrote poetry, but no one read it. Now no one writes it either'. The speaker is 'one of those people who believed that literature was in essence both unreadable and unwritable' (169). The stories of *Vermilion Sands*, with their complex repetitions, appear to be one segment of an otherwise infinite serial chain. 'Studio 5, The Stars' might appear to break the chain, to reinscribe the mythoi of inspiration and expressivity (Aurora acting out the legend of Melander and Corydon), but smashing the computers to return to expressive writing is itself a repetition of the myth of Melander, the Muse who demands sacrifice to reinvigorate poetry. This is no less programmed than computers.

Vermilion Sands is a sequence of nine stories linked by setting (an 'overlit desert resort as an exotic suburb of my mind' [Preface, 7]) and a repeated plot structure. Introduced as a retrospective narration of events, the narrator, differently named each time, details an entanglement with a desirable, but ultimately murderous *femme fatale*. Internally, each story is also, very precisely, about repetition compulsion; the narrators or other male characters find themselves, too late, inserted into a sequence of murderous events which has already been enacted previously, and will be re-enacted again. They are only one male in a series, objects apparently of female compulsion.

The women are standardly enigmatic, beautiful and quite insane. Their names are chosen for their powerful iconic resonance: Leonora Chanel (invoking Coco Chanel and Leonora Carrington, surrealist painter, mystic, chronicler of her own insanity and Ernst's partner), Emerelda Garland (an obvious reference to the fated Judy), Hope Cunard (recalling the modernist writer, patron and iconoclast Nancy Cunard), Raine Channing (perhaps an echo of Dorothea Tanning, Max Ernst's wife from 1946), Gloria Tremayne (the atmosphere of 'Stella-vista', the final story, clearly makes this a reference to Gloria Swanson's role as the egomanical Norma Desmond in *Sunset Boulevard*). Nearly all are possessed of a charismatic infamy, resulting from deaths in the past: Leonora Chanel lives in the wake of the 'mysterious' death of her husband, 'officially described as suicide' (18); Emerelda Garland is married to Van Stratten, whose mother died 'in circumstances of some mystery' (51); Lorraine Drexel had a brief affair with a pop-singer 'later killed in a car crash' (112); Raine Channing survives after 'the death of her confidant and impresario' (132); Howard Talbot hires the house where Gloria Tremayne was alleged to have shot her husband (194).

The stories concern compulsion, but the question is whose compulsions are to be dealt with. In many ways, these narratives are case histories, but ones which have failed to draw the lesson from Freud's conclusion to the incomplete analysis of Dora: 'I did not succeed in mastering the transference in good time' (160). In Freud's 'Papers on Technique' repetition, in the sense of acting out, re-enaction, is the enemy of analysis, that process of *remembering* and *working through*. 'This struggle between the doctor and patient . . . .between understanding and seeking to act, is played out exclusively in the phenomena of transference' ('Dynamics', 118). Failing to control this transference, the doctor may be inserted 'into one of the psychical "series" which the patient has already formed' ('Dora', 157). In this fictional realm, Freud's textual figure is to be recalled: 'What are transferences? They are the new editions or facsimiles of the impulses and phantasies which are made conscious during the process of the analysis' ('Dynamics', 100).

In this sense, the narrators' psychoanalytic 'explanations' come too late, cannot control the compulsion, as in 'The Screen Game' or 'Stellavista'. What is peculiar, however, is that whilst the (male) narration is in effect a remembering to counter (female) repetition, this remembrance is forgotten each time a story closes, and each narrator must begin again, *repeat* the remembering. Whose compulsion, then, is it? The women repeat trauma, but the narrators are also compulsive; traumatophiles, perhaps, actively seeking situations of trauma that they cannot control?

The narrators' attempts to master female compulsion come clumsily; they court hilarity. Even if their explanations are to be taken seriously Ballard's later story, 'A Host of Furious Fancies', serves as a warning. The deliciously named Dr Charcot[4] steps in to authoritatively 'solve' the Cinderella complex of an orphaned heiress, by repeating the father's incestuous relationship with her. This jargonistically rationalized account, however, is finally revealed as the fantasy of a decrepit old man, utterly controlled by his daughter. The authority of the 'explanation' is ruthlessly undercut, enmeshed as it is in the trap of countertransference.

Further, the 'explanations' in *Vermilion Sands* fail to grasp the extent of repetition. In 'Say Goodbye to the Wind', Samson is enraptured by a somnambulating woman and discovering her name, he recalls the death of Gavin Kaiser. He becomes unwittingly transferred into repeating Kaiser's role, although he escapes death. Samson proposes that: 'She had come back to Lagoon West to make a beginning, and instead found that events repeated themselves, trapping her into this grim recapitulation of Kaiser's death' (143). The reason for Kaiser's paroxysm and death remains unclear: 'What he saw, God knows, but it killed him' (142). There is in fact nothing to suggest Kaiser is not himself repeating a prior death, just as Samson nearly repeats his: the sequence is open to extension. To be strictly psychoanalytic, this must be the case: trauma must presuppose two events, the first prepubertal, a sexual event lying unrecognized until a second, postpubertal event, however obliquely or associatively, sparks off and reinscribes the first as sexually traumatic. However, Freud warns that: 'We must not expect to meet with a single traumatic memory and a single pathogenic idea as its nucleus; we must be prepared for successions of partial traumas and concatenations of pathogenic trains of thought' ('Psychotherapy',

373). Since this lies beyond the purview of the text and the purblind narrators, the repetition cannot be limited or mastered.

Vermilion Sands, however, is not a set of psychologically realist stories; it has strange science fictional elements. It is populated by plants that sing arias, sonic sculptures, psychotropic houses, photosensitive canvases and bio-fabrics, all of which respond to emotional surrounds. These function as the sites on which trauma is written. They become, in effect, objects embodying the psyche, have scored on them the lines of trauma which will be repeated by the next owner. Initially, the women seem to have a calmative effect (there is repetition here: as Jane Cyclacides enters the shop full of neurotically oversensitive screeching plants, they die down: 'They must like you' (35); when Raine enters the clothes shop full of neurotically oversensitive bio-fabrics, they are soothed: 'You've calmed everything down . . . They must like you' [133]). Dénouements, however, tend to revolve around the betrayal of their murderous pasts in the evidences left as writing traces on these objects. This version of trauma as writing means that compulsion can continue in the absence of its actors. In 'The Thousand Dreams of Stellavista' this continues beyond death, with Talbot and his wife repeating the violence between Miles Vanden Starr and Gloria Tremayne. The wife frozen out, Talbot enters into a sole relation, playing Miles to the convulsing, vaginal house. Once the scene of death is recapitulated, however, Talbot stays on: the story (and the text) ends: 'I know that I shall have to switch the house on again' (208).

To end on 'again' is to disrupt the security of closure; to open with 'again' ('The Singing Statues', 'Cry Hope, Cry Fury!') is to undercut by implying prior, inaccessible repetitions. There is a quite deliberate coding and overcoding involved: it is interesting to compare 'Venus Smiles' (a title repeated in or repeated from *Atrocity*) with its original version, 'Mobile', written in 1957. The plot is kept, but 'Mobile' was not set in *Vermilion Sands* and centred on a male sculptor, Lubitsch. The enigma of the furiously self-generating sculpture is coded into female obsession in its revision, as a perverse memorialization of her dead lover.

To say that repetition is a mark of recognition of a signature in the text before the text is undersigned is perhaps not to say anything until what is repeated is considered. However, textual repetition, abstractly and in itself, effectively cuts out the paratextual apparatus. Entering the Ballardian oeuvre is like entering a chain whose seriality severs any visibility of beginning or end. This is repetition understood not as secondary, copying a prior 'original', but as primary and instituting:

these repetitions are 'controlled by no centre, origin, or end outside the chain of recurrent elements . . . Such a sequence is without a source outside the series' (Hillis Miller, 142). Each text resonates not in itself but in the overdetermined tangle of lines of repetitive elements. This, to emphasize again, is a *textual* event; just as the male narrators of *Vermilion Sands* cannot control or bring to termination the sequence, quite beside explaining what instituted it, the reader can immediately recognize, by textual elements, a Ballardian fiction, but can do little to articulate its power or divine its meaning. In that sense, these stories remain *unreadable.*

So far I have analysed the 'empty' form of repetition—repetition *itself*—in *Vermilion Sands.* But repetition is also, of course, the condition of recognizability of specific idiomatic traits. The text is repetitive not only at the level of plot and plot-mechanism (compulsion), but it is also the most extreme example of Ballard's overloading of his text with abstruse figurations. Similes, in particular, pile up on page after page.

I want to keep for the moment with that naive view of figuration—of rhetoric as a whole—as an addition, as the detachable ornament to a delimitable 'literal' language. Ballard's 'bijou adjectives—"cerise," "vermilion" ' (Thomson) have been criticized as 'descriptive encrustations' (Strawson) that mar his work. This accords with the still largely pejorative sense of rhetoric: writings which are too 'rhetorical' equate with bad writing. 'Bijou' is in fact the perfect adjective for *Vermilion Sands,* because the text is studded with 'ornamental' tropes which precisely refer to jewels. Leonora Chanel is persistently referred to as having 'jewelled eyes' (16,17,18,19); Hope Cunard has 'opal hair' (100, 103) and 'opal hair, like antique silver' (93); in 'Venus Smiles', Carol's eyes flash 'like diamonds' and there is Lorraine Drexel's 'diamond heel' (114); Raine Channing has 'jewelled hands' (127) and carries 'a sonic jewel, like a crystal rose' (134); Emerelda already names a jewel, and has her army of jewelled insects.

Rhetoric is classically coded as feminine: the 'best dress of thought', 'clothing' language. The allegorical figure of Rhetoric is presented as 'a beautiful woman, her garments . . . embellished with all the figures, she carries the weapons intended to wound her adversaries' (Barthes, 'The Old Rhetoric', 32); these figures were also represented as jewels. This allegory combines both the figural and suasive elements of rhetoric, what Derrida in *Spurs* terms style and stylus (meaning dagger or stiletto). If clusters of figures tend to proliferate around the women in *Vermilion Sands* in an attempt to catch their truth, the veil of rhetoric is poisonous: 'Say Goodbye to the Wind', in which Raine presents the bio-fabric suit to Samson in which Kaiser had died, recalls the myth of Deianira, who give the coat poisoned by Nessus' blood to Hercules. The 'Muses' of *Vermilion Sands* may give a language that could return the narrators from a literature 'both unreadable and unwritable'(169), but that language, as will be seen, is also more than occasionally entirely unreadable.

Rhetoric, of course, has been re-established in literary studies, not least by Paul de Man. It is no longer naively perceived as an addition to a zero degree 'literal' language: the difficulty of dividing figural and literal levels is exactly the question. Much work can be found on metaphor, but there is little on simile. Simile is the most dominant trope employed in the Ballardian text, and it is alarmingly pervasive in *Vermilion Sands*. Almost any page will present numerous examples. Only Colin Greenland has attempted to determine its effect, and his comments are excellent. Greenland discovers a Surrealist strategy smuggled into an apparently simple device of explicit analogy: the forcing of a conjunction in a 'like' of terms which are entirely unlike. These 'pseudo-similes' offer a 'comparison which mystifies instead of elucidating', 'there is no discoverable parity between terms' (103) and Greenland offers a prime example from 'My Dream of Flying to Wake Island': 'Laing had not been particularly interested in Melville, this ex-pilot who had turned up here impulsively in his expensive car and was now prowling relentlessly around the solarium as if hunting for a chromium rat'. Greenland lets this example speak for itself, but it is possible to analyse its combination of, in effect, two devices. If the first is a simile that fails to elucidate a comparison, the comparing term 'chromium rat' can only be read as hypallage—but from where is this epithet transferred? The nearest candidate is the 'expensive car', but this is on the other side of the comparison. Effectively, an initially incomprehensible simile can only have a meaning offered by negating the simile. This is what Greenland means when the device 'keeps the relation but blurs the distinction, so that the two halves of the simile, the actual and the virtual, can be swapped over' (103).

Such abuse of tropes and tropes of abuse are consistently encountered in *Vermilion Sands*. Indeed, finding oneself in the role of the 'close reader' can tempt madness, for the closer the text is read the more unreadable it gets, the more bemusing it is that any meaning can 'leak' from its dense weave. Take, for example, the description of landscape in the opening pages of 'The Screen Game'. The mesas rise 'like the painted cones of a volcano jungle'(47) (painted?), the reefs are 'like the tortured demons of medieval cathedrals'(47) and towers of obsidian are 'like stone gallows'(47). The passage continues:

> The surrounding peaks and spires shut out the desert plain, and the only sounds were the echoes of the engine growling among the hills and the piercing cry of the sand-rays over the open mouths of the reefs like hieratic birds. (47–48)

The simile, 'like hieratic birds', refers back to the cry of the sand-rays, but this 'piercing cry' is confused with the 'open mouths' of the reefs. The analogical axis is confused by the metonymic contiguity of 'cry' to 'mouths'. And in what sense can birds be 'hieratic'? Does this moves back over the sentence as a kind of metatextual comment, hieratic in the sense of 'the cursive form of hieroglyphs', declaring its private language? The passage through the landscape continues, following the road ('like a petrified snake' [48]) where 'fragments of light haze hung over the dunes like untethered clouds' (48). How could a cloud ever be *tethered*? A few pages later: 'we barely noticed the strange landscape we were crossing, the great gargoyles of red basalt that uncoiled them-selves into the air like the spires of demented cathedrals' (52). Gargoyles 'uncoil' simply because of the euphony of the words, and 'gargoyles like spires' imposes an analogy between the terms where there evidently is none; gargoyles may be a synecdoche for spires, but they cannot be compared. The 'strange landscape' is more to do with the strangeness of the tropes used to describe it; de Man is right to suggest that 'there seems no limit to what tropes can get away with'. Another more readable cluster surrounds Emerelda: her face 'like an exotic flower withdrawing into its foliage' (61). However, when the narrator suggests that 'Talking to her was like walking across a floor composed of blocks of different height' (61), this is meaningless without the immediately following description of the squares of the terrace, once more negating the simile by literalizing it. No wonder that Charles Van Stratten 'smiled bleakly, as if aware of the slenderness of the analogy' (64)!

These knots in the text can be found throughout *Vermilion Sands*. Is it simply bad writing? Is 'eyes crossed by disappointment' (93) intentio-nal or just inept? When it comes to simile the issue seems prejudged: in recent discussions simile is posited as the 'low' equivalent of the heights of metaphor. Culler states: 'It is not easy to explain why the idea of a conference on metaphor seems perfectly natural, while the idea of a conference on simile seems distinctly bizarre and unlikely' (188). This bars simile from consideration as a form of metaphor, which is certainly how De Man (whose analysis Culler is partly glossing) sees it in his reading of Proust. Both work by analogy, but cannot be simply related: Davidson criticizes the view of metaphor as 'elliptical simile', which argues that any metaphor can be 'translated' back into simile, which reveals, through the 'like', the terms of comparison. Metaphor is more complex than the 'trivial' analogies of simile.

In what follows—in attempting to say what the Ballardian simile is *like*—I am aware of Culler's warning: 'One can never construct a position outside tropology from which to view it; one's terms are always caught up in the processes they attempt to describe' (209). Flatness is an apt, metaphorical, term to describe the prose. The landscapes of *Vermilion Sands* are horizontal: wide expanses of sand, infinitely receding horizons like Dali paintings. Flatness also has a pejorative sense, and this has been a consistent criticism of the prose style (of *Kindness* it was said the writing was 'slow, stately, curiously flat' [Margaret Foster]). Flatness seems to be induced by the rhetorical devices used. There is, in the multiple taxonomies of rhetoric, a distinction sometimes made between figures and tropes. Figures keep the sense of the words, but works effects by distribution, by syntactical devices (anaphora, parallelism, and so on). Tropes alter the meaning of a word or phrase from its 'proper' meaning. I want to suggest that simile, as an analogical trope, is used here figurally. In Jakobson's opposition, metaphor is vertical, whilst metonymy is flat, horizontal. When a metaphor is read, the reader has to 'make a leap', to discover the basis of comparison; in simile, the terms are laid out, and the reader is lulled by the connecting 'like'. The grammatical presence of 'like' or 'as' distributes the terms on either side of it, visibly, in conventionalized form. So pervasive is the simile in *Vermilion Sands* that it becomes hypnotic; the reader is flattened by its repetition. Lulled by the distributive function of the 'like', the *abuse* of its role, the dissimilarity or negation of the analogy, is all the more jolting.

Simile is not the sole device by which the awkwardness of the text is found. It would be necessary to consider the 'clumsy' clause constructions, the clashing of different registers, from hard science to soft conventionalized 'poeticisms', and the repetitive vocabulary. But this is to say nothing of another idiomatic chain that, in keeping with the abyssal slides of the text into unreadability, also constantly recurs. If the 'signature' and 'idiom' are two problematically distinct forms, then Ballard's recourse to the metaphor of the signature effectively elides them: 'hieroglyphic shadows, signatures of all the strange ciphers of the desert sea', 'signatures of a separate subject', 'the tomb that enshrined the very signatures of her soul' (96, 100, 196). Figures of writing pervade the text from the inscriptions in the cloud at Coral D to the writing of trauma that operates throughout.

What holds these together are their encryption, their status as hidden languages—like the ciphers and cryptographics that I have analysed in other texts. To discover their insistence in *Vermilion Sands* as well is to realize that they refold the text back on itself. Is it possible that so persistent a group of figures, one idiomatic trait, itself concerns the unreadability of pure idiom, a kind of idiom of idiom? It is not the case that these idiomatic figures of writing are simply metafictional moments of self-reflexivity. Rather, attention to their enfolding of the unreadable into the texts operates according to De Man's proposal that 'any narrative is primarily the allegory of its own reading' and that 'the allegory of reading narrates the impossibility of reading' (76–77).

'Coming along to sign, all by itself', idiom operates as a textual signature, the mark of a unique writing. But this has not yet broached the countersignature. Derrida proposes that:

> the signature becomes effective—performed and performing— not at the moment it apparently takes place, but only later, when ears will have managed to receive the message. In some way the signature will take place on the addressee's side . . . it is the ear of the other that signs (*The Ear of the Other*, 50–51)

To read is to countersign; the text's affirmation takes place on the other's side. This structure is open to risk: 'a countersignature comes both to confirm, repeat and respect the signature of the other, of the 'original' work; and to lead it off somewhere, so running the risk of *betraying* it' ('This Strange Institution', 63) . I want to suggest that parody is a form of countersignature that imitates the 'original' signature such that it problematizes the latter's authority.

As Hutcheon suggests, parody of its nature steals—even ridicules— but also, of necessity, monumentalizes its sources by dependence on them. For science fiction, parody, homage, collective conventions (forms, concepts, plots) remain vital. Of the New Wave writers, Harry Harrison and Philip José Farmer could be said to have gained their reputations as parodists. With a culture that has parody and self-parody at its heart, Ballard's texts did not survive long before entering this circulation. New Worlds published James Cawthorn's brief 'Ballard of a Whaler', playing on the frequent Moby Dick references, and puncturing the familiar elegiac tone. A later *New Worlds* collection also contained Disch's mock interview with G. G. Allbard, author of *Rash* (who talks so obsessively about his bodily fluids that the interviewer is incapable of posing any questions). Sladek also wrote a brief parody of the catastrophe novels, 'The Sublimation World', which accurately picks up on stylistic tics ('The whole city was a gibbous dune, once a mercury refinery, now frozen into a single gaseous crystalline chrysalid, depended from what had once been a flaming bloodfruit tree, now gone to iron, ironically'; 'He was barely visible, a slash of red among the yellow balloons, like a wound' [105]). Most intriguing, however, are the series of stories published by *Fantasy and Science Fiction* that were eventually collected under the title *Aventine*. There is no framing reference anywhere to the fact that they are parodies of *Vermilion Sands*. This is a delicious opportunity: parody is monumentalization, but equally it is a stealing of the signature from the unique signatory. In that latter sense it is a kind of death. The writer of these stories is Lee Killough. Should that be pronounced 'killer' or 'kill-off'? The kindness of women does not extend to her; when asked by Pringle Ballard tersely refused to read them.

Killough's borrowings are extensive. 'The Siren Garden' shifts from the singing plants of Ballard's 'Prima Belladonna' to crystals, which, like many of the objects in *Vermilion Sands*, are sensitive to extremes of emotion. Lorna Dalridian exploits them to ensnare the narrator into a murder of her husband. Lorna's eyes, incidentally, move through the range of silver, violet and obsidian. The garden is borrowed from another Ballard text, 'The Crystal Garden'. 'Tropic of Eden', with psychotropic houses, synthesizes elements of 'The Singing Statues' and 'Venus Smiles', whilst the series of portrait-sittings before psychically reactive materials recalls 'Cry Hope, Cry Fury!'. 'A House Divided' uses props from 'Stellavista', as does 'Broken Stairways, Walls of Time'. 'Menage Outré', meanwhile, has a narrator who writes computer-generated novels and becomes ensnared with a mysterious female neighbour, just as in 'Studio 5, The Stars'. 'Menage' begins: 'At night the sound of flutes and drums pulsed across the lawns' (5); 'Studio 5' opens: 'At midnight I heard the music playing from the abandoned nightclub' (145). Verbal echoes are constant, as is the (less obsessive) use of simile and the opening paragraphs which structure the narrative as retrospection. The women tend to have suitably mysterious and tragic pasts (one narrator remembers reading of Cybele's husband's 'death in a hovercraft accident'! ['Broken Stairways', 51]). A compulsive narrative unleashed by *Vermilion Sands* cannot be contained between its covers; distorted, perhaps, but with the same compulsion, it arises elsewhere.

That there is no acknowledgment of 'borrowing', no obvious sign of homage (although it may be significant that Cas refuses to sign his sculpture ['Tropic', 152], or that the objectionable Jason Ward loses his sister by going on a book-signing tour: a book which is computer-generated and thus not, in a loose sense, his? ['Menage', 14]) clearly irritates David Pringle. His review of the book with Colin Greenland, however, is written in the form of a parody, a parodying of the parodist.

In a highly complex move, Pringle and Greenland insert Killough's relation to Ballard into the plot of 'Stellavista', where parody is figured as the occupation of a psychotropic house inscribed with Ballard's personality. Reversing the gender structure, the *femme fatale* figure is disempowered and resituated into the psychical series of male victims. But the compulsion is intensified here: Killough is destroyed by the power of the Ballardian psychotrope. Murderous revenge: Killough is killed, the parodist evacuated from her upstart occupation of the text.

It is a strange defence of *Vermilion Sands*, however, to figure its parody in terms of a compulsion imposed by the personality of *Ballard*. Why take revenge on Killough when, in this scenario, she is a victim of a repetition that she cannot control? It is even stranger to perform this as a parody itself, for it becomes difficult to separate what is parodistic attack and what is parodistic defence. In effect, what Pringle and Greenland's review demonstrates is how inimitable idiom easily loses its singularity, its guarantee of uniqueness, to become bewilderingly disseminated across any number of imitative texts.

Killough's parody offers a countersigning of Ballard's text; Pringle and Greenland give a reading of that reading. But since they all tend to repeat the text, they perform nothing other than the compulsions set in train by Ballard's stories. Parody as reading is, as repetition, also non-reading: the ensnaring of the reader into structures of the text that cannot get beyond them.

The repetitive predictability of Ballard's texts allowed Martin Amis, in a review of *The Day of Creation*, to summarise the book through a parodic exchange between two Ballard fans: ' "I've read the new Ballard." "And?" "It's like the early stuff." "Really? What's the element?" "Water." "Lagoons?" "Some. Mainly a river." "What's the hero's name? Maitland? Melville?" "Mallory." ' Amis goes on to adjudge the book 'boring and frequently ridiculous'. But this conclusion needs to be set in the context of what, in actuality, is a narrative of *seduction*. In his long career of reviewing Ballard, Amis began by condemning the 'vicious nonsense' of *Crash* (cited, Pringle, *Bibliography*) and has always sniped at Ballard's sham portentousness. In a television discussion, he dismissed Ballard's claim that science fiction is the literature of the twentieth century by pointing out that science fiction, for all its self-promotion, has remained 'a minority pursuit—like train-spotting' (a very English insult). By the time of the review of *The Day of Creation*, however, his dismissal had modulated. To quote in full: 'Ballard's novel is occasionally boring and frequently ridiculous . . . You finish the book with some bafflement and irritation. But this is only half the experience. You then sit around waiting for the novel to come and haunt you. And it does'. In the preface to *Einstein's Monsters*, Amis even had to admit that he had begun to *write* like Ballard (x). For all the predictability, for all the endlessly re-rehearsed plotting, it is this, it is precisely this haunting remainder that survives ridicule. *Something* survives, *something* remains, no matter how exhaustive an attempt to fix his haunting work is, whether by trying to decode it autobiographically, or by an atomizing analysis of the texts sentence by sentence. The haunting remainder slips between these two approaches: once again, it occupies that strange and impossible angle between two walls.

Vermilion Sands in particular, it seems to me, reveals the way in which Ballard's texts effectuate their seduction. An obsessively repetitive text enchains an obsessively repetitive reading. You open a Ballard text, knowing once again you will be haunted, knowing that the compulsions it fosters will enfold you again, knowing that to read Ballard is to be held by a lure that is generated by an irreducible core of unreadability.

This lure compels critics, as we have seen, to become ensnared in Ballard's cycles of repetition. As I come to conclude, my principal anxiety is to what extent I have managed to evade collapsing into an obsessive reading myself, one which loses all critical distance and merely reiterates textual perversities that have failed to be mastered. This sequence of readings of Ballard's work, which has focused on his disruptions to the distributions of mainstream/science fiction, high/low, modernist/postmodernist, fiction/autobiography, interrogated the ability to discern a final ground to the circulating theories of the catastrophe and apocalypse, and sought ways to read Ballard's most experimental fictions outside the glazed world of postmodern nihilism, ends with an announcement that even by turning away from all of these approaches to adopt the role of the close reader results in the critic being trapped between the fiction of authorial truth and the maddening unreadability of idiom. I hope this is not taken as a fashionable display of critical incapacity. My aim has been to been to describe and analyse, as precisely as possible, the sense of unease generated by a recurrent topography—the weird effects of being left in a space between, a space that insistently erodes, although in a highly productive way, gestures of critical mastery. Jean Baudrillard, closing his discussion of Ballard's novel *Crash* ends by asking: 'Is it good or bad? We will never know. It is simply fascinating' (*Simulacra and Simulation*, 119). For him, 'Beyond meaning, there is fascination, which results from the neutralization and imposion of meaning' (*In the Shadow of the Silent Majorities*, 104). If I too have remained fascinated by Ballard (the flip-side of irritation and rejection), I hope that this book is a testament to the refusal of Baudrillard's ecstatic surrender: fascination should not be the bar to thought. It should, rather, be the very impetus to continue the process of critical thinking and writing, to pursue those peculiar border effects and strange (non-)spaces which generate the very possibility of meaning. May Ballard continue to hover at the edges, haunt the suburbs of our critical thinking; however frustrating, his work forces us to pay attention to the frames in which our literary judgments operate.

Notes

Preface

1. Aside from the interesting links to be made between the work of Angela Carter and J. G. Ballard—an alliance that seems to begin with the literary magazine *Bananas* in the 1970s—Ballard's fiction, and the responses to it, resonate strongly with the American 'blank' generation. Kathy Acker has acknowledged Ballard as an influence, whilst Bret Easton Ellis' *American Psycho* is the *Crash* of the 1990s.

2. Capitalizing 'the Zone', and delineating its weird state of suspension, is intended to recall The Zone of Tarkovsky's film, *Stalker*, in which travellers enter the magical, alien, technicolor pocket of terror and revelation in a contemporary, monochrome Russia. The Zone of Thomas Pynchon's *Gravity's Rainbow* is another key reference point in my articulating the 'space of the between'.

3. The oxymoron of a 'thetic literature' does not only apply to J. G. Ballard's work. My reading is informed in Chapter Three by Noel King's comments on Don DeLillo's *White Noise*. King describes the feeling of redundancy when reading a novel which has seemingly fully imbibed its Walter Benjamin, Roland Barthes and Jean Baudrillard, and mocks you for your incapacity to cap its own sophistication. DeLillo's novels are ungainly, awkwardly theoretical things: novels pretending to be novels. The response to Angela Carter's *The Passion of New Eve* often evokes a similar response. This is 'thetic literature', where the fiction seems overly theorized, but the theory undercut by the ludic play of the fictive.

Chapter One

1. An 'anthropological' theory of popular culture is passingly criticized by Gayatri Spivak, who cites a research proposal arguing 'that science fiction . . . may be considered, so to speak, the Third World fiction of industrial nations' ('Poststructuralism', 223). If Spivak's

reasons for citing this moment are different from mine, the quotation crystallizes a near 'Orientalist' approach to science fiction when critics claim that speak its silence, penetrate its surface, or brutally re-function it for their own critical ends.

2. The following reading of the way Ballard's texts trouble and expose framings is not the only available route to interrogate the assumptions of genre. Christine Brooke-Rose has noted that genre, gender and genius all have the same etymological root (255). As many other critics have noted, the gender of genius is usually assumed to be masculine; the gender of genre is feminized. The anxieties of science fiction, that masculine-identified genre, could be fruitfully read through this embedded gendering of genre; it gives a whole new resonance to the legitimation of science fiction by seeking the isolated masterpiece of the genius who transcends the generic.

3. This was also the time of Robert Silverberg's first retirement from the genre. These announcements of departure all come from male writers, just at the moment when science fiction is gaining interest from feminism, and women writers are entering the field in notable numbers. The death of the genre is often announced in suspicious proximity to the entry of women writers. I have argued elsewhere that the ecstatic reception of William Gibson's *Neuromancer* became the occasion for announcing either the final transcendence of the genre, or its re-masculinization after the wayward, 'feminine' 1970s. Gibson's Nebula and Hugo Awards in 1984 also conveniently allowed the eclipse of the short-story awards given in first recognition to science fiction's most extraordinary voice in the 1980s, Octavia Butler. See my essay, 'Horror and Beauty in Rare Combination'.

Chapter Two

1. See Freud, 'Civilization and its Discontents'. That Freud's specu-lations have influenced Ballard is made plain when Ballard inserts the final paragraph of Freud's text into the marginal commentary notes to the Re/Search edition of *The Atrocity Exhibition*, 72–73.

2. On the crisis of mimesis, see Maurice Blanchot, *The Writing of the Disaster*: 'The disaster, unexperienced. It is what escapes the very possibility of experience—it is the limit of writing. This must be repeated: the disaster de-scribes' (7). This does not bar writing, Blan-chot suggests, but means that one 'should write out of failure, in failure's intensity' (11). Mary Anne Doane and Patricia Mellencamp

have also analysed how the catastrophic both destroys representation, blasts out of the containment of history, and yet compels narrativizations. Reference, too, needs to be made to Lyotard's theory of the 'Sign of History'—signs which mark the *paralysis* of the conventional genre of historiography, demanding new modes of 'witness'. This is analysed in detail in relation to the 'sign' of Auschwitz in *The Differend*.

3. Ballard's refusal might be compared to Doris Lessing's subsequent novel in the catastrophe genre, *The Memoirs of a Survivor*. Here, the self-consciousness about the unrepresentability of the catastrophe becomes an explicit element of the narrative. 'It', whatever 'It' is, is 'like invisible ink between the lines, which springs up, sharply black, dimming the old print we knew so well' (136). The 'cause' of the catastrophe in this novel is never explained or examined and, echoing Ballard, there are only proliferating narratives of what it *might* be.

4. The 'impossible' demand that fictions of disaster, particularly of nuclear disaster, must be absolutely 'literal' and always admonitory, is asserted by Paul Brians in his *Nuclear Holocausts: Atomic War in Fiction*. To explore the paradox of demanding literal representation of that which has not (yet) taken place, which has no precedent, and which would in itself destroy all capacities of representation, would take time. I have explored this in my 'Nuclear Criticism: Anachronism and Anachorism'.

5. Dennis Walder has suggested that the disputes caused by *Empire of the Sun* over its 'fictionalization' of the truth is a result of Ballard's failure to write the 'correct' ideological imperial history. One of Ballard's co-internees, incensed by Ballard's apparent praise of the Japanese and implicit criticism of the British, accused Ballard of 'fashionable national self-denigration' (cited Walder, 83).

6. Taking the existential framework of *The Drought* seriously, following its links to the philosophy of Camus, Heidegger and Jaspers, might seem to court incredulity that such a context could have informed its writing. If critics have deployed a loosely 'existential' reading, my concern is to consider whether Ballard's text can sustain a more rigorous reading. This is fully in accord with Derrida's attempts to go beyond the 'doubling commentary'. To cite again: 'this indispensable guardrail has always only protected, it has never *opened*, a reading' (*Of Grammatology*, 158).

Chapter Three

1. All quotations from this text, for reasons that will become clear, derive from the Re/Search edition.

2. The decision to use 'T-cell' is partly for convenience, partly for its dubious evocation of the use of depletion of T-cells to measure the advance of the HIV virus. The main figure of *The Atrocity Exhibition* also undergoes 'depletion' until finally disappearing. Although this is in questionable taste the medical reference (and the question of 'taste' itself) is in keeping with the logic of the book. 'Cell' is also useful in that it implies both a singular entity as well as a close-knit collective (a 'terrorist cell' for instance). This seems more effective than using each version of the name, even if that means certain resonances are lost: the name Traven must be a reference to the reclusive American novelist, B Traven; Travis now wonderfully echoes with Travis Bickle, the 'psychotic' hero of Martin Scorsese's film, *Taxi Driver*.

3. Ballard's use of his own signature as 'brand name' on adverts could be compared to the objects Richard Hamilton embossed with 'Richard' in parody of the familiar 'Ricard' logo. The use of billboard art by Daniel Buren is discussed by Hal Foster in 'What's Neo about the Neo Avant Garde?' Jacqueline Rose has also referred to Jenny Holzer's use of billboards: 'There is a violence in these slogans that works at the level of content, but also, and more crucially, in the disruption caused by their presence and by the very mode of address. They add to the confusion of city space and then appropriate that confusion for a blatant political intention. What would it mean to ask that we are able, in any simple sense, to *orientate* ourselves in relation to them' ('The Man who Mistook His Wife for a Hat', 247).

4. Only Jonathan Benison, it seems, makes one brief comment on this question, and that in parentheses. Benison queries Ballard's 'apparently overfacile adoption of a woman figure to act as cipher, as key object' ('In Default of a Poet in Space', 414)

5. A useful extension to this, in terms of Sadeian writing, are Pierre Klossowski's comments: 'Dealing with a personal experience condemned by its very nature to remain incommunicable, Sade chooses to translate this experience into the conventional form characteristic of all communication. Then the conventional becomes "unreadable" each time the incommunicable experience asserts itself, but becomes all the more readable when this experience disappears again . . . This ecstasy cannot be conveyed by language; what language describes are the ways to it, the dispositions that prepare for it' (*Sade My Neighbour*, 39). Hence,

Klossowski explains, the need for endless reiteration in writing of the violent, pornographic act of possession, one that always slides away from the Sadist. My thanks to Julie Crofts for pointing out this source.

6. Those impatient with such attempts to negotiate with texts by Sade and Bataille, where they can see only misogyny, violently acted out, inevitably have a point, and Sontag's strategy of legitimation here is difficult to sustain or comply with. Sontag and Ballard belong to that generation which were bound up with 'liberation' narratives in the 1960s, and thus have wholly different attitudes to 'pornographic' writing just emerging from the cachet of censorship. Nevertheless, my reading, full of risks, is indirectly in the spirit of reassessments such as Angela Carter's *The Sadeian Woman*.

Chapter Four

1. 'Psychoanalysis in reverse' is a phrase adopted by Adorno from Lowenthal to indicate that 'somehow the psychoanalytic concept of a multilayered personality has been taken up by cultural industry, and that the concept is used to ensnare the consumer' (*The Culture Industry*, 143). This evidently informs Packard's formulations of the effects of advertising.

2. 'Taylorism' is the name given to the early twentieth-century time and motion studies of factory efficiency; it was often adopted by Leftist critics informed by Marx's analysis of the alienation of labour as evidence of the approaching apotheosis of capitalist alienation in advanced capitalist societies.

3. For the violent reaction of critics associated with science fiction to Baudrillard's essay on *Crash*, see the responses to it on its first English translation in *Science Fiction Studies*, 18:3, 1991. Both Katherine Hayles and Vivian Sobchack cite Ballard's 'Introduction' to the novel as clearly marking it out as admonitory. They fail to record, however, Ballard's retraction of the introduction: 'I felt I was not altogether honest in this introduction because I did imply that there was a sort of moral warning which I don't really think is there'. Perhaps because this retraction is so difficult to find, it has failed to register in discussions of *Crash* My source is in a footnote from Jonathan Benison's 'Jean Baudrillard and the Current State of SF', although the retraction has now been restated to Will Self: 'I went wrong in two ways in that introduction. First, in the final paragraph, which I have always regretted, I claimed that in *Crash* there is a moral indictment of the sinister marriage between sex and

technology. Of course it isn't anything of the sort. *Crash* is not a cautionary tale. *Crash* is what it appears to be. It is a psychopathic hymn'. (Self, 348). There can be no final determination of Ballard's intent, however. As I write these footnotes, reports are arriving from the 1996 Cannes film festival, where David Cronenberg's film of *Crash* caused much outrage. *The Independent* newspaper reports a press conference where Ballard suggests the moral of the film is 'Always wear a seat belt, and if you have sex, do it in the back seat'. 'He delivered it perfectly straight', the reporter notes (Chris Peachment, 'It's Raining in the Fast Lane', *The Independent*, Section Two, 23 May 1996, 10).

4. There is a highly *seductive* convergence, at times, between Baudrillard and Ballard. Sometimes, one text seems to respond to another: Ballard asks a question, Baudrillard answers it:

> There was the Queen in a fantasy/fancy dress uniform followed by all these real soldiers dressed up in costume to look like 17th century soldiers, being fired on by a man with a replica pistol! . . . I mean, how could you have possibly arrested a young man for doing that? I wondered: if you held up a sign with the word 'Pistol' on it, would that constitute an offence? (Vale and Juno, 7)

> Simulate a robbery in a large store: how to persuade security that it is a simulated robbery? There is no 'objective' difference: the gestures, the signs are the same as for a real robbery, the signs do not lean to one side or the other. To the established order they are always the order of the real . . . Parody renders submission and transgression equivalent, and that is the most serious crime (Baudrillard, *Simulacra and Simulation*, 20–21)

One has to respect this convergence, but one has also to respect the superabundance of thetic registers in Ballard's texts—this has been my whole point. To pinpoint this register seems to accord suspiciously with trying to legitimate Ballard by forcing his texts into the sole frame of postmodernism. If the space between touches on this logic, it is also traversed by many other, competing theses.

5. This criticism has been aided by the critique of Baudrillard offered by Meaghan Morris in *The Pirate's Fiancée*. For Morris, Baudrillard's trajectory of the sign ultimately reveals him as a simple Realist, because the whole structure rests on a first order of the sign which is one of originary plenitude, an absolute correspondence of word and world. Further, the sign-system Baudrillard volatizes is iconic, even indexical,

and any process of signification based on arbitrary signs (i.e. all verbal language) is rendered by Baudrillard in the language of 'murder'. And yet the 'murder of the real' is where meaning in language *begins* rather than ends, since it must be structured on the absented object-world. For Morris, then, third order simulation constructs its edifice on precritical notions of sign as resemblance and truth as correspondence to a really real. The traduction of the notion of the simulacra is merely another aspect of Baudrillard's shaky conceptual model.

6. This 'uncanniness' thus recalls the demonic doubles of stories like Henry James' 'The Jolly Corner' and Guy de Maupassant's 'The Horla'.

Chapter Five

1. This logic of detachment and reattachment might also be related to the anxiety of *restitution* that Derrida analyses in 'Restitutions of the Truth in Pointing', *The Truth in Painting*. There, Derrida finds a 'secret correspondence' in the argument between Martin Heidegger and Meyer Schapiro over the status of Van Gogh's paintings of peasant shoes. Both are anxious to find a proper place, a rightful owner, for the shoes—somewhere, some home, must be pointed to beyond the frame. That the problems of identifying the 'proper place' relate to Van Gogh's *series* of paintings on a theme might also be useful to consider in relation to Ballard's own serial oeuvre.

2. Angela Carter, however, cannily anticipated the logic of such readings in her own review of *Empire of the Sun*: 'Ballard's thirty-odd-year career as a cult classic is, however, about to come to an end. He has, in his mid-fifties, produced what they call a 'breakthrough' novel. No doubt the 'literary men' (and women) will now treat Ballard as the sf writer who came in from the cold. Who finally put away childish things, man-powered flight, landscapes of the flesh, the erotic geometry of the car crash, things like that, and wrote the Big Novel they always knew he'd got in him' (*Expletives Deleted*, 47).

3. Once more, Dennis Walder's analysis is a valuable source for a consideration of this element of *Empire of the Sun*. Perhaps here is the place to regret the absence of any sustained treatment of the novel in the nexus of colonial and post-colonial concerns. The potential for such analysis, hinted at in relation to *The Drowned World* and *The Crystal World* in chapter two, and the final reading of *Hello America* in chapter four, clearly indicates the space for such a reading—one more traversal of the peculiar zones of Ballard's work.

4. For a perverse psychoanalyst, being named after Jean-Martin Charcot, Freud's teacher in 1885–86, is a perfect choice. Charcot, with the sublime confidence of Victorian psychiatry, worked on the assumption of physiological disease as the source of all psychiatric problems; Freud had to break with his teacher in order to found the non-physiological project of psychoanalysis.

Bibliography

Primary Bibiography: J. G. Ballard

A: Fiction

The Wind From Nowhere (1962). Harmondsworth: Penguin, 1967.

The Voices of Time (originally published as *The Four Dimensional Nightmare*, 1962). London: Everyman Fiction, 1984.

The Drowned World (1962). Harmondsworth: Penguin, 1965.

The Terminal Beach (1964). London: Victor Gollancz, 1964.

The Drought (1965). London: Triad/Panther, 1978.

The Crystal World (1966). London: Triad/Panther, 1978.

The Day of Forever (1967). London: Panther, 1967.

The Disaster Area (1967). London: Triad/Panther, 1979.

The Venus Hunters (originally published as *The Overloaded Man*, 1967). London: Granada, 1980.

The Atrocity Exhibition (1970). London: Triad/Panther, 1979.

Vermilion Sands (1971). London: Everyman Fiction, 1985.

Crash (1975). London: Panther, 1975.

Concrete Island (1974). London: Triad/Panther, 1985.

High-Rise (1975). London: Triad/Panther, 1977.

Low-Flying Aircraft (1976). London: Triad/Panther, 1978.

The Unlimited Dream Company (1979). London: Triad/Panther, 1981.

Hello America (1981). London: Triad/Granada, 1983.

Myths of the Near Future. Harmondsworth: Penguin, 1988.

Empire of the Sun (1984). London: Panther, 1985.

The Day of Creation (1987). London: Grafton, 1988.

Running Wild, London: Hutchison, 1988.

War Fever, London: HarperCollins, 1990.

The Atrocity Exhibition (with added commentary notes). San Francisco, CA: Re/Search Publications, 1990.

The Kindness of Women. London: HarperCollins, 1991.

Rushing to Paradise. London: Flamingo/HarperCollins, 1994.

Cocaine Nights. London: HarperCollins, 1996.

B: Cited Non-Fiction

'Which Way to Inner Space?, *New Worlds*, 40:118 (1962): 2–3, 116–18.
'Myth-Maker of the 20th Century'. (1964). J. G. Ballard issue, *Re/Search* 8–9 (1984). Edited Vale and Juno: 105–07.
'The Coming of the Unconscious'. *New Worlds* 50:164 (1966): 141–46.
'Notes From Nowhere: Comments on a Work in Progress'. *New Worlds* 50:167 (1966): 147–51.
'Salvador Dali: The Innocent as Paranoid'. *New Worlds* 187 (1969) 25–31.
'The Alphabets of Unreason'. *New Worlds* 196 (1970): 26.
'A Personal View' (review of Aldiss, *Billion Year Spree*). *Cypher* 11 (May 1974): 7–11.
Two Letters. *Foundation* 10 (1976): 50–52.
'Introduction to Crash'. J. G. Ballard issue, *Re/Search* 8–9 (1984). Edited Vale and Juno: 96–98.
'In the Voyeur's Gaze'. *The Guardian*. 25 August 1989: 23.

A collection of Ballard's non-fiction, *A User's Guide to the Millennium* (London:HarperCollins, 1996) appeared after the completion of the main body of this text.

Secondary Bibliography

Abraham, Nicolas. 'Notes on the Phantom: A Complement to Freud's Metapsychology'. Trans. Nicholas Rand. *Critical Inquiry* 13 (1987): 287–92.
Abraham, Nicolas and Maria Torok. 'Introjection—Incorporation: Mourning or Melancholy'. Trans. Nicholas Rand. *Psychoanalysis in France*, ed. Serge Lebovici and Daniel Widlocher. New York: International UP, 1980: 3–16.
———*The Wolf Man's Magic Word: A Cryptonymy*. Trans. Nicholas Rand. Theory and History of Literature 37. Minneapolis: U. of Minnesota Press, 1986.
Ades, Dawn. *Dali*. London: Thames and Hudson, 1982.
Adorno, Theodor. *Aesthetic Theory*. Trans. C. Lenhardt. London: Routledge, 1984.
———*The Culture Industry*, ed. Jay Bernstein. London: Routledge, 1991.
Aldiss, Brian. *Billion Year Spree*. London: Wiedenfeld & Nicolson, 1973
Alexandrian, Sarane. *Surrealist Art*. Trans. Gordon Clough. London: Thames and Hudson, 1970.

Alloway, Lawrence. 'Pop Art since 1949'. *The Listener* LXVIII:1761, 27 December 1962: 1085–87.

Amis, Kingsley. 'ARRGH!', *Cypher* 4 (1970): 5–6.

——*New Maps of Hell*. London: Victor Gollancz, 1961.

Amis, Martin. 'Author's Note'. *Einstein's Monsters*. Harmondsworth: Penguin, 1988.

——Review of *The Day of Creation*. *The Observer*, 13 September 1987.

Anonymous. Review of *Crash*. *Times Literary Supplement*, 13 July 1973: 1466.

Augé, Marc. *Non-Places: Introduction to an Anthropology of Supermodernity*. Trans. John Howe. London: Verso, 1995.

Barber, Lynn. 'Sci-Fi Seer'. Interview with J. G. Ballard. *Penthouse* 5:5 (1970): 26–30.

——'Alien at Home'. Interview with J. G. Ballard. *Independent on Sunday*, 15 September 1991: 2–4.

Barlow, George. 'J. G. Ballard'. *Twentieth Century Science Fiction Writers*, ed. Curtis C. Smith. 2nd edition. London: St James Press, 1986: 32–33.

Barthes, Roland. *A Lover's Discourse: Fragments*. Trans. Richard Howard. New York: Hill and Wang, 1977.

——'The Metaphor of the Eye'. In Bataille, *The Story of the Eye*: 119–27.

——'The Old Rhetoric: An Aide-Memoire'. *The Semiotic Challenge*. Trans. Richard Howard. Oxford: Basil Blackwell, 1988: 11–93.

——*Roland Barthes*. Trans. Richard Howard. London: Macmillan, 1977.

Bataille, Georges. *Eroticism*. Trans. Mary Dalwood. London: Marion Boyars, 1987.

——*The Story of the Eye*. Trans. Joachim Neugroschal. Harmondsworth: Penguin, 1982.

Baudrillard, Jean. *America*. Trans. Chris Turner. London: Verso, 1988.

——*Fatal Strategies*. Trans. Philip Beitchman and W. G. J. Niesluchowski. London: Pluto/Semiotext(e), 1990.

——*In The Shadow of the Silent Majorities*. New York: Semiotext(e), 1983.

——*Simulacra and Simulation*. Trans. Sheila Faria Glaser. Ann Arbor: U. of Michigan Press, 1994.

——'Symbolic Exchange and Death'. *Jean Baudrillard: Selected Writings*, ed. Mark Poster. Cambridge: Polity, 1988: 119–48.

——'The Year 2000 Has Already Happened'. *Body Invaders: Sexuality and the Postmodern Condition*, ed. Arthur and Marilouise Kroker. London: Macmillan, 1988: 35–44.

Bellmer, Hans. 'Memories of the Doll Theme'. Trans. Peter Chametzky, Susan Fellerman and Jochen Schindler. *Sulfur* 26 (1990): 29–33.

Benison, Jonathan. 'Jean Baudrillard and the Current State of SF'. *Foundation* 32 (1984): 25–42.

———'In Default of a Poet in Space: J. G. Ballard and the Current State of Nihilism'. *Just the Other Day*, ed. Luk Van Der Vos. Antwerp, 1985: 405–24.

Benjamin, Walter. *Charles Baudelaire: A Lyric Poet in the Era of High Capitalism*. Trans. Harry Zohn. London: Verso, 1983.

———'Surrealism'. *One Way Street and Other Writings*. Trans. Edmund Jephcott and Kingsley Shorter. London: Verso, 1985: 225–39.

———'Theses on the Philosophy of History'. *Illuminations*. Trans. Harry Zohn. London: Fontana, 1992: 245–55.

Bhabha, Homi. *The Location of Culture*. London: Routledge, 1994.

Blanchot, Maurice. *The Writing of the Disaster*. Trans. Ann Smock. Lincoln: U. of Nebraska Press, 1986.

Blish, James. *More Issues at Hand*. Chicago: Advent, 1970.

Bogdanor, V. and Robert Skidelsky. *The Age of Affluence*. London: Macmillan, 1970.

Blow, David. 'Bloody Saturday and After'. Interview with J. G. Ballard. *Waterstone's New Books Catalogue*, Winter 1991: 35–37.

Brantlinger, Patrick. *In Crusoe's Footsteps: Cultural Studies in Britain and America*. London: Routledge, 1990.

———*Rule of Darkness: British Literature and Imperialism 1870–1914*. Ithaca, NY: Cornell UP, 1988.

Bretnor, Reginald (editor). *Modern Science Fiction: its meaning and its future*. Chicago: Advent, 1979.

Breton, André. *What Is Surrealism? Selected Writings*, ed. Franklin Rosemont. London: Pluto, 1978.

Brians, Paul. *Nuclear Holocausts: Atomic War in Fiction 1895–1984*. Kent, Ohio: Kent State UP, 1987.

Brigg, Peter. *J. G. Ballard*. Starmont Reader's Guide 26. Mercer Island, WA: Starmont House, 1985.

———'J. G. Ballard: Time Out of Mind'. *Extrapolation*. 35:1 (1994): 43–59.

Bristow, Joseph. *Empire Boys: Adventures in a Man's World*. London: HarperCollins, 1991.

Broderick, Damien. *Reading By Starlight: Postmodern Science Fiction*. London: Routledge, 1995.

Bronfen, Elisabeth. *Over Her Dead Body: Death, Femininity and the Aesthetic*. Manchester: Manchester UP, 1992.

Brooke-Rose, Christine. *Stories, Theories and Things*. Cambridge: Cambridge UP, 1991.

Brooks, Peter. 'Freud's Masterplots'. *Yale French Studies* 55–56 (1977): 280–99.

———'The Body in the Field of Vision'. *Paragraph* 14:1 (1991): 46–67.

Buck-Morss, Susan. *The Dialectics of Seeing:Walter Benjamin and the Arcades Project*. Cambridge, MA: MIT Press, 1989.

Buchloh, Benjamin H. D. 'Allegorical Procedures: Appropriation and Montage in Contemporary Art'. *Artforum* (September 1982).

———'Andy Warhol's One Dimensional Art'. *Andy Warhol: A Retrospective*, ed. McShine. New York: Museum of Modern Art for Hayward Gallery, London, 1989: 39–57.

Budrys, Algis. 'Galaxy Bookshelf'. Ballard review. *Galaxy* 25:2 (1966): 128–31.

Bukatman, Scott. *Terminal Identity: The Virtual Subject in Postmodern Science Fiction*. London: Duke UP, 1993.

Burger, Peter. *The Theory of the Avant-Garde*. Trans. Michael Shaw. Manchester: Manchester UP, 1984.

Caillois, Roger. 'Mimicry and Legendary Psychasthenia'. *October: The First Decade 1976–86*, ed. Rosalind Krauss et al. Cambridge, MA: MIT Press, 1987: 58–74.

Camus, Albert. *The Myth of Sisyphus*. Trans. Justin O'Brien. Hamondsworth: Penguin, 1975.

Carter, Angela. *Expletives Deleted*. London: Chatto and Windus, 1992.

Carter, Dale. *The Final Frontier: The Rise and Fall of the American Rocket State*. London: Verso, 1988.

Cawthorn, James. 'Ballard of a Whaler'. *New Worlds* 50:120 (1966): 157.

Chadwick, Whitney. *Women Artists and the Surrealist Movement*. London: Thames and Hudson, 1985.

Christopher, John. *The Death of Grass*. Harmondsworth: Sphere Books, 1978.

Clareson, Thomas (editor). *SF: The Other Side of Realism*. Ohio: Bowling Green UP, 1971.

Cohen, Margaret. *Profane Illumination: Walter Benjamin and the Paris of the Surrealist Revolution*. Berkeley: U. of California Press, 1995.

Conan Doyle, Arthur. *The Lost World and The Poison Belt*. San Francisco: Chronicle Books, 1989.

Connington, J. J. *Nordenholdt's Million*. Harmondsworth: Penguin, 1946.

Conquest, Robert. 'Science Fiction and Literature'. *Science Fiction*, ed. Mark Rose, 30–43.

Cooper David E. *Existentialism: A Reconstruction*. Oxford: Basil Blackwell, 1990.

Csicsery-Ronay Jr., Istvan. 'The Science Fiction of Theory: Baudrillard and Haraway'. *Science Fiction Studies* 18:3 (November 1991): 387–404.

Culler, Jonathan. 'The Turns of Metaphor'. *The Pursuit of Signs*. London: Routledge, 1981: 188–209.

Davidson, David. 'What Metaphors Mean'. *Critical Inquiry* 5:1 (1978): 29–46.

de Beauvoir, Simone. 'Must we Burn de Sade?' Introduction to Marquis de Sade, *The One Hundred and Twenty Days of Sodom*. London: Arena, 1989: 3–64.

Debord, Guy. *The Society of the Spectacle*. London: Rebel Press, 1987.

de Camp, L. Sprague. 'Imaginative Fiction and Creative Imagination'. *Modern Science Fiction*, ed. Reginald Bretnor: 120–57.

de Certeau, Michel. *The Practice of Everyday Life*. Trans. Steven Rendall. Berkeley: U. of California Press, 1988.

de Duve, Thierry. 'Andy Warhol, or the Machine Perfected'. Trans. Rosalind Krauss. *October* 48 (1989): 3–14.

de Man, Paul. *Allegories of Reading*. New Haven: Yale UP, 1979.

Delany, Samuel. 'Reading Modern American Science Fiction'. *American Writing Today*. Ed. Richard Kostelanetz. Troy, NY: Whitson Publishing Co., 1991: 517–28.

Deleuze, Gilles. 'Plato and the Simulacrum'. *October* 27 (1983): 45–56.

Derrida, Jacques. *The Ear of the Other*. Trans. Peggy Kamuf. Lincoln: U. of Nebraska Press, 1985.

——' "Fors": The Anglish Words of Nicolas Abraham and Maria Torok'. Trans. Barbara Johnson. In Abraham and Torok, *The Wolf Man's Magic Word*, xi–xlviii.

——*Glas*. Trans. John P. Leavey and Richard Rand. Lincoln: U. of Nebraska Press, 1984.

——'The Law of Genre'. Trans. Avital Ronell. *Glyph* 7 (1980).

——'Living On: Border Lines'. *Deconstruction and Criticism*, ed. Harold Bloom. New Haven: Yale UP, 1979: 75–176.

——'No Apocalypse, Not Now (Full Speed Ahead, Seven Missiles, Seven Missives)'. *Diacritics* 14:2 (1984): 20–31.

——'Of an Apocalyptic Tone Recently Adopted in Philosophy'. Trans. John P Leavey. *Oxford Literary Review* 6:2 (1984): 3–37.

————*Of Grammatology*. Trans. Gayatri Spivak. Baltimore: John Hopkins UP, 1974.

————*Spurs: Nietzsche's Styles*. Trans. Barbara Harlow. Chicago: U. of Chicago Press, 1979.

————' "This Strange Institution Called Literature": An interview with Jacques Derrida'. *Acts of Literature*, ed. Derek Attridge. London: Routledge, 1992: 33–75.

————*The Truth in Painting*. Trans. Geoffrey Bennington and Ian McLeod. Chicago: U. of Chicago Press, 1987.

Disch, Thomas. 'The Eternal Invalid'. *New Worlds*, Vol. 10, ed. Hilary Bailey. London: Corgi, 1976: 223–26.

Doane, Mary Ann. 'Information, Crisis, Catastrophe'. *Logics of Televison*, ed. Patricia Mellencamp. Indiana: Indiana UP/BFI, 1990: 222–39.

Durham, Scott. 'The Technology of Death and Its Limits: The Problem of the Simulation Model'. *Rethinking Technologies*, ed. Verena Andermatt Conley. Minneapolis: U. of Minnesota Press, 1993: 156–70.

Eagleton, Terry. 'Capitalism, Modernism and Postmodernism', *New Left Review* 152 (1985): 60–73.

Ebert, Theresa. 'The Convergence of Postmodern Innovative Fiction and Science Fiction', *Poetics Today* 1:4 (1980): 91–104.

Eco, Umberto. *Travels in Hyperreality*. Trans. William Weaver. London: Picador, 1986.

Ellison, Harlan. *Dangerous Visions*. Combined edition. London: Victor Gollancz, 1987.

Ellul, Jacques. *The Technological Society*. Trans. John Wilkson. London: Cape, 1965.

Ernst, Max. 'What is the Mechanism of Collage?'. *Theories of Modern Art*, ed. Herschel Chipp. Berkeley: U. of California Press: 1968: 427.

Evans, I. O. (editor). *Science Fiction Through the Ages*. London: Panther, 1966.

Fiedler, Leslie. *The Collected Essays Volume II*. New York: Stein and Day, 1971.

Finkelstein, Haim. ' "Deserts of Vast Eternity". J. G. Ballard and Robert Smithson'. *Foundation* 39 (1987): 50–62.

Foster, Dennis. 'J. G. Ballard's Empire of the Senses: Perversion and the Failure of Authority'. *PMLA* 108:3 (May 1993): 519–32.

Foster, Hal. 'Armor Fou'. *October* 56 (Spring 1991): 65–98.

————*Compulsive Beauty*. Cambridge, Mass: MIT Press, 1993.

————'What's Neo About the Neo-Avant-Garde?' *October* 70 (Fall 1994): 5–32.

Foster, Margaret. Review of *The Kindness of Women*. *Evening Standard*, 19 September 1991.

Foucault, Michel. 'What is an Author?'. *The Foucault Reader*, ed. Paul Rabinow. Harmondsworth: Penguin, 1986: 101–20.

Freud, Sigmund. 'Beyond the Pleasure Principle'. *Pelican Freud Library*, Volume 11. Harmondsworth: Penguin, 1984: 269–338.

———'Civilisation and Its Discontents'. *Pelican Freud Library* Volume 12. Harmondsworth: Penguin, 1985: 243–340.

———'Dreams and Delusions in Jensen's Gradiva'. *Pelican Freud Library* Volume 14. Harmondsworth: Penguin, 1985: 27–118.

———'The Dynamics of Transference'. *Standard Edition*, Volume 12. Trans. James Strachey. London: Hogarth Press, 1958: 99–108.

———'The Ego and the Id'. *Pelican Freud Library* Volume 11. Harmondsworth: Penguin, 1984: 339–407.

———'Fragment of an Analysis of a Case of Hysteria' ('Dora'). *Pelican Freud Library*, Volume 8. Harmondsworth: Penguin, 1977: 31–164.

———'The Psychotherapy of Hysteria'. *Pelican Freud Library*, Volume 3. Harmondsworth: Penguin, 1974: 337–93.

———'Mourning and Melancholy'. *Pelican Freud Library* Volume 11. Harmondsworth: Penguin, 1984: 245–68.

———'Remembering, Repeating and Working Through', *Standard Edition* Volume 12. Translated James Strachey. London: Hogarth Press, 1958: 147–56.

———'The Uncanny'. *Pelican Freud Library* Volume 14. Harmondsworth: Penguin, 1985: 335–76.

Frick, Thomas. 'The Art of Fiction: J. G. Ballard'. Interview. *The Paris Review* 94 (1985): 133–60.

Genette, Gerard. 'Introduction to the Paratext'. Trans. Marie Maclean. *New Literary History* 22:2, (1992): 261–72.

Glover, Edward. *Freud or Jung?* London: Allen and Unwin, 1950.

Goddard, James. 'Interrogation'. Interview with Ballard. *Cypher* 3 (December 1970): 23–27.

Goddard, James and David Pringle. *J. G. Ballard: The First Twenty Years*. London: Bran's Head Books, 1976.

Greenberg, Clement. *Art and Culture*. Boston, MA: Beacon Press, 1961.

Greenblatt, Stephen. *Marvelous Possessions: The Wonder of the New World*. Oxford: Clarendon, 1991.

Greenland, Colin. *The Entropy Exhibition: Michael Moorcock and the British 'New Wave' in Science Fiction*. London: Routledge, 1983.

Greenland, Colin and David Pringle. Review of Lee Killough's *Aventine*. *Foundation* 25 (1981): 77–79.

Grosskurth, Phyllis. *The Secret Ring: Freud's Inner Circle and the Politics of Psychoanalysis*. Reading, MA: Addison-Wesley Publishing, 1991.

Gusdorf, Georges. 'Conditions and Limits of Autobiography'. Trans. James Olney. *Autobiography: Essays Theoretical and Critical*, ed. James Olney. Princeton, NJ: Princeton UP, 1980: 28–48.

Haggard, H. Rider. 'About Fiction'. *The Contemporary Review* 51 (1887): 172–80.

Hall, Stuart et al. *Resistance Through Rituals: Subcultures in Postwar Britain*. London: Hutchinson/Centre for Contemporary Cultural Studies, 1976.

Hayles, N. Katherine. 'The Seductions of Cyberspace'. *Rethinking Technologies*, ed. Verena Andermatt Conley, Minneapolis: U. of Minnesota Press, 1993: 173–90.

Heidegger, Martin. *Being and Time*. Trans. John Macquarrie and Edward Robinson. Oxford: Basil Blackwell, 1962.

Heinlein, Robert. 'Introduction: Pandora's Box'. *The Worlds of Robert Heinlein*. London: New English Library, 1978: 7–25.

———'Science Fiction: It Nature, Faults and Virtues'. *The Science Fiction Novel: Imagination and Social Criticism*, ed. B. Davenport. Chicago: Advent, 1959: 14–45.

Hennessy, Brendan. 'J. G. Ballard'. Interview. *Transatlantic Review* 39 (Spring 1971): 60–64.

Hewison, Robert. *Too Much: Art and Society in the Sixties 1960–75*. London: Methuen, 1986.

Hobsbawm, Eric. *The Age of Empire: 1875–1914*. London: Weidenfeld and Nicolson, 1987

Hubert, Renée Riese. *Surrealism and the Book*. Berkeley: U. of California Press, 1988.

Hutcheon, Linda. *A Theory of Parody*. London: Methuen, 1985.

———*The Politics of Postmodernism*. London: Routledge New Accents, 1989.

Huyssen, Andreas. *After the Great Divide: Modernism, Mass Culture and Postmodernism*. London: Macmillan, 1986.

Iser, Wolfgang. 'The Reading Process: A Phenomenological Approach'. *Modern Criticism and Theory*, ed. David Lodge. Harlow, Essex: Longman, 1988: 211–28.

James, David E. 'The Unsecret Life: A Warhol Advertisement', *October* 56 (Spring 1991): 21–42.

Jameson, Fredric. *Postmodernism, or the Cultural Logic of Late Capitalism*. London: Verso, 1991.

————'Postmodernism, or the Cultural Logic of Late Capitalism'. *New Left Review* 143 (1984): 53–94.

————'Progress Vs. Utopia; or, Can we Imagine the Future?', *Science Fiction Studies* 9:2 (1982): 147–58.

Jaspers, Karl. *Philosophy 3: The Metaphysics*. Trans. E B Ashton. Chicago: Chicago UP, 1971.

Jefferson, Ann. 'Autobiography as Intertext: Barthes, Saurrate, Robbe-Grillet'. *Intertextuality: Theories and Practices*, ed. Michael Worton and Judith Still. Manchester: Manchester UP, 1990: 108–29.

Jenny, Laurent. 'From Breton to Dali: The Adventures of Automatism'. *October* 51 (1989): 105–114.

Jung, Carl et al. *Man and His Symbols*, London: Aldus Books, 1964.

Kamuf, Peggy. *Signature Pieces: On the Institution of Authorship*. Ithaca, NY: Cornell UP, 1988.

Keating, Peter. *The Haunted Study: A Social History of the English Novel 1875–1914*. London: Fontana, 1989.

Kemp, Peter. 'Atrocity as Art-Object'. Review of *The Kindness of Women*. *The Times Literary Supplement*, 20 September 1991: 22.

Killough, Lee. 'Broken Stairways, Walls of Time'. *Fantasy and Science Fiction* 56 (March 1979): 8–21.

————'A House Divided'. *Fantasy and Science Fiction* 54 (June 1978): 82–99.

————'Menage Outré'. *Fantasy and Science Fiction* 60 (February 1981): 5–19.

————'The Siren Garden'. *Fantasy and Science* Fiction 46 (March 1974): 62–78.

————'Tropic of Eden'. *Fantasy and Science Fiction* 53 (August 1977): 141–56

Kimberley, Nick. 'The Sage of Shepperton'. Review of *The Kindness of Women*. *New Statesman and Society* 27 September 1991: 52.

King, Noel.'Reading *White Noise*: Floating Remarks'. *Critical Quarterly* 33:3 (1991): 66–83.

Klossowski, Pierre. *Sade My Neighbour*. Trans. Alphonso Lingis. London: Quartet, 1992.

Krauss, Rosalind. 'Corpus Delicti'. *L'Amour Fou: Photography and Surrealism*, ed. Krauss and Jane Livingstone. London: Hayward Gallery, 1986: 57–100.

————*The Optical Unconscious*. Cambridge, MA: MIT Press, 1993.

————*The Originality of the Avant-Garde and other Modernist Myths*. Cambridge, MA: MIT Press, 1985.

————'Photography in the Service of Surrealism'. *L'Amour Fou*, ed.

Krauss and Jane Livingstone. London: Hayward Gallery, 1986: 14–42.

Kristeva, Julia. 'Why the United States?' Trans. Sean Hand. *The Kristeva Reader*, ed. Toril Moi. Oxford: Basil Blackwell, 1986: 272–91.

Kuhn, Annette (editor). *Alien Zone: Cultural Theory and Contemporary Science Fiction*. London: Verso, 1990.

Lacan, Jacques. *Ecrits: A Selection*. Trans. Alan Sheridan. London: Tavistock, 1977.

Laing, R. D. *The Divided Self*. Harmondsworth: Penguin, 1965.

———*The Politics of Experience*. Harmondsworth: Penguin, 1967.

Lang, Andrew. 'Realism and Romance'. *The Contemporary Review* 52 (1888): 683–93.

Laplanche, Jean. *Life and Death in Psychoanalysis*. Translated Jeffrey Mehlman. Baltimore: John Hopkins UP, 1976.

Laplanche, Jean and J. B. Pontalis. *The Language of Psychoanalysis*. Trans. Donald Nicholson-Smith. London: Institute of Psychoanalysis/ Karnac Books, 1988.

Lawson, Thomas. 'Bunk: Eduardo Paolozzi and the Legacy of the Independent Group'. *Modern Dreams*, ed. Brian Wallis: 19–29.

Lejeune, Philippe. *On Autobiography*. Trans. Katherine Leary. Theory and History of Literature 52. Minneapolis: U. of Minnesota Press, 1989.

Lessing, Doris. *Memoirs of a Survivor*. London: Picador, 1976.

Lippard, Lucy. *Pop Art*. London: Thames and Hudson, 1988.

Loesberg, Jonathan. 'Autobiography as Genre, Act of Consciousness, Text'. *Prose Studies* 4 (1981): 169–85.

Louit, Robert. Interview with Ballard. Trans. Peter Nicholls. *Foundation* 9 (1975): 49–54.

Luciano, Patrick. *Them or Us: Archetypal Interpretations of Fifties Alien Invasion Films*. Bloomington: Indiana UP, 1987.

Luckhurst, Roger. ' "Horror and Beauty in Rare Combination": The Miscegenate Fictions of Octavia Butler'. *Women: A Cultural Review*. 7:1 (Spring 1996): 28–38.

———'Nuclear Criticism: Anachronism and Anachorism'. *Diacritics* 23:2 (1993): 89–97.

Lyotard, Jean-François. 'Anamnesis of the Visible, or Candour'. Trans. David Macey. *The Lyotard Reader*, ed. Andrew Benjamin. Oxford: Basil Blackwell, 1989: 220–39.

———*The Differend: Phrases in Dispute*. Trans. George Van Den Abbeele. Manchester: Manchester UP, 1988.

———The Postmodern Condition: A Report on Knowledge. Trans. Geoffrey Bennington. Manchester: Manchester UP, 1984.

Maine, Charles Eric. Thirst. London: Sphere Books, 1977.

Malzberg, Barry. 'Rage, Pain, Alienation and Other Aspects of the Writing of Science Fiction'. Fantasy and Science Fiction (April 1976): 103–08.

Mandell, Barrett. 'Full of Life Now'. Autobiography: Essays Theoretical and Critical. Ed. James Olney. Princeton, NJ: Princeton UP, 1980: 49–72.

Mann, Paul. The Theory Death of the Avant-Garde. Bloomington: Indiana UP, 1991.

Marcuse, Herbert. An Essay on Liberation. London: Allen Lane, 1969.

———One Dimensional Man. London: Ark Paperbacks, 1986

Massey, Anne. 'The Independent Group: Towards a Re-definition'. The Burlington Magazine no. 1009 (April 1987): 232–42.

Massey, Anne and Penny Sparke. 'The Myth of the Independent Group'. Block 10 (1985): 48–56.

Mathy, Jean-Philippe. Extrême-Occident: French Intellectuals and America. Chicago: U. of Chicago Press, 1993.

McCaffery, Larry. 'Introduction: Storming the Desert of the Real'. Storming the Reality Studio. London: Duke UP, 1991: 1–16.

McHale, Brian. Constructing Postmodernism. London: Routledge, 1992

———Postmodernist Fiction. London: Methuen, 1987.

McLuhan, Marshall. Understanding Media. London: Ark Paperbacks, 1987.

McShine, Kynaston (editor). Andy Warhol—A Retrospective. New York: Museum of Modern Art, 1989.

Mellencamp, Patricia. 'TV Time and Catastrophe, or Beyond the Pleasure Principle of Television'. Logics of Television, ed. Patricia Mellencamp. Bloomington: Indiana UP/BFI, 1990: 240–66.

Merril, Judith. 'Books'. Ballard Review. Fantasy and Science Fiction. (January 1966): 39–45.

———'What Do You Mean Science? Fiction?'. SF: The Other Side of Realism, ed. Clareson : 53–95.

Miller, J Hillis. Fiction and Repetition: Seven English Novels. Oxford: Basil Blackwell, 1982.

Moorcock, Michael. 'New Worlds: A Personal History'. Foundation 15 (January 1979): 5–18.

———'Ballard: The Voice'. New Worlds 50, 167 (1966): 2–3, 151.

Morgan, Kenneth. Labour in Power 1945–51. Oxford: Clarendon, 1984.

Morris, Meaghan. The Pirate's Fiancée: Feminism, Reading, Postmodernism. London: Verso, 1988.

Morse, Margaret. 'An Ontology of Everyday Distraction: The Freeway, the Mall, and Television'. *Logics of Television*, ed. Patricia Mellencamp. Bloomington: Indiana UP/BFI, 1990: 193–221.

Murray, Charles. 'Psychic Alien Aloft in Suburban Eyrie'. Review of *The Kindness of Women*. *Literary Review*, September 1991: 9–10.

Nadeau, Maurice. *The History of Surrealism*. Trans. Richard Howard. Harmondsworth: Penguin, 1973.

Nead, Lynda.*The Female Nude: Art, Obscenity and Sexuality*. London: Routledge, 1992.

Neale, Steve. 'Questions of Genre'. *Screen* 31:3 (1990): 45–66.

Nichol, Charles. 'J. G. Ballard and the Limits of Mainstream SF'. *Science Fiction Studies* 3:2 (July 1976): 150–57.

Nicholls, Peter. 'Jerry Cornelius at the Atrocity Exhibition: Anarchy and Entropy in New Worlds Science Fiction'. *Foundation* 9 (1975): 22–44.

———(editor). *The Encyclopedia of Science Fiction*. London: Granada, 1979.

Olney, James. *Metaphors of the Self: The Meaning of Autobiography*. Princeton NJ, Princeton UP, 1972.

Osborne, Peter. 'Aesthetic Autonomy and the Crisis of Theory: Greenberg, Adorno, and the Problem of Postmodernism in the Visual Arts'. *New Formations* 9 (Winter 1989): 31–50.

Parrinder, Patrick (editor). *Science Fiction: A Critical Guide*. London: Longman, 1979.

Perry, Nick and Ray Wilkie. 'The Atrocity Exhibition'. *Riverside Quarterly* 6:3 (1975): 180–88.

———'Homo Hydrogenesis: Notes on the the Work of J. G. Ballard'. *Riverside Quarterly* 4:2 (1969): 98–105.

———'The Undivided Self: J. G. Ballard's The Crystal World'. *Riverside Quarterly* 5:4 (1970): 268–77.

Pfeil, Fred. *Another Tale to Tell: Politics and Narrative in Postmodern Culture*. London: Verso, 1990.

Pickering, Paul. 'Out of the Shelter'. Interview with J. G. Ballard. *The Sunday Times* 22 September 1991, books section: 5.

Pohl, Frederik. 'The Tunnel Under the World'. *The Penguin Science Fiction Omnibus*, ed. Brian Aldiss. Harmondsworth: Penguin, 1973: 337–76.

Porush, David. *The Soft Machine: Cybernetic Fiction*. London: Methuen, 1985.

Pratt, Mary Louise. *Imperial Eyes: Travel Writing and Transculturation*. London: Routledge, 1992.

Priest, Christopher. 'British Science Fiction'. *Science Fiction*, ed. Parrinder: 187–200.

———'Landscape Artist: The Fiction of J. G. Ballard'. *The Stellar Gauge*, ed. Michael J. Tolley and Kirpal Singh. Australia: Nostrilia Press, 1980: 189–96.

Pringle, David. *Earth is the Only Alien Planet*. San Bernadino, CA: Borgo Press, 1979.

———'Introduction'. *J. G. Ballard: A Primary and Secondary Bibliography*. Boston: Hall and Co., 1984: xi–xxxi.

———*J. G. Ballard: A Primary and Secondary Bibliography*. Boston: Hall and Co., 1984.

———'J. G. Ballard'. Interview. *Interzone* 22 (1987): 13–16.

Pringle, David and James Goddard. 'An Interview with J. G. Ballard'. *Vector* 73 (March 1976): 28–49.

Punter, David. 'J. G. Ballard: Alone Among the Murder Machines'. *The Hidden Script*. London: Routledge, 1985: 9–27.

Rand, Nicholas. 'Psychoanalysis with Literature: An Abstract of Nicolas Abraham and Maria Torok's The Shell and the Kernel'. *Oxford Literary Review* 12:1–2 (1990): 57–62.

Ratcliff, Carter. 'Swallowing Dali'. *Artforum* (September 1982).

Revell, Graham. Interview with J. G. Ballard. *Re/Search* 8–9 (1984). Edited Vale and Juno: 42–49.

Rønnov-Jessen, Peter. 'Science Fiction in the Market Place: The Incorporation of "New Wave" Science Fiction into the Literary Established Considered as a Downhill Motor Race'. *The Dolphin* 11 (April 1985): 73–91.

Rose, Jacqueline. 'The Man Who Mistook His Wife for a Hat or A Wife is Like an Umbrella—Fantasies of the Modern and the Postmodern'. *Universal Abandon? The Politics of Postmodernism*, ed. Andrew Ross. Edinburgh: Edinburgh UP, 1989: 237–50.

Rose, Mark (editor). *Science Fiction: A Collection of Critical Essays*. Englewood Cliffs, NJ: Prentice–Hall, 1976.

Rosmarin, Adena. *The Power of Genre*. Minneapolis: U. of Minnesota Press, 1985.

Ross, Andrew. 'Getting Out of the Gernsback Continuum'. *Critical Inquiry* 17:2 (Winter 1991): 411–33.

———*No Respect: Intellectuals and Popular Culture*. London: Routledge, 1989.

Ryan, Anthony. 'The Mind of Mr. J. G. Ballard'. *Foundation* 3 (1973): 44–48.

Saintsbury, George. 'The Present State of the Novel'. *Fortnightly Review* 49 (1888): 410–17.

Samay, Sebastian. *Reason Revisited: The Philosophy of Karl Jaspers.* Dublin: Gill and Macmillan, 1971.

Sartre, Jean-Paul. 'American Cities' and 'New York, Colonial City'. *Literary and Philosophical Essays.* Trans. Annette Michelson. London: Rider and Co., 1955: 107–17, 118–24.

Scholes, Robert. 'The Roots of Science Fiction'. *Science Fiction,* ed. Mark Rose: 46–56.

Scholes, Robert and Eric Rabkin. *Science Fiction: History-Science-Vision.* Oxford: Oxford UP, 1977.

Segal, Lynn. *Straight Sex.* London: Virago, 1994.

Self, Will. Interview with Ballard. *Junk Mail.* London: Bloomsbury, 1995: 329–71.

Shiel, M. P. *The Purple Cloud* (1901). London: Alison and Busby, n.d.

Shippey, Tom. 'The Cold War in Science Fiction 1940–60'. *Science Fiction,* ed. Patrick Parrinder: 90–108.

Sladek, John. 'The Sublimation World'. *Fantasy and Science Fiction* (July 1968): 103–06.

Sinclair, Iain. *Radon Daughters.* London: Jonathan Cape, 1994.

Sinfield, Alan. *Literature, Politics and Culture in Post-War Britain.* Oxford: Oxford UP, 1989.

Sobchack, Vivien. 'The Virginity of Astronauts: Sex and the Science Fiction Film'. *Alien Zone,* ed. Annette Kuhn: 103–15.

Sontag, Susan. *Against Interpretation and other essays.* London: Deutsch, 1987.

————'The Pornographic Imagination'. In Bataille, *The Story of the Eye*: 83–118.

Spinrad, Norman. *Science Fiction in the Real World.* Carbondale, IL: Southern Illinois UP, 1990.

Spivak, Gayatri. 'Post-Structuralism, Marginality, Post-Coloniality and Value'. *Literary Theory Today,* ed. Peter Collier and Helga Geyer-Ryan. Cambridge, Polity Press, 1990: 219–44.

Stephenson, Gregory. 'J. G. Ballard and the Quest for an Ontological Garden of Eden'. *Foundation* 35 (Winter 1985–86): 38–47.

————*Out of the Night and Into the Dream: A Thematic Study of the Fiction of J. G. Ballard.* Westport, CT: Greenwood Press, 1991.

Stevenson, Randall. 'Postmodernism and Contemporary Fiction in Britain'. *Postmodernism and Contemporary Fiction,* ed. Edmund Smyth. London: Batsford, 1991: 19–35.

Stone, Albert E. 'Introduction: American Autobiographies as Individual Stories and Cultural Narratives'. *The American Autobiography: A Collection of Critical Essays*. Englewood Cliffs, NJ: Prentice-Hall, 1981: 1–10.

Strawson, Galen. 'Difficulties with Girls'. Review of The Kindness of Women. *The Independent on Sunday*, 29 September 1991: 31.

——'Welcome to Ballardland'. Review of *War Fever. The Independent on Sunday*, 11 November 1990.

Suleiman, Susan Rubin. *Subversive Intent: Gender, Politics and the Avant-Garde*. Cambridge, MA: Harvard UP, 1990.

Sutherland, John. 'Fiction and the Erotic Cover'. *Critical Quarterly*, 33:2 (1991): 3–18.

Sutherland, J A. 'American Science Fiction since 1960'. *Science Fiction*, ed. Parrinder: 162–86.

Suvin, Darko. 'On the Poetics of the Science Fiction Genre'. *Science Fiction*, ed. Mark Rose: 57–71.

——*Positions and Presuppositions in Science Fiction*. London: Macmillan, 1988.

Tagg, John. 'Postmodernism and the Born-again Avant-Garde'. *Block* 11 (1984): 3–7.

Tate Gallery. *Richard Hamilton*. London: Tate Gallery, 1992.

Theroux, Paul. Review of *Love and Napalm*: *Export USA* (American version of *The Atrocity Exhibition*). *New York Times Book Review*, 29 October 1972.

Thomson, Ian. 'A Futurist with an Urge to Exorcise'. Interview with J. G. Ballard. *The Independent*, 21 September 1991.

Todorov, Tzvetan. *The Conquest of America*. Trans. Richard Howard. New York: Harper Perennial, 1992.

——*The Fantastic: A Structural Approach to a Literary Genre*. Trans. Richard Howard. Cleveland: Press of Case Western Reserve University, 1973.

——'The Typology of Detective Fiction'. *Modern Criticism and Theory*, ed. David Lodge. Harlow, Essex: Longman, 1988: 157–65.

Towers, Robert. 'Believe it or Not'. Review of *The Kindness of Women*. *New York Review of Books*, 24 October 1991: 37–38.

Tsai, Eugenie. 'The Sci-Fi Connection: The IG, J. G. Ballard and Robert Smithson'. *Modern Dreams*, ed. Brian Wallis: 71–75.

Vale, V. Interview with Martin Bax. *Re/Search* 8–9 (1984): 36–41.

Vale, V. and Andrea Juno. 'J. G. Ballard'. *Re/Search* 8–9 (1984).

——'Interview with J. G. Ballard'. *Re/Search* 8–9 (1984): 6–36.

Vidler, Anthony. *The Architectural Uncanny: Essays in the Modern Unhomely*. Cambridge, MA: MIT Press, 1994.

Virilio, Paul. 'The Third Interval: A Critical Transition'. Trans. Tom Conley. *Rethinking Technologies*, ed. Verena Andermatt Conley. Minneapolis: U. of Minnesota Press: 1–12.

Wagar, Warren. 'J. G. Ballard and the Transvaluation of Utopia'. *Science Fiction Studies* 18:1 (March 1991): 53–70.

Walder, Dennis. 'J. G. Ballard: "Empire of the Sun" '. *Literature and History*. Block 8. London: Open UP, 1991: 71–92.

Wallis, Brian (editor). *Modern Dreams: The Rise and Fall of Pop*. ICA, New York/MIT Press, 1988.

Wallraff, Charles. *Karl Jaspers: An Introduction to His Philosophy*. Princeton, NJ: Princeton UP, 1970.

Webb, Peter. *Hans Bellmer*. London: Quartet Books, 1985.

Webb, W. L. 'An Educated Eye for Atrocity' (announcement of Ballard as winner of the 1984 *Guardian* fiction prize). *The Guardian*, 29 November 1984: 10.

Weber, Samuel. *The Legend of Freud*. Minneapolis: U. of Minnesota Press, 1982.

Webster, Duncan. *Looka Yonder: The Imaginary America of Populist Culture*. London: Routledge, 1988.

Williams, Linda. *Hard Core: Power, Pleasure and the Frenzy of the Visible*. London: Pandora, 1991.

Wilt, Judith. 'The Imperial Mouth: Imperialism, the Gothic and Science Fiction'. *Journal of Popular Culture* 14 (1981): 618–28.

Wollen, Peter. 'The Situationist International'. *New Left Review* 174 (1989).

Wymer, Rowland. 'How "Safe" is John Wyndham?'. *Foundation* 55 (1992): 25–36.

Wyndham, John. *The Kraken Wakes*. Harmondsworth: Penguin, 1955.

————*The Midwich Cuckoos*. Harmondsworth: Penguin, 1957.

Index